LUTON TOWN
AT KENILWORTH ROAD
A Century of Memories

DESERT ISLAND FOOTBALL HISTORIES

LUTON TOWN

AT

KENILWORTH ROAD

A Century of Memories

Series Editor: Clive Leatherdale

Roger Wash

DESERT ISLAND BOOKS

First published in 2005
by
DESERT ISLAND BOOKS LIMITED
7 Clarence Road, Southend on Sea, Essex SS1 1AN
United Kingdom
www.desertislandbooks.com

© 2005 Roger Wash

The right of Roger Wash to be identified as author of this work has been
asserted under The Copyright Designs and Patents Act 1988

British Library Cataloguing-in-Publication Data
A catalogue record for this book is available from the British Library

ISBN 1-905328-10-9

Printed in Great Britain
by
Biddles Ltd

The photographs in this book were kindly provided by Gareth Owen,
Bedfordshire Newspapers, and Aerofilms

CONTENTS

AUTHOR'S NOTE

What started out as a celebration of Luton Town's 100 years at Kenilworth Road expanded into a re-write and updating of the club's entire history, bearing in mind that it is now twenty years since *The Luton Town Story* was first published.

I have tried to concentrate on all things happening in and around Kenilworth Road over the past century, although some events elsewhere needed to be mentioned for sake of completeness. The 'Kenilworth Road Classic' matches featured throughout the book are all games that took place on the hallowed turf (or plastic).

When nominating the 'Kenilworth Road Heroes' I looked for players who made at least 300 league appearances, or other individuals who had given long service to the club in some other capacity. This meant that popular heroes such as Mick Harford and Malcolm Macdonald miss out, although their contributions are in no way belittled because of this.

Series editor Clive Leatherdale, as well as my wife Mary, have bullied me throughout this project to ensure that it has been finished in time for the centenary celebrations.

I am indebted to my long-standing friend and fellow Luton Town supporter Dave Cockfield who, together with his son Adam, made innumerable trips to Luton library to check facts, especially regarding the ground, and to photocopy many match reports.

Also, thanks are due to stalwart Luton supporters Les Miller, Frank Batt and Mick McConkey for their assistance, as well as David Ainsbury from the *Luton News*, for taking the trouble to source certain photos from the newspaper's archives.

Gareth Owen, Bedfordshire Newspapers and Aerofilms kindly provided, or gave permission for the use of most of the photographs in the book.

ROGER WASH
August 2005

Prologue

1880-1905

The earliest mention of organised football in Luton came when the creation was announced of the Luton Wanderers in September 1880. This followed a meeting at the Cricketers Arms in High Town Road. Its members, all working men, paid a shilling (5p) entrance fee and a subscription of twopence (1p) per week for the season.

The team played its matches on Bell's Close, then as now a public open space, and so were unable to collect any form of gate money. This changed in 1884 when a field – now the Dallow Road Recreation Ground – belonging to Mr W Deacon was hired. A paying gate watched the first FA Cup-tie to be played in the town. Old Etonians, then a big power in football, were the visitors and ran out 3-1 winners.

The only other nearby club with pretensions was Luton Excelsior, also comprising working-class men, but regarded as more rough and ready by their neighbours. Excelsior did, however, boast an enclosed pitch in Dallow Lane, a stone's throw from the Wanderers ground, and common cause suggested amalgamation of the two clubs. If successful, the new club could entice opponents from further afield, as passion for Association Football intensified among the population at large.

At a meeting called on 11th April 1885 it was proposed that Luton Town Football Club be established. Although the Excelsior delegates were in favour of the merger, some of the Wanderers quibbled: they had already proposed renaming their club 'Luton Town Football Club' at a meeting held at St Matthew's School some three months before. In the event, opponents of the merger were defeated. There should have been little or no bad feeling, as the joining of the two strongest local sides made eminent sense, especially when the Excelsior ground was thrown into the equation.

A poll elected the inaugural committee of nine gentlemen. To soothe any ruffled feathers it was agreed that six Wanderers would be selected for the inaugural fixture, just five from Excelsior, with the split reversing the following week and so on, throughout the season. Die-hard Wanderers officials, still a little aggrieved by the merger, persisted with fielding a side in the FA Cup over the following two campaigns. Its lack of success is indicated by the fact that no mention of Wanderers as a separate entity can be found past 1887.

Football was obviously unrecognisable to the game played today. In 1885 professionalism had only recently been legalised, but was confined to Northern and Midlands clubs. There were no goal nets and the penalty-

kick was still six years in the future. Players were both courteous and brutal, with little finesse being exhibited as the combatants kicked lumps out
of each other.

The Luton Town minute book famously confirms that the 'colors [note
the American spelling] of the club should be navy blue and pink with a
shirt and cap to be worn by each member when playing'. How players were
expected to race up and down while keeping a cap on is anyone's guess, but
they were still being worn the following year. It was reported that 'Messrs
Beecroft's were to be taken to task for overcharging for the new caps'.

Advertisements were placed in the popular *Pastime* and *Referee* maga-
zines seeking fixtures, and a list of likely opponents was drawn up and letters posted. Among the earliest invitations were to Old Etonians, Grove
House, Old Foresters, Old Wykehamists, Prairie Rangers, Hendon,
Hotspur and St Albans. Most of these names mean little to today's supporters, but they were, in fact, the Premiership of the day, boasting international players galore.

Negotiations were entered into with John Sanders, joint owner of the
Dallow Lane ground previously used by Excelsior, and an annual rent of
five guineas ($£5.25$) was agreed. The committee confirmed that a ball
should be purchased and scaffold poles erected for the goals. A hut was
erected for the convenience of members, and it was stipulated that one
police constable should be present at forthcoming games.

The ground at Dallow Lane (now Road) was sited behind what was
Dunstable Road School and was hemmed in by the railway line to
Dunstable. Steam trains chugged past while games were in progress.
During an early local derby against St Albans, star centre-forward Harry
Whitby missed a sitter and later claimed that smoke from a passing engine
got in his eyes.

In those formative years the season extended from October to Easter,
finishing with two games, both played on Bank Holiday Monday. Apart
from entry into the FA Cup, or English Cup as it was then known, and forays into local charity cup competitions, the remainder of the matches were
what would today be termed 'friendlies'. No league existed. As the game
grew, the committee was forced to dig deep into its pockets, offering bigger and bigger financial 'guarantees' to the opposition. The minutes reveal
that some clubs, particularly Northern professional outfits, sought sums
that simply could not be afforded on home gates of just a few hundred.

Although the birth of Luton Town had been problematic, its life might
have been short if the minutes from the first Annual General Meeting,
called for 15th May 1886, are to be believed. The AGM could not start on
time because so few were in attendance. 'The club was on its last legs,' both
support and money-wise.

Mercifully, although the committee was 'three bodies short', there was a stay of execution. By March of the following year, 1887, it was stated that the gate money for the 9th April game against Hanover United should be for the 'benefit of three players'. This suggests that the club had overcome its initial financial worries and, as an aside, had ventured into quasi-professionalism earlier than previously thought.

Although committee members paid an annual subscription, and could therefore be regarded as custodians of the club, they carried more clout as regards control of players than would be acceptable today, even to a benefactor with millions. Players were regularly summoned before the committee to be castigated over their 'selfish play' and failure to score enough goals, as well as warned over their future behaviour after being spotted 'taking the drink' in the fleshpots of Luton.

With many of the committee-men owners of the numerous hat factories in the town, they treated the players as they would their own employees, oblivious to the fact that the players were not being paid at all. This small fact did not prevent them from holding back with their criticisms. Nor, it must be said, did the players seem to take offence, touching their forelocks in deference to a perceived higher class of person.

Victorian morals also encouraged paternalism towards the players and unpaid officials of the club. Against London Caledonians over Easter 1887, McLennon, the visiting captain, was reported as going over after a heavy tackle. Although he twice tried to resume, two Luton doctors in the crowd confirmed he had broken his leg. They placed him on one of the duckboards surrounding the pitch and he was conveyed to St Mary's Hospital across the road. The contest was abandoned. In those days there was no state assistance for the incapacitated, so the Luton committee proposed that member HG Spratley provide the player with a pair of crutches out of club funds.

As attendances started to increase at Dallow Lane it was soon realised that spectators needed a few creature comforts to encourage them to return. A 'ground man' was taken on, at a wage of three shillings (15p) per match, urinals built (although nothing for ladies), and the goalposts painted white for ease of visibility. These changes to Dallow Lane appeared cosmetic, which gives the impression that even from the earliest days the committee was seeking an alternative venue. Every few months a deputation visited the Bury (Bury Park) to assess the football field there.

One of the main problems at Dallow Lane was the lack of adequate changing facilities. When the Fox public house, across the road from the ground, decided to cease offering a dressing room, the players had to change at the Crown and Anchor, a fair walk, even though 'towels and hot water' were available.

In spite of its shortcomings, the club decided to make a fist of it at Dallow Lane, signing a seven-year lease in July 1890 which all of a sudden seemed 'hardly long enough'. A small covered stand with some seating was erected on the Dallow Lane side. Unfortunately, it could not be utilised at the start of the 1890-91 season because the Luton Cricket Club, which had use of the ground during the summer as part of the agreement with the landowner, still had fixtures to play. The football team therefore borrowed Captain Carruthers' ground at Bury Park Farm for one game. Such was the state of the Dallow Lane pitch, which had been used by all and sundry over the summer, not just the cricketers, that the club then resorted to renting Mr Heley's ground, used by Luton Montrose 'at the back of the Bury' (between the present day Beech Road and Oak Road) until the end of November. It was in fact used for an FA Cup-tie against 93rd Highland Regiment in October 1890.

Although tying the club to a pitch that was often unusable smacks of folly, the committee had high ideas. In December 1890 the minutes state: it was 'resolved that 5/- [25p] a week be offered to brothers F and H Whitby and Read, failing this the Hon. Sec. to use his own discretion in the matter'.

By offering money to keep better players, the club had embarked on the slippery slope towards full professionalism. Less two months later, it was reported that Frank Whitby demanded one shilling (5p) a week more than his brother Harry, to cover travelling and loss of earnings. Not surprisingly, it dawned on the committee that 'if one or two [players] were paid, the remainder had a perfect right to ask for payment on the same lines'. That particular meeting concluded with the observation that 'enough money had already been spent on professionalism and that if continued it undoubtedly would prove disastrous to the club'.

Having considered the matter from all angles, Frank Whitby's request was turned down. Yet by August 1891 the club proposed to pay all players two shillings and sixpence per week for matches played at home, with sixpence (2.5p) extra for out (away) matches, while time lost before 12.00am would be made up to them on reasonable terms. The carrot also came with a stick: any player delaying the kick-off by fifteen minutes would receive a fine of one fifth of his remuneration, or thirty minutes two fifths. There is no mention of Frank Whitby's response to all this.

The advent of semi-professionalism had one obvious benefit: it ensured the players would turn up, and was hoped to put an end to little tales such as this, recorded in the minutes of 4th December 1890:

'One of the Harpenden men, Moore, could not play unless he could get back by 8pm. This being the case it was thought we ought to play Moore by some means. It was therefore proposed, seconded and carried unanimously that Mr Long [a committee member] should hire Mr Cannon's horse and trap, drive down gently early in the day and bring Mr Moore back at night.'

Semi-professionalism was a natural progression, considering all that was happening in the game at the time. A Southern League had been mooted as early as February 1890, as clubs such as Luton Town wearied of a procession of friendlies against a huge variety of opposing sides where the standard differed wildly. It was common for the Town to offer financial 'guarantees' to some of the big Northern clubs to play in Luton, only for the visiting team, on arrival, to contain few if any of its star players. On the other side of the coin, clubs pestered the Town's committee for a game, but when Formby visited they were thrashed 16-0. What were thought to be 'class opponents' turned out to be the 'biggest failure' ever to appear on the Town ground.

Despite this variance in opposition, crowds were on the up. For the big English (FA) Cup games up to 4,000 were present on a ground that lacked most of the basic amenities. The club's first good run in the competition, in 1891-92, ended with the Town paired with 'big boys' Middlesbrough at Dallow Lane.

Boro offered a huge financial inducement of £50 to switch the tie to Teesside, but the Town's committee refused and probably regretted it. A miserable 0-3 defeat followed, amidst spectator complaints of overcrowding and a lack of creature comforts.

The lesson learned, the committee made plans to erect a modern grandstand, but it was not until December 1893 that the new structure opened. Situated on the railway side of the ground with a direct entrance from Dunstable Road, the new stand was 120ft long, 18ft high, 13ft deep and had five tiers of seats as well as a Press table. At last the club had decent facilities on offer. The stand proved popular with spectators, luring them from the small pavilion behind the goal and the shed along the other touchline.

Other changes around this time included goal nets, recently sanctioned by the Football Association, and a large canvas sheet to be erected on the railway embankment to protect the ground from non-paying onlookers.

With regard to new players, an advertisement placed in *Athletic News* brought a healthy response. The committee plumped for JW Julian of Woolwich Arsenal. Bill Julian's signature was a coup. Not only was he a star, but Secretary Isaac Smith also convinced him to continue to live in Plumstead and work at the munitions factory there. This meant no outside job or house had to be provided for him in Luton.

Soon afterwards came the signing of Hugh Galbraith from Burnley. In no time, Galbraith established himself as the 'finest goalscorer in the south'. He and Julian formed the backbone of a new look Luton Town side that beat Old Westminsters at Wembley Park in the FA Cup in November 1893. Old Westminsters, whose eleven included six internationals, were a notable scalp and a 'great throng' was present at Luton railway station to greet the returning heroes. Unfortunately, although the Town won through to the first round proper once more, they went down 1-2 at the other Teesside club, Middlesbrough Ironopolis.

Galbraith, despite becoming a crowd favourite, was not immune from criticism. The Secretary was instructed to write to him 'drawing his attention to the way he hangs on to the ball instead of passing it when the opportunity presents itself'. Other players to receive formal advice included Jack Dimmock, who was to be advised to 'to put a little more heart and dash into his play', and John Finlayson, from whom a promise was extracted to 'try his best to keep himself from the drink'.

As well as cracking the whip, the committee also showed their gentler, more paternalistic side: 'on Gorman's expiration of his term in the army £5 be granted to him in order to obtain civilian clothing.'

With the club seemingly in fine fettle, on and off the pitch, the chance to become founder members of the Southern League came at an opportune moment. Only nine clubs participated in that inaugural season, but for Luton Town it finally meant truly competitive football in a professional league.

To celebrate, the new stand was extended by twelve yards at each end, advertising hoardings placed on every available space around the ground, and 'Match Cards' (programmes) were produced for the first time. Samuel Pride put in the highest tender of fifty shillings (£2.50) for the season.

The new campaign started with a home defeat by Millwall in front of a 5,000 crowd at Dallow Lane. These proved to be the strongest two sides in the league, with the Town finishing runners-up to the 'Dockers'. Another run in the FA Cup saw mighty Preston win 2-0 at Luton in the first round proper (equivalent to today's fourth round).

Towards the end of that 1894-95 season it became known that the lease on Dallow Lane, due to expire in 1897, would not be renewed. The owners wished to sell part of the land, in order that the future Dunstable Road school could be built. The club faced homelessness, so the committee approached a Mr Crawley regarding the possible sale of the Bury Park land and football pitch. The Town had used it before, and it was now in use by local rivals Luton Montrose. Mr Crawley was not keen to sell, but with time running out a deal was struck to rent the ground. This left the club in a precarious position for the future.

The 1895-96 season once again saw the Town finish second to Millwall in the Southern League. At the end of the campaign the decision was taken to resign from the Southern League, then apply to the Football League for membership of Division Two. Severing its membership of the Southern League was a risky strategy. It meant the club could easily find itself with no professional league to play in, especially as the Football League at that time remained a bastion for Northern and Midlands clubs. Woolwich Arsenal, for example, were the only Second Division club south of Leicester, so applying to the Football League can be seen as a radical step by Luton Town. In the event, those worst fears were realised. Blackpool, Walsall and Gainsborough Trinity were elected, leaving the Town and six other aspirants failing to gain the necessary votes.

Facing a season in the wilderness, the Town applied to join the new United League which was then being formed. The club's AGM noted that financial losses incurred during the previous season were due to lack of spectator interest in the Southern League, as well as the cost of travelling. This is curious, as those costs would not have been reduced by all those trips north as members of the Football League. It was argued that the smaller United League would enable costs to be minimised, although this is difficult to substantiate. The AGM made no mention of the abortive attempt to gain admission to the predominantly northern-based Football League. Face-saving seems the best explanation of this sudden enthusiasm for the United League.

Threatened on the one hand by not owing its ground, and on the other by a request for a £500 overdraft being refused by the club's bankers, it is a wonder that the club survived. Showing resilience both on and off the pitch, everyone pulled together. On the playing side, the Town finished runners-up once more, again to Millwall, and enjoyed another run in the FA Cup before being beaten 0-1 by West Bromwich Albion in front of a record crowd of 6,898 at Dallow Lane in January 1897.

Soon afterwards the club made the short move to Dunstable Road, Bury Park, for the next chapter in its history. The new ground was just across the railway track, only a goal-kick away from the old pitch. It offered the advantage of having ample room for expansion. It was originally intended to build a new stand on the Dunstable Road side of the ground, but this was refused by Luton Town Council. The intention was to build the new stand with dressing rooms underneath, but nine people living in the new houses opposite objected to its proposed height of 27 feet.

Consideration was then given to placing the stand along the opposite touchline (where Avondale Road now stands). This would mean that spectators would not face the afternoon sun in their eyes, but for ease of access the Dunstable Road side was favoured. It was decided that the Dallow Lane stand, erected only three years previously, should be dismantled and moved to the new site.

The club was living on borrowed time. They should have quit Dallow Lane at the end of 1896 and were on a month by month agreement with the owners, who were becoming increasingly agitated. The decision to relocate the old stand was taken only three weeks before the proposed opening of the new ground. Matters were exacerbated by long delays with the planning department, and one wonders what would have happened should the Council have found in the club's favour, and permitted them to erect a new stand after all.

Although games were scheduled for the new field from February 1897, no spectator facilities were yet available. The official opening was therefore put back to 3rd April, with Loughborough the visitors for a United League fixture. Remarkably, just about everything was in place when the big day arrived. The stand was strewn with bunting in the new club colours of red, white and black stripes (the club had changed from their original pink and blue to cardinal red in 1889) and a band led the procession of dignitaries from the Town Hall. These included the Duke of Bedford who was to carry out the official opening, as well as perform the kick-off.

A crowd of 5,000 had assembled, but presumably only a few would have heard the Duke express his long-held support of the club, his being honoured to be present on such an occasion, where all the inhabitants of Luton, all classes and all ages, appeared to take the greatest interest. He then declared the ground open. In a vote of thanks the local MP, Mr TG Ashton, thanked His Grace for coming and declared: 'Perhaps a Saturday half-holiday is not so precious to the Duke of Bedford as to some of those here?' Perhaps realising his faux-pas, he extricated himself from the hole he was digging by adding 'not that he is a less hard working man'. The Duke seemed unabashed and pledged £50 towards the £800 still outstanding to bring the ground completely up to scratch. He then set the ball rolling. For the record, the dreary contest finished 1-0 to the Town, with future manager John McCartney scoring the goal.

The old ground at Dallow Lane was within a year buried beneath Dunstable Road school. The rest of the site became a timber yard for Henry Brown, and the abandoned shed used by the Town for covered accommodation on the Dallow Lane side stored wood until the 1960s.

Within weeks of moving grounds, the committee agreed that the club be floated as a Limited Liability Company with capital of £2,000 in £1 shares. The Football League clubs would also be canvassed once more to gain the necessary votes for admittance to Division Two.

This time the Town gained the extra couple of votes needed. As before, the bottom three clubs sought re-election. Lincoln City and Burton Swifts were successful. The Town were next on the list with thirteen votes, which was enough for them to take the place of Burton Wanderers.

The Town had assembled a fair side for that first season in the Football League. Their opening-day draw at Leicester Fosse was par for the course. They finished eighth out of sixteen, winning thirteen and losing thirteen of their thirty matches. Crowds hovered around the 4,000-5,000 mark, with the central terraced section opposite the main stand covered to protect more spectators from the elements. The best crowd at Dunstable Road came on 29th January 1898, when 9,000 saw First Division Bolton win an FA Cup-tie 1-0. Wanderers were without their skipper, Jones, who had burnt his toe trying to cure a corn!

During the 1898 close season Second Division newcomers Glossop North End made a £300 bid for four Luton players – Jimmy McEwen, Robert Donaldson, Richard Williams and William Gallacher. Cash-strapped Town accepted. The departures provoked a minor stampede of other players leaving the club. The new-look side was not nearly as strong, finishing fifteenth in the expanded eighteen-team division, missing the need to apply for re-election by one place. Glossop, incidentally, had invested wisely, finishing second behind Manchester City to earn promotion to Division One at the first attempt.

With regard to personnel, trainer Billy Lawson was offered a wage of thirty shillings (£1.50) a week with an additional 2s 6d (12.5p) for washing the kit. In November 1898 three players were summoned before the Board to answer charges of 'immorality and misconduct'. The misconduct referred to drunkenness but details of the other charge are frustratingly not recorded. All three players were severely censured, fined, and suspended for fourteen days. In months to come, the Board received a report that Messrs Lawson, Lindsay, Sharp and Blessington were drunk on the return journey from Oxford after the friendly match at City. All were suspended for a week, with trainer Lawson threatened with dismissal unless he consented to becoming teetotal.

The Town's third season in the Football League was disastrous. A thin squad of young, inexperienced players won only five league games out of 34. Crowds dropped to around 1,500 as defeat followed defeat, and the huge costs of travel to everywhere except Woolwich Arsenal left the Board facing massive financial losses With the team finishing next to bottom, it was decided not to seek re-election but to go cap in hand to the Southern League and ask for re-admittance. The Southern League was becoming progressively stronger, but it duly accepted Luton's application.

The 1900-01 season saw the Town back amongst old friends. On the opening day Southampton, adversaries from the club's earliest days, were the visitors. A healthy crowd of around 5,000 saw the Town lose 3-4 but they improved to finish in a comfortable position. Behind the scenes it was a case of repairing the club's parlous financial position.

It was not long, though, before it was necessary for the club to uproot yet again. The owners of the Dunstable Road site could see the developmental potential, especially as the area was enjoying a building boom alongside the rapid growth of the town. This time the Board was determined to acquire ownership of a ground of its own, to enable the club to put down roots. A 'Ground Committee' was set up in September 1903 so that as many new sites as possible could be explored.

After exploring various sites the Board finally plumped for another slice of land bounded by the Luton to Dunstable railway, and again only a goal-kick from their existing home. The site – at the end of the newly developed Ivy Road – was smaller than the one on Dunstable Road, it was handicapped by a slope from one corner to the other, and had a chunk sliced off by the railway line. Little did anyone foresee that this site, far from ideal even then, would be the club's home for over a century.

At the time, industry was being encouraged to relocate to Luton on the promise of cheap land, and it is pretty clear that the club's directors acted on the expectation that workers attracted to the area would need spectator sports for their relaxation. That the club chose such an unprepossessing site, when most of the alternatives offered so much more, was obvious. Cost!

The Ivy Road site was purchased for £300 by six directors, Messrs Arnold, Squires, Allen, Smith, Gibbs and Smart. It was then rented back to the club on a seven-year lease at £160 per annum. In fairness, a sizeable sum was needed to bring the new ground up to scratch, but as the land was purchased a year before occupation, and a 'New Ground Fund' had been set up for supporter contributions, the final cost to the directors was probably not as high as it might have been.

It was reported at a supporters meeting at the Plait Hall in April 1905 that the cost of levelling and preparing the new site, plus the moving of the Dunstable Road grandstand, amounted to £1,000. At the club's AGM in July, these costs were stated as being £2,000! It is not revealed how much the 'New Ground Fund' raised, nor the extent of the advertising revenue obtained after erecting ten-foot high fences at the Dunstable end (Oak Road) of the ground.

Chapter One

The First Quarter-Century
1905-1930

At last Luton Town had a ground to call their own. Part of the purchase agreement was that the land would only be used for football, and everyone connected with the club was content in the knowledge that it would not be asked to move again – at least not in the short term. The old ground at Dunstable Road gave way for the development of Hazelbury Crescent and Avondale Road, with Kenilworth Road itself further developed. Strangely, the land fronting Dunstable Road, which presumably was the most valuable, was not built upon until the late 1930s, when the Odeon cinema was erected. In the interim, it appears to have functioned as a car park, with motor car-owning football-goers taking advantage of it when big matches were staged.

The new ground was formally opened on Monday, 4th September 1905 at 5.00pm sharp to allow kick-off at 5.15pm, which would then enable the Southern League visitors, Plymouth, enough time to catch their train home that evening. That inaugural fixture became known as the 'Green Game'. The Pilgrims, then as now, played in green, the referee was a Mr A Green, the formal opening was conducted by Mr JW Green of local brewery fame, and the whole event had been orchestrated by Secretary Charles Green. The pitch, of course, was green.

KENILWORTH ROAD CLASSICS: **Luton v Plymouth** – 0-0

Southern League, 4th September 1905

The first game at Kenilworth Road was played on a warm, late summer evening and attracted a crowd of over 6,000, who paid £120 for the privilege of taking part on an historic occasion. Mr JW Green formally opened proceedings by kicking off the contest, after announcing that he would be donating 25 guineas (£26.25) to the club. The contest was end to end, with both sides hitting the goalframes. The Town had a point to prove, having finished second bottom the previous season (fortunately they were re-elected with little fuss), and had recruited better players to replace those 'not able to withstand the rigours of competitive football'. In other words, the long ball and muscle were to be the order of the day. The referee had trouble preventing the game deteriorating into a 'rough and tumble affair', and more than once he had to separate brawling players.

LUTON: *Platt, Blackett, McCurdy, F Hawkes, White, R Hawkes, Gallacher, Warner, Brown, Pickering, Barnes.*

PLYMOUTH: Sutcliffe, Saul, A Clark, Leech, C Clark, Mortimer, Briercliffe, Buck, Willcox, Buchanan, Corrin.

~~~~~~~~~~

The new enclosure was smaller than the one left behind. It was already hemmed in by new houses in Ivy, Beech and Oak Roads, not to mention the railway line. Behind the Oak Road goal was wooden terracing backed by a high wooden fence, while at the Kenilworth Road end clinker banking had been built up to provide a reasonable vantage point.

Beech Hill Path served as a natural boundary for the ground. Along this side more wooden terracing was erected, with a roof extending over the rear steps. On the opposite side stood the wooden Main Stand, which had followed the club from site to site. With a standing 'paddock' in front of it, this side of the ground was reckoned to accommodate 1,500 out of a total capacity of 10,000. To finish off, a 'stout wooden fence' enclosed the pitch, something that had not been present at either of the other two grounds. The general reaction can be gauged by this letter to the *Luton News*:

'Sir – I was one of those who witnessed the very fine opening football match upon the new Town ground on Monday last. My pleasure, and that of many others was, however, spoiled by the foul, disgusting language of two men of the baser sort who stood near me. Their swearing was vile in the extreme. Their mouths needed washing and their hearts needed changing. Two or three remonstrances only made them worse. It is a great pity and shame too, that one of our national games should be spoiled by men such as these. This gentleman who stood near me remarked "no wonder people do not come to the matches". I am sure there are scores if not hundreds of good clean living men, who take pleasure in witnessing a good match, whose consciences will condemn them if they are obliged to listen to such language as I have referred to. I am soliciting the help of the Press, believing it to be the best way to expose this great evil. I sincerely hope the Directors will take immediate steps to deal with such offenders in a very decided manner. Unless this is done the game is bound to suffer, and the "gates" too.'

Yours &c.
Mr A Hill
Chapel Street
Luton

After the poor showing during the 1904-05 season, the team were greatly improved in their first campaign at their new home, and finished fourth in a strong division. They were also top goalscorers, aided in no small part by ex-Scottish international centre-forward Sandy Brown, 'The Glenbuck Goalgetter,' who weighed in with eighteen of the Town's 64 goals.

Fourth position was repeated the following season, but the novelty of the new ground had passed, prompting a dip in match receipts but no such drop in players' wages. As such, new recruits were of lesser calibre, and in 1907-08 the team slipped down the table to eighteenth.

Shortly after the ground opened, a new entrance to the Lane Stand (Beech Hill Path) was made at the top of Beech Road, while a large advertising hoarding was erected over the Ivy Road entrance, which was let to Freeman, Hardy & Willis for seven years. In time, another plot of land adjacent to the railway line (where the club shop now stands) was purchased, while the National Telephone Company erected a pole at the ground, which allowed the club to have its first direct telephone line. Five shillings a season was earned by giving sole rights to a Mr Stevens to take charge of bicycles at the ground.

KENILWORTH ROAD CLASSICS: **Luton v Sunderland** – 0-0

FA Cup Round Two, 2nd February 1907

After Luton had beaten Gainsborough Trinity in a replayed first round tie, cup fever arrived when the Strawplaiters were drawn against mighty Sunderland in the equivalent to round four today. This was the first serious test of the new ground's capacity and although Sunderland offered £150, plus half of the gate to switch the tie, the Town's directors stood firm.

Some 10,500 turned up, generating receipts of £571, both of which were then records for football in Luton. Apparently, there was still spare capacity, with the Kenilworth Road banking the only section 'full'. With so many visitors, 'Beware of Pickpockets' signs were posted on all approaches. Twenty constables were engaged and 'special arrangements for keeping the players under control in the evenings leading up to the match were to made by the secretary and a suitable hotel found'.

A huge hat in blue and white plait, bearing the words 'Play up Luton', was placed in front of the Main Stand, with the crowd whipped into a frenzy as the game kicked off.

Sunderland, members of Division One since 1890, and four times champions, fielded a team full of internationals. One – England centre-forward George Holley – saw his fierce shot well saved by Peter Platt in the Luton goal. Home half-back Bob Hawkes had to call upon his experience in robbing Angus McIntosh, who was 'conspicuous by reason of his very short knickers', when the Sunderland forward raced clear.

It was not all Sunderland. William Barnes fired wide from a free-kick and then just failed to connect with a cross from Brown. At the end, the Luton directors were happy with the prospect of more gate money. In the replay, the Town lost 0-1 in front of 18,000 at Roker Park. Sunderland fell to the eventual winners, Sheffield Wednesday, in the next round.

LUTON: Platt, Hogg, McCurdy, F Hawkes, White, R Hawkes, Murphy, Gittins, Brown, Fitzpatrick, Barnes.

SUNDERLAND: Ward, Rhodes, Watson, Tait, McGhee, McConnell, Raine, Gemmell, McIntosh, Holley, Bridgett.

~~~~~~~~~~~

A month after the Sunderland Cup-tie, the club's Secretary was instructed to post a notice in the dressing room, stressing that no players' dogs were permitted on the premises during training. It was followed by an appeal to all players to refrain from rough play. In November 1908 special dispensation was received from the Football Association for a collection to be taken at a forthcoming match for the benefit of old player Hugh Galbraith, who was suffering from rheumatics of the spine. The eventual collection made £9 12s 9d.

The aftermath of the Sunderland defeat was disheartening. A gale took off part of the roof of the Lane Stand, causing damage to a nearby house, and attendances tailed off severely. Facing yet another parlous financial position, in March 1909 the directors proposed two separate turnstiles to be set aside for supporters willing to pay one shilling for entrance, rather than the normal admission fee of half that. Unsurprisingly, the idea was shelved two weeks later due to lack of use.

As matters worsened, with the very existence of the club at stake, a special Board meeting resolved that 46 players would be placed on the open to transfer list. All players would be asked to forego part of their wages for the remainder of the campaign. The only substantial bids were for the club's few jewels. The sale of John Quinn and John Smith to Millwall for a 'considerable sum' gave rise to the directors being tagged with a selling club mentality for the first (and certainly not the last) time.

Paradoxically, the sale of the two players seemed to lift a dark cloud from over Kenilworth Road, and the 1910-11 season started with a bang. By October the team were top, and although the momentum could not be sustained, a final position of ninth was better than expected. Extra income from the gate raised a rare profit. Rather than use the money to strengthen the squad, the directors instead merely re-signed most of the existing players on increased wages.

The ploy was misguided, and the Town struggled from the start of the 1911-12 campaign, which culminated in relegation to Division Two. A crop of injuries did not help, but the death of 24-year-old Sammy Wightman, who had been kicked in the stomach at Brighton, as the season drew to a close, brought an abrupt end to a sad chapter in the club's history. The full-back appeared to be winded from the blow and had to leave the field with the Town losing 0-1. There were no substitutes, of course, nor would there be until 1965. Wightman was given the all-clear to travel back with the squad, but on the train from Brighton to London his condition worsened. He was rushed across the capital in a horse-drawn cab and put on a train to Luton, from where he was taken to the Bute Hospital for immediate surgery. Whiteman never regained consciousness and died a day later.

Much soul-searching took place that summer at Kenilworth Road, and at one stage it was touch and go whether the club would condescend to participate in Division Two of the Southern League. One problem was that this division seemed packed with Welsh clubs, and to offset the drain on travel expenses Luton tried to impose a travel subsidy of £20 per match played in the Principality. The argument went back and forth between the Town and the Southern League management committee, before a comprise figure of £12 10s was reached. What action the club would have taken, had the Southern League refused to entertain the principle of a subsidy, is not recorded.

Around this time the Town's first organised Supporters Club – probably one of the first in the country – was formed. Its members made £60 immediately available for the club's coffers. Add the fact that substantial transfer fees were received for those players who did not wish to step down a division, plus the Southern League's travel subsidy, and it seems that the Town's finances were not too bad. Pity the poor players, though. They had to accept the cheapest rail seats to far-flung footballing outposts in Wales, and then be expected to turn on the style against agricultural footballers on pitches little better than cow pastures.

The team made heavy weather of their first season at basement level, 1912-13, and could only finish fifth. The Supporters Club was not only expected to find volunteers to act as unpaid stewards and gatemen, but also provide income to pay for players' summer wages, not to mention contribute to a transfer fee pot.

For once, this pot was spent wisely. Two players were signed for the combined sum of £50 and proved integral to the club's attempts to climb back to Southern League Division One. Ernie Simms was signed from Barnsley for £10, while Frank Rollinson came from Portsmouth for £40. Together they might give the Town the firepower lacking in the previous campaign. Between them they struck 45 goals as the Town won promotion, finishing runners-up on goal-average behind Croydon Common. This was just as well. That season, 1913-14, the Southern League's Division Two had only four English representatives – Luton, Croydon, Brentford and Stoke. Every other club was Welsh.

Reports from that season speak of poor pitches and less than friendly opposition. Mid-Rhondda was typical: 'an undersized pitch, on a slope and full of lumps.' Despite everything, the goals flowed. A 7-0 home win over Aberdare was bettered by an 8-1 victory over Mid-Rhondda at Kenilworth

Road and a 9-0 thrashing of Caerphilly in Wales. A poor spell in November, with defeats suffered at Llanelly and Pontypridd, was followed by a 0-2 'disaster' at Newport on Christmas Day. But these were the only reverses of the campaign. In the second half of the season the defence was stiffened, with the outcome that no team scored more than once against the Town and the perfect home record was maintained until the end.

Kenilworth Road Classics: **Luton v Stoke** – 2-1

Southern League, Division Two, 10th April 1914

Mardy, Abertillery, Treharris, Barry, Llanelly, Pontypridd, Ton Pentre, Mid-Rhondda, Aberdare, Newport, Swansea, Caerphilly and Stoke! The old Stoke, founder members of the Football League in 1888, had resigned from the competition in 1908 and entered into liquidation, having finally run out of money. The new Stoke Football Club (1908) Ltd had risen from the ashes and initially joined the Birmingham and District League before joining the Southern League. Stoke had avoided the Town over the previous two seasons, having won promotion to Division One as the Town dropped out and were then relegated to Division Two.

Luton looked to extend an unbeaten run that began on Christmas Day and now extended to twelve games. A record crowd of 12,000 turned up for the Good Friday fixture and were treated to a stirring struggle. Frank Rollinson scored for the Town midway through the first half and then netted twice more, only to see both efforts disallowed. Outside-right Arthur Durrant then limped off and the ten men remaining were suddenly not so prominent. Stoke missed two simple chances, but it was the Town who increased their lead when Simms thundered in shortly after the interval. Stoke immediately replied through Dick Smith, but the Luton defence held firm to secure a result that virtually ensured promotion.

Stoke strolled to the championship the following season, and successfully reapplied for their place back in the Football League.

Luton: Mitchell, Elvey, Robinson, F Hawkes, Frith, R Hawkes, Durrant, Wileman, Simms, Rollinson, Hoar.

Stoke: Gadsden, Turner, Milne, Jones, Parker, Bradley, Hargreaves, Herbert, Smith, Ellis, Tempest.

~~~~~~~~~~~

While the Town were building up a head of steam towards promotion, an agreement was struck with the Palace Theatre. In return for an advertisement of forthcoming Luton Town matches displayed on the theatre screen twice a week, theatre staff bearing an advertising banner would be permitted to parade around the pitch at half-time of each game.

Promotion was celebrated with a special dinner and a bonus of £125 handed out to the players, to be split based on appearances. Also, a glossy photographic souvenir was published by the *Luton News*, which included the text of congratulatory telegrams, most of which were sent by clubs in Southern League Division One, who seemed genuinely pleased to have the Town back in the fold.

With hindsight, it appears an oddity that the 1914-15 season was concluded, given that the Great War was raging across the Channel, claiming an untold toll of young males. At the end of April 1915 it was announced that professional football would be suspended for the duration of the hostilities. Unlike in World War II, when competitive football was seen as vital to keep spirits up, it was the opposite during the Great War. Sports were frowned upon as frivolous diversions to the objective of victory.

KENILWORTH ROAD CLASSICS: **Luton v Great Yarmouth** – 15-0

FA Cup, 4th Qualifying Round, 21st November 1914
The absurdity of the English Cup authorities in pitching Luton – back to the first division of the Southern League – into the fourth qualifying round, 'led to a sort of "game" that can only take place when two sides are in such absolutely different classes that they ought not to be put together unless they both want a vacant date filled. When the better club has to re-arrange first-class matches to make room for such a fixture, then the affair is ridiculous.' So wrote a very miffed 'Crusader' (JJ Hunt) in the *Luton News*.

A crowd of 4,000, including 1,000 soldiers, paid £88 on a cold day to see this one-sided rout, which remains the Town's record score in any competition. Yarmouth were handicapped from the start, with three of their regulars away with the Norfolk Cyclists Battalion, whose duty it was to guard the East Coast, but in the eyes of the reporter they gave in rather too easily and, after conceding an early own goal – when Housego deflected a cross into his own net after ten minutes – heads dropped.

The Town were five up at the interval. The crowd willed Yarmouth to cross the halfway line, but apart from two early corners and a couple of long shots, Joe Mitchell in the Luton goal was a spectator. The players used the second half as shooting practice but most of the goals were tap-ins as the forwards took turns to set each other up. The crowd went wild when Ernie Simms and Arthur Wileman ran through with the ball shoulder to shoulder 'like a pair of horses attached to the same pole'. Other spectators were saddened to see the players show such disrespect.

The scorers were Simms (four, including a penalty), Frank Rollinson (four, including a genuine hat-trick), Wileman (two), an own-goal, and singles for Fred Hawkes, Robert Frith, Hugh Roberts and Sid Hoar.

After beating Oxford C and Bromley, Luton lost 0-3 at Southampton.

LUTON: Mitchell, Elvey, Dunn, F Hawkes, Frith, R Hawkes, Roberts, Wileman, Simms, Rollinson, Hoar.

GT YARMOUTH: Gay, Housego, Malachowski, Watts, Adams, Wade, Turner, Millican, Perkins, Harris, Newson.

~~~~~~~~~~~

In September 1914 the club's directors resolved that the players should attend the shooting range at the Luton Rifle Club once a week, with the club paying the membership fee of 10s 6d (53p). The players would have to pay for their own ammunition. Whether or not this had anything to do with the ongoing conflict is not made clear.

Charles Green, the Town's long-serving secretary, kept the club afloat throughout the war almost single handed. Having arranged friendlies in the autumn of 1915, following the refusal of the hastily formed London Combination to admit clubs more than eighteen miles from the capital, he persuaded them to reconsider for the back end of that season, in which Luton had a run of fourteen games.

Due largely to Green's efforts, the Town participated in the London Combination for the whole of the 1916-17 season. They notched 101 goals in only 39 games. Ernie Simms made an even bigger name for himself when netting forty times from thirty starts. This not only made him the record goalscorer for the season but also, apparently, in football history at that time.

Not even Green's persuasive powers could convince the authorities that the Town should take part in the London Combination over the following two seasons. It was decreed that on grounds of security and travel the competition should be restricted to clubs in the London area. Friendlies were all that could be arranged, but Green tried to make them as varied, competitive and interesting as possible. He did not always get it right, with Simms scoring six in four consecutive games in March 1919.

Sadly, the Town's players did not escape the 'war to end all wars'. Ernest Dodd, Arthur Wileman and Frank Gilder were all killed in action, while Ernie Simms, Frank Lindley, Westby Heath and Arthur Roe were injured and Sid Hoar gassed. Two ex-players – Jack Jarvie and George Porter – were also killed in action.

With the Great War finally over, all at Kenilworth Road were geared up to make 1919-20 a season to remember. Unfortunately, the season became one to forget. The Town finished third from bottom with a team that on paper was as good as anything else in the division. Although ex-Dunstable Road schoolboy forward Jimmy Chipperfield was sold to Tottenham for £1,000 in June 1919, he was quickly replaced by Louis Bookman, an Irish international, from West Brom. Bookman signed for Luton for £250 in what must have been one of the first deals to include a sell-on clause. Should he ever command a future fee in excess of £250, then the profit would be split between the Town and Albion. It is interesting to note that the Supporters Club was still active, with £50 being donated towards meeting Bookman's transfer fee.

The deprivations of war seemed to affect the players. For example, Simms looked a pale shadow of his former self, but gradually fitness returned and by the start of 1920-21 everyone was raring to go.

KENILWORTH ROAD CLASSICS: **Luton v Liverpool** – 0-2

FA Cup, Round Two, 31st January 1920

An FA Cup run was seen as just the tonic to brighten up a dismal season. After beating Brighton in the sixth qualifying round, the Town entertained Coventry City of Football League Division Two. A crowd of 10,054 witnessed a thrilling 2-2 draw. In the replay, Luton took the lead in the twelfth minute, when Sid Hoar, seemingly offside, centred to Ernie Simms, whose goal stunned the crowd of 21,893. It was now a case of hanging on, with full-backs Jack Elvey and John Dunn successfully buttoning up the Coventry wingers.

Cup fever hit Luton when First Division Liverpool, losing finalists in 1914, were the next visitors. Another record crowd, 12,640, braved the rain to see the Town almost net in the first minute. A blocked clearance by Don McKinlay provoked a mass free-for-all before the ball was hacked clear.

Dunn was cautioned for fouling Billy Lacey for the third time in as many minutes. But Lacey got his own back when heading in Jackie Sheldon's corner in the tenth minute. Luton goalie Percy Summers – who had fainted in the bath after being kicked on the head in the first Coventry tie – tipped a Harry Lewis shot onto the bar.

In the second period the rain clouds lifted and the sun shone. The game turned on a decision by the referee. Sid Hoar 'scored' for Luton direct from a corner with the goalie and defenders shielding their eyes from the sun. The Town players felt that Kenneth Campbell in the Liverpool goal had touched the ball, but the referee thought otherwise and ruled it out. A rule change seven years later would have allowed the goal to stand, but in 1920 a corner-kick was tantamount to an indirect free-kick.

Lacey netted a second with twenty minutes left. Liverpool reached the quarter-finals, where they were knocked out by Huddersfield.

LUTON: *Summers, Elvey, Dunn, Urwin, Rutherford, Parker, Hoar, Roe, Simms, Dodd, Bookman.*

LIVERPOOL: *Campbell, Longworth, McKinlay, Bamber, Wadsworth, Bromilow, Sheldon, Lacey, Miller, Lewis, Pearson.*

~~~~~~~~~~

Talk of amalgamating the Football League and Southern League dated back to 1909. Now, in 1920, the deed was done and the First Division of the Southern League became Division Three of the Football League. At the same time, out went Luton's light blue shirts and white shorts, and in came the black and white which supporters have come to associate with the Town. For two Kenilworth Road stalwarts, however – Fred and Bob Hawkes – Football League status came too late. They were fast approaching forty.

KENILWORTH ROAD HEROES: **Fred Hawkes**

Born in Luton in April 1881, Fred Hawkes was the original schoolboy football star. After turning out for the Town's junior side, Stanley, where he played alongside his namesake Bob, it was no surprise when he signed for the Strawplaiters. After two seasons in the reserves he made his first-team debut as an inside-forward as the club dipped out of the Football League in 1900. In the Southern League it was not long before Fred made a half-back position his own, and he formed a partnership with Bob Hawkes and Fred White which was the mainstay of the side for several seasons.

Although not tall, Fred compensated with good anticipation, a firm tackle, coolness in tight situations, and excellent distribution. A model of consistency, Fred was also lucky with injuries and did not miss a Southern League game for over six seasons. His tally of over 500 Southern League appearances is remarkable when four years' actions were denied to him by the Great War. A one-club man, with only a bid from Chelsea slightly turning his head, Fred bowed out in 1920 but continued playing into his fifties.

~~~~~~~~~~

KENILWORTH ROAD HEROES: **Bob Hawkes**

Bob, no relation to Fred, was born in Breachwood Green in October 1880 and played junior football in Luton before signing for the Town on amateur forms in 1900. He took time to make his breakthrough in the first team, but once established there was no looking back. Bob looked nothing like a footballer, but his slight frame belied a rare talent and it was not long before he was regarded as the best left-half in the country.

A true amateur for most of his career, Bob rejected overtures from Football League clubs and remained loyal to the Town throughout. Picked for England, Bob won many amateur international caps as well as playing a part in England's gold medal winning football side in the 1908 Olympic Games. His caps are still on display at Kenilworth Road.

It was always thought that his aversion to heading the ball was down to a gold plate under his ginger hair which protected an old skull fracture. Bob, though, thought that football should be played with the feet and preferred to bring the ball down before playing an inch-perfect pass out of defence. On the occasion of Bob's wedding in September 1909 the club's directors asked him what he wanted as a present (something they had never done for any other player). After much thought he decided upon a piano.

After the wedding Bob wrote a letter giving thanks for the 'splendid instrument' which was a 'beautiful present'.

Bob eventually turned professional in 1911-12 and was at once made the highest paid player at the club. Like his namesake Fred, he also finished his Luton career at the end of 1919-20, and after a short period at Bedford, retired from playing and went back to his old hat-making trade.

~~~~~~~~~~

At the start of the first season in Football League Division Three, 1920-21, supporters could be forgiven for doubting the ambitions of the directors when the full-back pairing of Jack Elvey and John Dunn were transferred to Bolton and Sheffield Wednesday respectively, especially when the team then lost 1-9 at Swindon on the opening day.

Ex-Dunstable Road schoolboy (where the author also went) Elvey was looked on as a future England international, having already played for the FA on a tour to South Africa, and the massive fee of £2,500 reflected this. Elvey was paid half that figure by way of benefit, but later the Football Association made him donate 50 per cent to charity. Sadly, his career was cut short after a botched cartilage operation. This was common enough in the days before laser and keyhole surgery.

As it turned out, the full backs were not missed. Ready-made replacements George Lennon and Alf Tirrell stepped in, and with Ernie Simms back to his best – he banged in 28 goals – the club finished a creditable ninth out of 22 and also enjoyed their best FA Cup run to date.

An indication of security concerns can be seen in the club's request for takings from each Saturday's home game to be lodged with Luton police station over the weekend. The request was agreed to.

Another sign of changing times can be seen when Harry Higginbotham became the first Luton player to be sent off in the Football League. It happened at Portsmouth on 8th September 1920 and was followed by Allan Mathieson being expelled at Southampton on Christmas Day. 'Mathieson's offence cannot be disputed, but the decision was autocratic and reflected a pettish disposition. What happened was this. Parker [Southampton], in order to stop Simms and Mathieson, deliberately handled the ball within three yards of the goal. Simms made an attempt to force the ball through, but it rebounded to Mathieson who shot over. Mathieson and Simms appealed for a penalty but the referee waved for play to continue. The exuberant Mathieson, in a determined effort to get the referee to reconsider, took hold of the official's coat and was promptly ordered off.'

In the days when sendings off were so infrequent that players could more or less get away with murder, the word of the referee could never be questioned. To actually touch the official was a heinous crime as Mathieson found out when he received a massive two-month ban.

KENILWORTH ROAD CLASSICS: **Luton v Preston** – 2-3

FA Cup, Round Three, 19th February 1921

Luton's record FA Cup run began at Second Division Rotherham County, predecessors to today's United, in the sixth qualifying round. A 3-1 win – a Simms hat-trick – was rewarded with a home tie against Division Two leaders, and eventual champions, Birmingham City in the first round proper. A record crowd of 12,700 saw Simms and Louis Bookman score the goals in a 2-1 win. Controversially, when City were given a penalty, Luton full-back George Lennon stood by a goalpost as Blues' Jack Jones drove his kick wide. A complaint was later made by Birmingham to the Football Association and Lennon was called to account as the dispute hit the national press. The matter seems to have been brushed under the carpet, as far as the Town were concerned, although the referee was eventually censured by the FA. There appears to be no further instance of a player distracting a penalty taker in such a way, and presumably the present law, which states that all players must be on the field of play and that no outfield player may be behind the goal-line, possibly stemmed from that incident.

In the second round Luton went to Second Division South Shields, where a record crowd of 21,003 gathered at the Horsley Hill ground. The players had stayed at a Whitley Bay hotel over the previous week and, suitably relaxed, tore into their opponents. Harry Higginbotham opened the scoring against his old club in a 4-0 win.

The Town were through to the last sixteen for the first time, and were pitched at home to First Division Preston, who had thrashed Watford in the previous round. Such was the huge interest that parts of Kenilworth Road were made all-ticket, and when the turnstiles stopped clicking all previous gate records had been smashed. The final figure was 17,754 beating the previous best by over 5,000, and it is difficult to see how so many could have squeezed into the ground as it was then.

The only area with crush barriers, installed before the Birmingham tie, was the clinker banking behind the Kenilworth Road goal. Their flimsy structure was confirmed when one gave way before the kick-off, as did part of the perimeter fence. Spectators perched on roofs and up telegraph poles and some two dozen with Lane stand tickets were unable to get through the crowds. It is a marvel that no one was injured or even killed in those far off days before Health and Safety legislation.

The game was a cracker, with England international centre-half Joe McCall cancelling out Ernie Simms. Luton had more chances but could only put away two – both coming from Harry Higginbotham – while at the other end Preston had four efforts, with Tommy Roberts netting three and hitting the bar. The pressmen bemoaned Luton's luck, but the club could count record receipts of £2,226.

LUTON: Bailey, Lennon, Tirrell, Molyneux, Parker, Lamb, Hoar, Higginbotham, Simms, Butcher, Bookman.

PRESTON: Causer, Doolan, Speak, Waddell, McCall, Mercer, Rawlings, Jefferis, Roberts, Holland, Quinn.

~~~~~~~~~~

The police tracked down an airman from RAF Henlow and arrested him for taking a ball from Kenilworth Road after the Preston Cup-tie. He was up before the local magistrates the following week.

It was hoped that the 1921-22 season, now with Third Divisions South and North, would see a tilt at the title. The new campaign opened well, with the Town amongst the leading pack from the start. So highly was their forward line regarded that an unprecedented three players were picked for international duty. On 22nd October 1921, Ernie Simms was chosen to lead the English front line against Northern Ireland in Belfast. Opposing him were Luton's right-flank pairing of Louis Bookman and Allan Mathieson.

Belfast-born Bookman, who had changed his name from Buckhalter to disguise his Jewish origins, was a dazzling winger. His partner, the bulky but twinkle-toed Mathieson, was a goal-taker of class. Both had been capped previously, though for Simms this was to be his international debut. None of the Luton trio covered himself in glory – to the glee of the London press, who demanded representatives from Arsenal, Tottenham and Chelsea – and none was capped again

At Kenilworth Road the Town fielded a team shorn of three of their better players, as there were no postponements for international call-ups in those days. The depleted side still overcame fellow title-chasers Portsmouth 1-0, with reserve centre-forward Billy Walsh scoring the all-important goal.

KENILWORTH ROAD CLASSICS: **Luton v Swindon** – 2-1
Football League Division Three (South), 27th December 1921
With only the champions promoted, the fate of most clubs was clear by Christmas. The 1921-22 season, however, was closely fought and by the turn of the year a dozen teams were still in contention. The Town had gone ten games without defeat and had drawn 1-1 at promotion rivals Swindon on Boxing Day. Although Luton were without the injured Sid Hoar, Jimmy Walker, John Foster and Ernie Simms, the return game the following day enticed a record league crowd of 15,761. They saw the Robins score after ten minutes through future Hatter Bert Davies. Luton struck the bar twice before Harry Higginbotham headed in a Bill Molyneux cross just on half-time. Ten minutes later a cross from George Butcher was fumbled into his own net by Swindon keeper Len Skiller. Although they pushed forward, Swindon could not find a way past the Luton defence.

LUTON: Bailey, Lennon, Tirrell, Molyneux, Walsh, Roe, Bassett, Higginbotham, Mathieson, Butcher, Bookman.

SWINDON: Skiller, Weston, Maconnachie, Ing, Archer, Dawe, Denyer, Davies, Metcalfe, Johnson, Turner.

~~~~~~~~~~

The 1921 FA Cup run had bought home to the directors the fact that the ground lacked the necessary facilities to accommodate a large crowd. In particular, the thirty-year-old grandstand was nowhere near big enough. In March 1921 a deputation of directors paid a visit to Southend United's Kursaal Stadium to inspect the new stand erected there by Humphries of Knightsbridge. Liking what they saw, they asked the builders to quote for a new stand at Kenilworth Road, only to turn white when given a figure of £9,000. The project was quietly shelved, the directors citing the poor industrial outlook for the country.

But a year later, on the night of Saturday, 11th March 1922, the main grandstand was consumed by fire, despite the efforts of the Fire Brigade.

'Charles Green, the club's long serving secretary who lived in Hazelbury Crescent, was in bed when he was notified of the fire by a Mr King of Kenilworth Road. Mr King had seen a small blaze, but by the time Mr Green arrived on the scene seven or eight minutes later the whole of the stand, offices and dressing rooms were well alight and it was impossible for the Fire Brigade, who arrived soon afterwards, to get the flames under control until every part of the stand and rooms underneath were destroyed. There was hardly a bootlace left. The Fire Brigade had been notified from three street alarms, the final communication being received from Walsh, the Town half-back, who was informed of the outbreak when returning from a whist drive at the Commercial Cars premises. Chief Officer Andrew saw at once that the only useful work the Brigade could do was to prevent the fire spreading to other parts of the ground, and in this they were successful. Nothing of any value was recovered from the debris.'

On the Monday following, the players needed to acquire new boots and equipment, and as the club's bath had been destroyed they had to use the public baths. The visit of Brighton scheduled for Saturday, 18th March, was re-arranged and played at Brighton, while the reserves played their Brighton counterparts at Kenilworth Road. The club filed an insurance claim amounting to £3,481 – presumably the cost of replacing the stand like for like – to Royal Exchange, of which Luton director Ernest Gibbs happened to be an agent. The claim was settled at £2,100 within a month of the fire.

A quarrel arose as to who was entitled to the insurance money, the landlords or the club? The former agreed that, provided they received the claim money, they would ensure the construction of a new stand.

For as long as this writer can recall, it was common knowledge that the 'new' stand arrived 'second hand' from Kempton Park racecourse. The club's minutes do not mention this, the local press is silent, and the minutes of Kempton Park show that no stand was taken down, demolished or sold at any time around this period. Although the Kempton Park rumour would appear to be an urban myth, aerial views of Kenilworth Road soon after the new stand went up show that it was not purpose built, but was a rectangular box with a piece sliced off to fit the contour of the railway line. Perhaps the stand had been ordered ready for erection elsewhere, only for the buyer to pull out, leaving the Town's landlords to pick up the tab for a knock-down price. The truth is anyone's guess.

In any event, the new stand, which according to reports cost £8,227, was ready for the start of the following season. At a grand opening ceremony prior to the visit of Charlton on 26th August 1922, Mr J McKenna, President of the Football League, hoisted a flag in front of almost 12,000 spectators before toasting the King.

In the same month as the fire, the Town's directors declined an invitation to tour Sweden in the summer, on the stated grounds that the itinerary would have required playing games on Sundays.

Neither the fire nor the tour (supposing they knew of the invitation) appears to have affected the players, who finished fourth in 1921-22, albeit nine points adrift of champions Southampton. The summer saw the departure of Bassett, Bookman and Mathieson. Together with the loss of Simms, who had moved to South Shields in March, it meant that Luton's forward line was somewhat threadbare.

New season, new stand, and a new crowd favourite in the shape of young Welshman Sid Reid who, although only 5ft 6in, netted eighteen goals as the Town enjoyed another useful season, finishing fifth. The youngsters introduced had settled in well, and spectators sensed better times ahead.

KENILWORTH ROAD HEROES: **Billy Lawson**

At the end of the 1922-23 season came news that trainer Billy Lawson, a fixture at the club for thirty years, was to retire. A larger than life character – a boxer of no mean ability in his youth, as well as an athlete of renown – Lawson's sunny disposition lit up Kenilworth Road as he trained and treated several generations of Luton Town players.

Born in Luton, Lawson arrived as reserve team trainer in 1893 before taking charge of the first team four years later at a wage of thirty shillings (£1.50) a week. He survived several skirmishes with the committee in his early years, some probably over wages, and some certainly over alcohol, but matters settled down and he proved not only loyal – turning down moves to larger clubs – but also good at his job. On retirement from Kenilworth

Road he was awarded a benefit against Arsenal in December 1923, which raised over £100. He later set up business as a masseur in the town.

~~~~~~~~~~~

Despite optimism that 1923-24 would see a crack at the championship, a very poor start – with only one win in seven games – meant that the team was always playing catch-up. By the end they could only climb to seventh. Reid was unable to maintain the form of the previous campaign, leaving the goalscoring mantle on the shoulders of new man Andy Kerr, who had been recruited from Scottish junior football.

Discipline problems also raised their head, with two Luton Town players dismissed, both at Kenilworth Road. First to go was full-back Joe Till, sent off during a tempestuous match against Exeter, then ex-boxer George Butcher was dismissed against Norwich. Butcher's punishment was a month's suspension.

Supporters began to question the ability of the Board to scout for players, sign them and then pick the team. Most clubs by this time had a manager (often termed a secretary-manager) in charge of team affairs, but when this was mooted at Kenilworth Road one director, Ernest Gibbs, who looked upon himself as a judge of no mean ability where players were concerned, threatened to resign.

In 1924-25 the team got off to another slow start. This time it was Kerr who was unable to repeat his goalscoring prowess of the previous season. By February 1925 the Board bowed to the inevitable and appointed the club's first proper manager, although they still reserved for themselves the right to pick the team!

George Thompson seems a strange choice inasmuch as he had no managerial experience. He arrived after a career as a journeyman right-winger for Sheffield United and Derby. Aged forty at the time of his appointment, Thompson – who was to be paid £300 per annum salary – set about adding weight and height to the team and conducted a major clear-out at the end of the 1924-25 campaign.

Billy Lawson's replacement as trainer was Fred Westgarth, who appears no less colourful. He was summoned before the Board to explain reports that he had struck one of his assistants. Such was his impassioned plea for leniency that he was told 'to be more careful next time'. The reprieved Westgarth did not last long in Luton, for the new manager wanted his own man and appointed Billy Barr, whose experience extended not only to training teams in Britain but also in Germany and Switzerland.

In October 1924 a local benefactor offered the club the loan of a billiard table. It was to be placed in the players 'recreation room', where it was hoped to engender a better team spirit. Unfortunately, the club had so such recreation room, so had to go to the expense of kitting one out.

Season 1925-26 saw four new players make their debuts. They appeared no better than those released in the summer and, following five defeats in six games through September into October, Thompson was relieved of his duties. His departure left the directors, who were in no hurry to appoint a replacement, back in full control of the playing side of the club.

One lasting legacy of George Thompson's short reign was the signing of his namesake, the charismatic Jimmy, who turned out to be a goalscorer of rare ability. Thompson's goals enabled the Town to finish seventh, and only one place lower the following season, 1926-27.

KENILWORTH ROAD CLASSICS: **Luton v Millwall Athletic** – 6-0

Football League Division Three (South), 25th December 1926

The Town were a footballing side, playing the ball along the ground rather than launching it down the pitch. This approach did not always work in Division Three, at a time when the game was more 'robust', but if a strong referee clamped down on thuggery, Luton could turn on the style.

Millwall were the visitors on Christmas Day 1926. With both clubs in the leading pack, 9,447 came to see the Lions thrashed. Although Millwall resorted to 'unfair tactics', the referee was having none of it. Luton took a 3-0 interval lead with goals from John Black, Norman Thomson and Sid Reid. In the second period the Town toyed with the opposition. Reid completed his hat-trick, with the sixth goal coming from Harry Woods.

Luton had, they thought, avenged a 0-7 hiding at The Den the previous season, and travelled there again two days later intent on giving the Lions another lesson. 'Crusader' of the *Luton News* takes up the story: 'For some time I have wondered how long it would be before opponents were found who would take mean advantage of the Town's sporting style of play. By the irony of things it came in the season of goodwill, for on Christmas Day Millwall Athletic could not accept defeat as sportsmen should and several of their players were guilty of the meanest tricks yet conceived. In spite of that we saw skill triumph over brute force, largely because the official in charge insisted on literal interpretation of the rules. Alas! The same official could not take the return match at New Cross (the new referee came from London!) and from the kick-off it was clear that several of the Millwall players were out to win by means without any qualification to fairness at all. Kicking, hacking, brutal charging, kneeing, elbowing and in two cases blows – such was the so called play that there was not one of the players required by the Town that did not show severe damage on his body. In thirty years experience of serious football I have never seen a team suffer to the extent that Luton suffered and take it so meekly.'

Luton were kicked off the park. Reid had to retire, injured, and the ten men capitulated to the tune of 0-7 for the second season running.

LUTON (both games)*: Harper, Graham, Till, Black, Rennie, Millar, Pointon, Thomson, Reid, Woods, Thompson.*

MILLWALL: Lansdale, Fort, Hill, Amos, Bryant, Graham, Chance, Moule (Gomm), Parker, Phillips, Gore (Black). (At The Den in brackets).

~~~~~~~~~~

Following the installation of the new stand at Kenilworth Road, little was done to the rest of the ground throughout the 1920s, other than erect 6ft netting behind the Oak Road goal to prevent the ball from breaking nearby windows.

As has been stated before, Health and Safety left a lot to be desired in those days, so the smell must have been overpowering for the local Sanitary Inspector to condemn the urinals at the ground, as happened on two separate occasions during the decade. It is hoped that HRH The Prince of Wales, who presented colours to the 2nd Battalion of the Beds and Herts Regiment at Kenilworth Road in November 1926, had no need to use the facilities.

Alcohol problems continued to rear their head. The Town's directors tried to put the Eight Bells and Granville public houses out of bounds for players, after tales of misbehaviour filtered back to them, but after taking legal advice they found they could not impose such a restriction. They were on stronger ground when trying to prevent players from driving those new fangled motor cars, but only to the extent of being able to withhold wages should any player be unable to play due to a motor accident.

With Jimmy Thompson taking his shooting boots to Chelsea in the summer of 1927, Luton were left toothless in front of goal. Once the team lost the first four games of the new season, the directors once again decided to divert the flack by appointing a team manager.

The appointment of John McCartney was both brave and bizarre. No stranger to these parts, having played for the Town with distinction in the 1890s, McCartney had gone on to make a name for himself as manager of Barnsley, St Mirren, Hearts and finally Portsmouth, who he had lifted from Divisions Three to One. He had resigned from Fratton Park only three months earlier, on the grounds of ill health, but presumably the 61-year-old felt sufficiently recuperated to resume his career.

He was appointed as secretary-manager on a three-year contract at £416 per annum. Long-serving secretary Charles Green had his nose put out of joint when asked to step aside to become financial secretary and company secretary. Both were grand titles but everyone knew they represented a demotion and a curtailing of powers he had enjoyed for years.

To accommodate McCartney, the directors purchased the house at 24 Kenilworth Road for £875, which they then rented out to him for £1 per week. His immediate task was to lift the club from the re-election positions.

The centre-forward problem was solved when, out of desperation, centre-half Andy Rennie – who had scored one goal in 53 league appearances – was moved up front and responded by banging in 24 goals. His strike partner, Jimmy Yardley, a recruit from Clapton Orient, netted 23 times as the Town rattled in 94 goals. That sharpshooting enabled the Town to finish thirteenth, by which time McCartney's ill health had returned and he was hospitalised, manager in name only.

Part of Luton's revival might have been down to the decision to generate passion in the crowd by including a 'chorus' in the match programme.

'Zee-la-zee-baa! / Zee-la-zee-baa!
Luton bella! Luton bella! / Ching! Ching! A-Chinga!
And we shall be for Luton! / For Luton! For Luton! For Lu-ton!
Wa-a-ah!'

The days of innocence on the terraces!

With no sign of McCartney returning to work, the club reduced his salary by 50 per cent in May 1928 and, that summer, appointed a new trainer-coach in ex-Bolton and West Ham stalwart George Kay. This meant the club had two trainers. Horace Pakes – who had been assistant trainer for over thirty years – had been promoted the previous summer, but now found his authority usurped by the new recruit. Pakes accepted the new situation with good grace. Not so Charles Green, who decided to retire just short of his sixtieth birthday. For his services to the Southern League he was presented with a medal, and from the Town the proceeds of a testimonial game against Hearts.

KENILWORTH ROAD HEROES: **Charles Green**

A career administrator, Luton-born Charles Green had participated in local football from his youth and was involved with Luton Wanderers before becoming caught up with the affairs of the newly formed Luton Town. He became secretary in 1901 and was the administrative rock who bore the brunt of the move to Kenilworth Road. He ensured the club survived the Great War, no easy task given the Government's views on spectator sports. Living in nearby Hazelbury Crescent, Green was always on call and after his retirement in 1928 continued to support the club he loved.

~~~~~~~~~~

As the 1928-29 season commenced, with McCartney back at the club on part-time duties, makeshift forward Andy Rennie demanded that he be returned to the half-back line. It is as well that McCartney and his lieutenant George Kay managed to talk sense into him, as Rennie went on to break all records when scoring 43 goals, leaving the Town within an ace of promotion. Not only was Rennie, obviously, the club's top scorer, but he shared with Sunderland's Dave Halliday top billing for the Football League.

KENILWORTH ROAD CLASSICS: **Luton v Gillingham** – 8-0

Football League Division Three (South), 13th April 1929

Luton were early leaders, with six straight wins, but a pre-Christmas slump saw them overtaken by Plymouth. Apart from a week in March 1929, when they went top after a 5-2 home thrashing of Newport, Luton were always in the chasing pack. But then, after losing at Charlton on Good Friday, three undefeated games saw them just two points off the top.

The visit of Gillingham attracted a reasonable crowd of 7,278. A penalty given for handball was converted by hot-shot Rennie. The Gills were then reduced to ten men when defender Harry Bruce had to retire injured. From that moment it was The Andy Rennie versus George Hebden Show. Hebden shone in the Gillingham goal, but according to match reports could do nothing about the eight goals that flew past him, which 'would have beaten any goalkeeper'. Rennie's five took him to 41 for the season and eleven from five games, as teammates teed him up. By the end, Luton were only one point off the top. Sadly, only one point was picked up from the final four games, and Charlton sneaked through on the blind side.

LUTON: Banes, Kingham, Richards, Clark, Fulton, Millar, Daly, Yardley, Rennie, Woods, Bedford.

GILLINGHAM: Hebden, Wilson, Tyler, Bruce, Crawford, Forsyth, Legge, Taylor, Hanney, Dowell, Poxton.

~~~~~~~~~~

Season's end saw McCartney's contract cancelled 'by mutual consent' but strangely he was retained for three months at a salary of £6 per week, when the position would be reviewed. No explanation was given, particularly as McCartney wrote the minutes, but the decision was presumably taken on health grounds. Boardroom changes were announced, with Chairman Harry Arnold stepping down to become Club President and Life member. He had joined the Board in 1893 and been Chairman since 1897. Another long server, Harry Smart, was also made a Life Member, while the chair was taken up by Ernest Gibbs, who had shadowed Arnold since Victorian times. Of greater significance was the appointment of a younger breed of director, including local builder Charles Jeyes, who was set to oversee success for the club over the ensuing two decades.

The minutes note that in April 1929, terracing gave way during a game which prompted a compensation claim from a spectator for severe bruising. The claim was dismissed. Also, nine passes had been issued to players for their wives. 'Sweethearts could also be issued passes if applied for.'

1929-30 saw Luton in mid-table. The loss of Rennie through injury did not help, but the youth policy nurtured by McCartney did not bear fruit. He resigned on 31st December 1929, citing ill health. George Kay was named new manager on New Year's Day 1930.

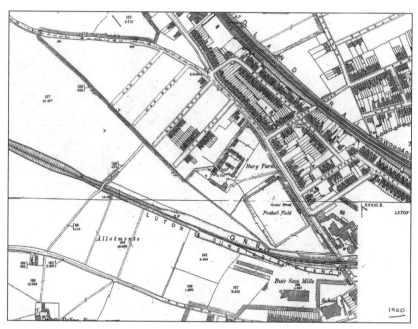

Ordnance Survey map from 1900 showing the future site of Kenilworth Road. Also
shown is the Dunstable Road ground, plus the remnants of the Dallow Road ground
(Bute Saw Mills)

A map of the same area 23 years later

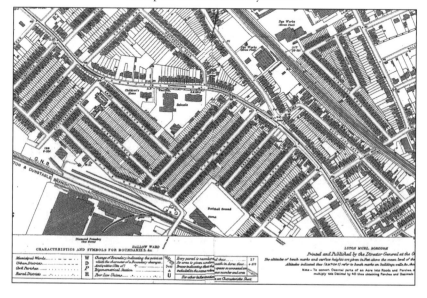

The Town players line up before the first ever game at Kenilworth Road

An Edwardian photograph looking towards the Kenilworth Road end

Cox, Luton.]

THE NEW LUTON TOWN ENCLOSURE AND GRAND STAND.
Luton v. Millwall, Southern League competition, 1905-6.

Another Edwardian photograph, this time looking towards the old main stand

Looking towards the Oak Road end in the Edwardian era

W. H. Cox, Luton.]

A CAPITAL VIEW OF THE NEW IVY ROAD ENCLOSURE, THE HOME OF LUTON TOWN
FOOTBALL CLUB.
Match, Luton v. Portsmouth, Southern League competition, season 1905-6.

An unusual view looking over the back of the Kenilworth Road terrace, around 1912

The wooden planks of the Oak Road end would be denied a Safety Certificate today

Chapter Two

The Second Quarter-Century

1930-1955

New manager George Kay could do little to resuscitate the 1929-30 season, which saw the Town finish a disappointing thirteenth, but during the summer he revisted his old club West Ham – who he had captained in the first FA Cup final at Wembley in 1923 – and signed Tom Hodgson for £100. Little did he know that Hodgson would stay involved with the club for over fifty years as player, director, chairman and finally president.

The new campaign, 1930-31, got off to another poor start but after Christmas things improved and, with Andy Rennie now fully fit, after an injury-hit period during the previous season, the team finished a creditable seventh. Supporters were right to wonder why the players could not have performed during the first part of the campaign as well as they had the second, for that season the division was there for the taking.

The Town and Clapton Orient really got to know each other that season. Paired in the FA Cup, the teams drew 2-2 at Luton but the Town were victorious in the replay at Highbury. Arsenal's ground was used because the authorities had decreed that the fence surrounding Orient's new Lea Bridge enclosure was too close to the pitch, leaving the playing area too small if the lines were re-drawn.

With Luton still in the Cup, the home league game with Orient was switched to Monday afternoon, 15th December, but no one appears to have told the officials, who failed to turn up. A local referee was eventually found and, after borrowing a whistle from a police officer, started the game almost an hour late. With the away side leading 4-3, bad light and fog eventually caused the contest to be abandoned with twenty minutes left, which was hardly a surprise, given the time of year.

When the game was finally played, the Town lost 0-1 in a bad-tempered clash which saw ace marksman Andy Rennie dismissed for the only time in his career. 'He dared me to pull his nose so I did,' said Rennie afterwards. For nose-pulling read 'thumping', which was not the thing to do right in front of the referee. Rennie's subsequent suspension meant that he missed the away league game at Clapton, which the Town lost 2-3.

KENILWORTH ROAD CLASSICS: **Luton v Thames Association – 8-0**
Football League Division Three (South), 11th April 1931
Thames Association Football Club enjoyed a brief, exciting, but ultimately unsuccessful life in the East End of London as a club formed to play at

the new West Ham Stadium at Custom House. Born in 1928, Thames was the brainchild of a quick-talking showman who wanted a football club to fit in alongside his speedway team and his greyhound racing. Immediately accepted into the Southern League, it was only two years before the club was voted into the Football League. Albeit situated in a densely populated area, Thames were on the doorstep of West Ham and Clapton Orient, with Arsenal and Tottenham not much further away, and it is little wonder that they struggled to attract big crowds from the off. This must have been particularly galling to the men in charge, who saw spectators dotted around a stadium that had accommodated 64,000 for speedway and 56,000 for greyhound racing. When the Town visited Thames in December 1930, only 469 turned up, which was a new low for a Saturday game, a Football League record which stands to this day. Luton received a postal order for 1s 8d in respect of their share of the gate, which was framed and hung on the boardroom wall.

Such was the Town's poor form in the first half of the season that they went down 0-1 to Thames in the East End fog, although in mitigation the players had just got through a tough FA Cup replay only two days before. By the time of the return, the Town were in a rich vein of form but were surprised when Thames took the initiative and were the stronger side for the opening fifteen minutes. George McNestry then opened the scoring against the run of play, before Archie Clark netted from the spot after a Thames defender handled the ball. Robert Bryce and Jimmy Yardley then scored before the interval and as the players left the pitch the crowd of 6,029 could hardly believe the scoreline.

The second half started the same as the first, with Thames having all the play, only for the Town to net four more in the final twenty minutes, with McNestry, Yardley, Jackie Slicer and Archie Heslop all on the scoresheet. For the record, Thames finished bottom of the table in the following, 1931-32 season, did not seek re-election and quietly folded never to be seen again.

LUTON: *Harford, Kingham, Hodgson, Clark, McGinnigle, Fraser, Heslop, McNestry, Yardley, Bryce, Slicer.*

THAMES ASSOCIATION: *Bailey, Donnelly, Smith, Warner, Spence, Igoe, Le May, McCarthy, Perry, Phillips, Mann.*

~~~~~~~~~~

As the 1930-31 season drew to a close, money problems re-surfaced, as they have done with glum regularity throughout the club's history. The upshot was to transfer half-back Archie Clark to Everton for £1,250. Clark had been the Town's record signing in 1928, but this counted for nothing as he became yet another of the 'family jewels' sold to keep the club afloat. Although the thoughts of manager Kay are not recorded, he was no doubt miffed at the transfer. Only a few days later he was on the point of signing a new contract himself when Southampton of Division Two stepped in to offer him the rewards of a buying club rather than a selling one.

The Town's directors acted quickly: just two weeks after Kay's departure they appointed Harold Wightman to the hot seat at a salary of £300 per annum plus the free use of the club-owned house at 24 Kenilworth Road. Wightman, who the previous season had been assistant manager at promoted Notts County, had garnered a reputation as one of the game's new breed of 'thinkers'.

Whether he questioned the Board's ambitions is not known, but only two months after pleading abject poverty they splashed out an extraordinary £1,800 on two Bolton Wanderers players, Fred Kean and Tom Tait. The arrival of ex-England international half-back Kean and highly regarded goalscorer Tait was seen as a major coup, and was perhaps an indication of the new progressive attitude of the Board.

Behind the scenes, though, it soon became obvious that the Town could not afford such an outlay. When the team failed to make a meaningful impact in the 1931-32 season, and it was realised that the bold bid to 'chase the dream' would not materialise, costs had to be cut and player sales became inevitable. In March 1932 centre-forward Jimmy Yardley was sold to Charlton for £850, and young winger George Turner, who had made only sixteen appearances in the first team since signing the previous summer, went to Everton for £1,000. On the face of it, the books had been balanced but the Town took a further eighteen months to finally pay off Bolton for the two buys, despite many threats by Wanderers of reporting the matter to the footballing authorities.

KENILWORTH ROAD CLASSICS: **Luton v Wolverhampton** – 1-2

FA Cup, Round Three, 9th January 1932

With all the off-field money problems facing the club, a good run in the FA Cup was vital, and after a 5-0 win at Swindon and a 4-1 replay victory over Lincoln, the reward was a home tie with Division Two leaders Wolves. A crowd of 16,945 turned up to see Wolves take the lead, when Wilf Lowton scored from the spot after Hugh McGinnigle handled a goalbound shot. This fifth-minute upset did not upset the Town unduly, and if they had taken their chances they would have been ahead at the interval.

Presumably something was said to the Wolves players at half-time, as during the second period they pulled the home defence all over the place before Charlie Phillips doubled the lead after showing clever anticipation to convert a cross. The game was not without its twists, though. With Wolves relaxing in the final quarter, the Town put on a grandstand finish. Jimmy Yardley volleyed in Andy Rennie's cross with five minutes to go and then saw a shot hit a defender on the goal-line, then a post, before going out of play.

LUTON: Imrie, Kingham, Hodgson, Kean, McGinnigle, Fraser, McNestry, Tait, Yardley, Rennie, Slicer.

WOLVES: Whittaker, Lowton, Lumberg, Rhodes, Hollingsworth, Richards, Phillips, Bottrill, Hartill, Deacon, Barraclough.

~~~~~~~~~~~

During the summer of 1932, boxing and wrestling tournaments were staged at Kenilworth Road in a bid to raise funds to pay the players' wages over the close season, as well as try to make inroads into the debt owed to Bolton. Any money raised, though, was spent on bringing Tom Mackey and Davie Hutchison from Sheffield Wednesday and Carlisle United respectively. It can be seen that the Board were clearly desperate for promotion, but their mishandling of the financial side of the club was worrying, and surely they would never have subjected their own companies to such mismanagement.

The next bombshell was the issue of greyhound racing at Kenilworth Road. In October 1932 a request was made from a Mr Lewis Cooper to bring dogs to the ground. Having first verified Mr Cooper's credentials with the National Greyhound Association, the club's directors then sent a deputation to Watford's Vicarage Road, which had a greyhound track, and Bristol Rovers' Eastville, another elliptical ground which offered plenty of room for greyhound racing.

The club put forward a business proposition that a lease be granted for seven, fourteen or 21 years on the basis of £4,000 up front, and then £500 per annum rent for the first seven years, £650 for the second seven years and £750 for the third. Also, any damage to the pitch to be made good at the track-owners' expense.

The greyhound consortium came back with a counter bid of £20,000 for the ground, lock, stock and barrel. This was accepted by the Board subject to approval and license by the National Greyhound Association. That approval was not forthcoming, presumably because it was obvious that Kenilworth Road was not suited for anything that involved a track being laid, unless, of course, the club decided to seek an alternative home.

On the pitch, if not the track, fortune smiled on Luton Town Football Club in the shape of a magnificent run in the FA Cup, which took the Hatters through to the quarter-finals for the first time in their history.

KENILWORTH ROAD CLASSICS: **Luton v Tottenham** – 2-0

FA Cup, Round Four, 28th January 1933

The Town's FA Cup first-round pairing with Isthmian League Kingstonian hardly caused much excitement, given that the Town had never previously got anywhere near the Twin Towers of Wembley. Kingstonian were just about the strongest non-league outfit around, as proved by their lifting of the Amateur Cup at the season's end, and their league championship the following year. A crowd of 7,701 gathered at Kenilworth Road to see the Town lucky to escape with a 2-2 draw. The replay was no easier, watched by a then record crowd at Richmond Road, but this time the Hatters scraped through 3-2.

It was off to uncharted territory in the next round, with the club's first ever meeting with Stockport County of Division Three (North). The final score of 3-2 to the Town flattered County, whose second goal only came in the last minute. Their goalkeeper, Thomas Gale, was blamed for two of the goals, including one from the Town's Fred Kean, which looked to be drifting wide, catching him unawares.

A 0-0 draw at Barnsley, again of Division Three (North), brought the Tykes back to Luton, where prolific marksman Andy Rennie bagged both Luton goals. FA Cup euphoria now swept through the streets of Luton, as mighty Tottenham would be the visitors for the fourth-round tie. Although 'only' a Division Two side, Spurs were on their way to promotion and boasted a proud FA Cup pedigree, having already won the trophy in 1901 and 1921.

Tottenham supporters, confident after their team's 6-0 win at Oldham in the previous round, started arriving early on match-day, having caught the first available trains out of London, and by 7.30am were staging an impromptu kickabout on the Moor. By noon queues stretched down Hazelbury Crescent and two hours later the gates were closed with 17,213 in the ground. Some 21 coaches from London were parked along Dunstable Road and the site of the old Town ground was used as an over-spill car park.

The pitch was hard and icy, and would doubtless be regarded as unplayable today, but the Town's groundstaff employed a steamroller in the morning to iron out the ruts and at least make the playing area flat. With the gates closed, exhibitionists paraded round the pitch in fancy dress, one using frying pans as cymbals. Such was the crush that youngsters were allowed to sit in front of the perimeter walls and fences.

Luton adapted better to the conditions, for within twenty minutes they were two goals to the good, courtesy of strikes from Tom Alderson and Tommy Tait. Both efforts had been set up by Arthur Mills, deputising for the injured Rennie. For Spurs, Taffy O'Callaghan's shot that hit the bar was the closest they came. During the final minutes the roar from the crowd became deafening, and on the final whistle thousands rushed onto the pitch to chair off their heroes. This match represents the earliest known film footage of a game at Kenilworth Road.

Luton: Harford, Kingham, Mackey, Kean, McGinnigle, Fraser, Mills, Nelson, Tait, Alderson, Roberts.

Tottenham: Nicholls, Felton, Whatley, Colquhoun, Levene, Meads, Howe, O'Callaghan, Hunt, Hall, Evans.

~~~~~~~~~~

The Town's reward was an anticlimactic trip to Halifax, 2,000 supporters travelling to the Shay to swell the crowd to a record 29,235. Halifax, another club new to Luton, had seen off Darwen, Workington, Doncaster and Chester and were confident of progressing to the quarter-finals for the first time ever.

Luton travelled up on the 9.02am train, due to arrive at 2.00pm, just an hour before kick-off. The Town had taken the trouble to write to the London, Midland & Scottish railway informing them of the importance of the engagement. Although the train arrived on time, snow was falling heavily and the lines of the pitch had to be swept. Tait fired Luton ahead on twenty minutes, but in blizzard conditions the referee soon called the players off. They were off for half an hour and there was a danger the game would not finish. At half-time the players changed round without any break, and with yet more snow falling Alan Nelson made the game safe by tapping in after a shot from Rennie was parried by the goalkeeper.

By now, it was felt that the Town could go all the way. Even when it was announced that Everton at Goodison Park were to be the opponents in the quarter-final, it was seen as merely a stepping stone on the inevitable march to Wembley. Three special trains, one of which had a huge boater mounted on the front of the engine, and countless motor coaches carried several thousand Luton supporters to Liverpool. When the turnstiles stopped clicking, 55,431 spectators were present, generating receipts of £4,143, a vast sum. This time the players travelled up on the Thursday and stayed at Southport.

With Alderson's injured shoulder ruling him out, Mills returned, but commentators did not feel this would affect the shape of the team. The choice of Rennie to play inside-forward rather than central striker did, however, raise eyebrows. As it turned out, Rennie was clattered early on and played out time limping on the wing. Everton were already one goal to the good, with the Town finding difficulty in adapting to the wide open spaces of Goodison. If the game had been staged at Kenilworth Road, doubtless Everton, like Tottenham, would have struggled within its cramped confines.

Although Kean had his sights on adding to the FA Cup winners medal he had earned with Bolton in 1929, Everton's forwards seemed to breach the Luton defence at will. It ended 6-0, and it was scant consolation to the Town that they received a handsome share of the huge gate, that the great

Dixie Dean only scored once, and that their cup run meant exemption to the third round next year. These were hollow rewards when the players felt they would win the Cup. That honour went to Everton, who overcame Manchester City 3-0 in the final.

To spur the Hatters on the road to Wembley a ditty was composed in rhyming couplets:

'O, *Play up the Town!' let spectators all shout,*
And let the team know there's Strawhatters about;
Let everything go with a cheer and a swing,
Encourage your forwards, and goals it will bring.
Let your shouting back up every movement to score,
Cheer up your defenders with many a roar.
Don't let the team think you don't care if they lose,
For this thing is certain, 'they' will win if 'you' choose.
So, 'Play up the Town!' let your shouts reach the sky,
If you back up your team, they'll never say die;
Don't grumble and grouse, meet reverse with a grin.
To boo your own team is a shame and a sin.

KENILWORTH ROAD CLASSICS: **Luton v Brentford** – 5-5
Football League Division Three (South), 1st February 1933
Four days after the historic FA Cup win over Tottenham came a rearranged league game against the Bees. Without floodlights, the game had to be played in the afternoon, and with many supporters convinced of a postponement – the previous Saturday's ice having turned to mud – only 3,044 turned up. They saw Tommy Tait's hat-trick help the Town to a 4-1 interval lead. Brentford, heading for the title, fought back and by the end the Town were hanging on at 5-5. Jack Holliday scored all five for Brentford, still a club record, while the scoreline represents the only 5-5 league draw for the Hatters.

LUTON: *Harford, Kingham, Mackey, Kean, McGinnigle, Fraser, Mills, Nelson, Tait, Alderson, Roberts.*

BRENTFORD: *Baker, Stevenson, Hodge, Ware, Bain, Burns, Hopkins, Walsh, Holliday, Scott, Crompton.*

~~~~~~~~~~~

Since the erection of the new stand in 1922, there had been no further changes to the ground, and by 1933 it was beginning to look tired. Behind the Kenilworth Road goal was a cinder bank, while along the Beech Hill Path side and behind the Oak Road goal was wooden plank terracing. All this was open to the elements, as was the Maple Road end of the Main Stand. This was another cinder bank known as 'Scotch Corner', in view of its proximity to the 'Scotch colony' in the streets off Dallow Road which had migrated to Luton from Falkirk with the Davis Gas Stove company.

As the ground was still not yet owned by the club, one of the first measures introduced by new chairman Charles Jeyes – who replaced the long-serving Ernest Gibbs in April 1933 – was to enter into negotiations with the landlords for its full and final purchase. The £8,037 originally agreed with the landlords back in 1923 had been whittled down to £5,000 by successive lump-sum payments by the club over the years, and an overdraft was now arranged with Westminster Bank to complete the transaction. At long last, the football club now owned the ground, subject, of course, to a bank charge.

Heartened by this news, the Supporters Club redoubled its efforts to improve the facilities. It raised the not insignificant sum of £690 needed to cover the Beech Hill Path side as far as Ivy Road and concrete the terracing. This was carried out during November and December 1933 and was christened the 'Bob Stand' later changed to 'Bobbers', as it cost a bob (one shilling = 5p) to stand there.

KENILWORTH ROAD CLASSICS: **Luton v Torquay** – 10-2

Football League Division Three (South), 2nd September 1933
During the summer of 1933 new chairman Charles Jeyes warned manager Harold Wightman that anything other than improvement on the fourteenth position in 1932-33 would not be tolerated. Wightman responded by culling his playing staff, retaining only ten from the previous campaign. Of the new intake, the majority had played in Division One at some time. George Martin, who had played alongside Dixie Dean at Everton – and who was later to manage the Hatters on two occasions – was the most famous of the new signings, but Bill Pease from Middlesbrough had played for England some seasons before.

The new season kicked off at neighbours Northampton, with the Town notching their first away win since Boxing Day. The 3-2 score was a personal triumph for centre-forward Tom Tait. His hat-trick took his Luton tally to 46 in only 70 starts since signing from Bolton two years previously. The first home game came two days later, on Bank Holiday Monday, against relegated Charlton. A crowd of 11,904 saw Tait on target again in a 2-1 victory, with that other prolific marksman, Andy Rennie, netting the other. This game marked the return of full-back Tom Mackey who, having reported for pre-season training, went off to apparently join the Police Force. The matter was eventually sorted out, with the Town writing to the Chief Constable of Durham to say that Mackey was under contract. The no-nonsense defender duly resumed his illustrious Town career, which continued in a coaching capacity once his playing days were over.

The second home game, the following Saturday, was to prove an attendance barometer as far as the directors were concerned. They were pleased when 10,745 paid to see if the good start could be maintained at the expense of Torquay. Tait was out, having injured a leg during training. His place was taken by Tom Bell, whose first professional club had been Torquay. Coincidentally, Torquay included Albert Hutchinson, who started his career with the Hatters.

Both sides had difficulty in controlling the bouncing ball, but Town were in control by the time Rennie tapped in after twenty minutes, following unselfish play by Bell. The Hatters were denied a penalty ten minutes later when Torquay's Don Welsh handled a shot from Martin, but a second goal arrived from Rennie after a strike from Bell rebounded off the bar. Bell headed against a post and shots from Rennie and skipper Fred Kean were well saved by Percy Maggs in the Torquay goal.

The Torquay players came out for the second half and soon reduced the arrears when Welsh scored direct from a free-kick after Martin had up-ended George Stabb on the edge of the box. For a time, Torquay had the upper hand, but when Welsh punched away a cross from Martin the referee allowed Kean to score from the spot.

Bell then got the goal his unselfish play deserved when he headed home a cross from Pease. Two minutes later, George Pearson set up a simple chance for Rennie. Straight from the restart, Bell took the ball past two defenders and the goalkeeper to walk it into the net. Luton had scored four goals in five minutes. After another five minutes Martin shrugged off a foul by Torquay's Lew Tapp to shoot past the advancing Maggs, and Martin backheeled number eight after a cross from Pearson rebounded off a defender.

Torquay then scored themselves when, with the Luton defence scattered, Hutchinson headed in a long cross. But in the last minutes Pease netted before Rennie knocked in his fourth and the Town's tenth. The 10-2 win was a record for the Town, but the exploits of Joe Payne, a couple of years later, erased it.

LUTON: Mittell, Kingham, Mackey, Kean, McGinnigle, Fraser, Pease, Martin, Bell, Rennie, Pearson.

TORQUAY: Maggs, Fowler, Tapp, Lievesley, Welsh, Pickersgill, Steele, Harker, Stabb, Hutchinson, Ryder.

~~~~~~~~~~

Sadly, the Hatters' promising start to the 1933-34 season could not be sustained and frustratingly inconsistent form saw crowds fall away. Although the Town stayed up with the fringes of the promotion chase, it was all too much. What was needed was another extended run in the FA Cup competition.

KENILWORTH ROAD CLASSICS: **Luton v Arsenal** – 0-1

FA Cup, Round Three, 13th January 1934

In view of their recent Cup exploits the Town were granted exemption to the third round for the 1933-34 competition. As a further reward they were pulled out of the hat to play mighty Arsenal, the team of the 1930s. Admission prices were hiked threefold, but this seems to have been grudgingly accepted by the supporters, such was the drawing power of the Gunners. In scenes reminiscent of the Tottenham tie twelve months earlier, visiting fans started arriving from London on the milk trains, waking up the good folk of Luton with their rattles and bells. The gates were closed before kick-off with a new record crowd of 18,641 present, and every vantage point, including the roof of the new Bobbers Stand, was seized. Those on the roof were moved both for their own safety and also for that of the spectators below them.

In the shock of the decade, Arsenal had lost at Walsall of Division Three (North) at this stage of the previous year's competition and were determined not to become headline news for the wrong reasons again.

Understandably, the game was tense. With few chances created by either side it seemed to be petering out, but with fifteen minutes left Luton half-back Charlie Fraser was hurt in a tackle. A gap appeared on the right, where Fraser would normally have been stationed. England winger Cliff Bastin took advantage and skipped down the flank before putting over a cross that was headed home by Jimmy Dunne. The Town could not reply and had to be content with their share of the £3,000 gate.

LUTON: *Harford, Kingham, Mackey, Kean, McGinnigle, Fraser, Pease, Martin, Bell, Rennie, Hutchison.*

ARSENAL: *Moss, Male, Hapgood, Jones, Roberts, John, Coleman, Bowden, Dunne, Bastin, Beasley.*

~~~~~~~~~~

With the growth in population in and around Luton, the club's Board was determined to provide Division Two football, as they felt that the support would be forthcoming. Although crowds had dwindled following the slump in form, the average attendance was still 2,500 higher than in 1932-33, which gave them the necessary confidence to 'go for broke' once more. Over the course of the 1934-35 season the seeds were laid for a side that would eventually be claimed as one of the club's finest. George Stephenson was signed from Aston Villa, Fred Roberts from Birmingham, goalkeeper Joe Coen from Bournemouth, and a promising wing-half from Bolsover Colliery by the name of Joe Payne.

Long-time servant and record scorer Andy Rennie had now reached the veteran stage and was replaced in October 1934 by prolific marksman Jack Ball. But not even Ball's thirty goals could fire the Town to promotion.

KENILWORTH ROAD HEROES: **Andy Rennie**

Andy Rennie was born in Baillieston, Glasgow in 1901 and played his early football for Paisley Waverley and Kilwinning Rangers, where he came to the attention of Luton trainer Billy Barr, who recommended him for trials. Originally a goalkeeper, Rennie had switched with considerable success to centre-half and it was in that position that he made his debut for the Town against Millwall reserves at Kenilworth Road just before Christmas 1925.

He was such a success that his retention was never in doubt and he signed professional forms long before his four-week trial was up. After a good grounding with the reserves, a full league debut came his way, at centre-half, in a 4-1 win against Swindon at Kenilworth Road in February 1926, and he retained his place until the end of the season.

Rennie made 35 appearances, all at centre-half, in the following campaign, scoring his first goal in the process. Then, early in 1927-28, when the Town were struggling to find a suitable centre-forward – following the departure of Jimmy Thompson to Chelsea – Andy was asked to have a go in that position and the rest, as they say, is history.

Andy scored in his first game as centre-forward and went on to become the club's top marksman that season with 24. He was just warming up, notching 43 goals in 1928-29! That was almost half the Town's total that season and included five against Gillingham, who were thrashed 8-0 at Kenilworth Road. This feat meant Rennie proudly topped the list of leading goalscorers in the country that season, alongside Halliday of Sunderland.

The following season began in the same vein and included a hat-trick at Watford as the Hatters trounced the Brewers 4-0. But in a 2-2 draw at Torquay at the end of October 1929 Andy was crocked as the result of a bad foul. He was on the injured list for almost four months – but still managed to end up as the Town's top scorer. It was generally reckoned that Rennie never truly recovered from that injury, with the result that he was eventually moved over to inside-left, where his passing abilities came to the fore. He set up numerous chances for the new owners of the No 9 shirt, including Tom Tait and, in later years, Jack Ball.

Despite all this, Rennie was still top goalscorer in 1930-31 and again in 1933-34. His left-foot drives were legendary and, according to my late grandfather, he had a habit of 'swinging his leg from the hip' before connecting with the ball.

Because of his goalscoring prowess, Rennie suffered at the hands of many crude defenders, and although he had a quick temper – earning him the nickname 'Ratty' Rennie – he was only sent off once during his career. On that particular occasion he said afterwards, 'He [the defender] dared me to pull his nose, so I did.' Obviously 'pull' and 'thump' had the same meaning pre-war.

Following a 0-1 defeat at Reading in December 1934, Rennie lost his place to Fred Roberts, and at the end of that campaign he was granted a free transfer. He had played a total of 385 games for the Town, in all competitions, scoring 184 goals which would have made him a multi-million pound player today. His goalscoring record is all the more remarkable when it is remembered that his early career at Kenilworth Road was spent in defence. Trials followed at both Walsall and Newport which came to nothing and he decided to hang up his boots and take a job at JW Green's brewery in Luton.

Three years later Rennie was admitted to the Bute (St Mary's) Hospital in Luton for a routine hernia operation. Although successful, complications set in and Andy died from pneumonia on 5th September 1938, aged 37, leaving a widow and two young children.

Tributes poured in and 'Crusader' of the *Luton News* divulged a couple of instances of his generosity. These included handing over a week's wages to a wizened old lady scouring the gutters in Merthyr, and on another occasion he paid the train fare from Exeter to London for some other poor unfortunate.

~~~~~~~~~~~

As the 1934-35 season approached its climax, a double bombshell hit the club. Billy 'Buster' Brown, who had finally come good after several seasons at Kenilworth Road, and top scorer Sam Bell – who had arrived at Luton from Norwich for £100 at the end of the previous season – were sold to Huddersfield and Tottenham respectively. Both transfer fees were over £2,000 and represented an outgoing record for the club.

Supporters were up in arms over the decision to sell these major assets at such a crucial time, and threats were made in the local press to boycott the club. The directors had, however, been canny. They realised that even if the Town won all their remaining games they still would still have missed out on promotion. So the decision was taken to cash in on nearly £5,000, which was added to the war chest ready for a fresh tilt at the title the following year. It gives no great pleasure to report that neither player set the world alight after leaving the Hatters.

The one sad departure that particular season for which the Board could not be blamed, was that of wing-half Charlie Fraser, then at the peak of his powers. His leg fracture during the Aldershot home game became folklore in Luton as the snap 'like a gunshot' could be heard all around the ground. Fraser would never play again, which made it three players in five years – the others being Sid Reid and Tommy Hodgson – who were forced into early retirement following injury.

During that season, in December 1934, there was an extraordinary fight-back at Southend. The home side were awarded a second penalty for handball shortly after the break. Luton skipper Tom Mackey disputed the decision to such an extent that he was first booked and then sent off. Southend scored from the spot to put them three up, but so aggrieved were the ten men of Luton that they fought back to level.

Sendings-off before the Second World War were extremely rare, and the Town were not untypical in having only seven dismissals during the period 1920-39 in first-team games. Most of these were for outright thuggery right under the nose of the referee.

KENILWORTH ROAD CLASSICS: **Luton v Chelsea** – 2-0

FA Cup, Round Three replay, 16th January 1935

In 1934-35 the Town enjoyed another bye into the third round of the FA Cup, and drew another plum tie in the shape of Division One Chelsea at Stamford Bridge. The Town were going through a topsy-turvy period where they would win by four goals one week, then lose by four the next. Chelsea were in comfortable mid-table.

A crowd of 46,492 saw the Town give one of their better performances and it was no real surprise when Sam Bell forced the ball home, following a corner, five minutes before the interval. The goal was disputed, as many in the ground felt that the ball had not crossed the line. The London press later tried to prove the impossible by dangling a ball from the crossbar to demonstrate how photographs can be deceiving, especially when taken from anywhere other than on the goal-line. The goal stood and it was not until the last ten minutes that Chelsea pushed everyone forward in an effort to equalise. This they did, when James Argue shot through a crowd of players to take the tie back to Luton.

Despite the midweek afternoon kick-off, there was huge interest in the game, as realised by the town's major employers who anticipated a major walkout. Skefco, George Kent, Vauxhall, Electrolux, Davis Gas Stove Co and all the hat factories bit the bullet and closed from mid-day. Only the first two companies asked employees to return after the match to make up for lost time.

The gates at Kenilworth Road were closed thirty minutes before kick-off, but such was the pressure of those outside that the Kenilworth Road end gates were forced open and many hundreds gained admission without paying, which added to the crush inside. A posse of police officers had to force a way through to allow the Chelsea players and directors in, while hundreds of spectators perched on the roof of the Bobbers Stand. This time the police were unable or unwilling to remove them, nor the hardy individual who had climbed to the top of a telegraph pole. The official attendance was 23,041, which smashed the previous record by over 4,000, but this figure did not account for those who got in for nothing. The ground was dangerously overcrowded and it is a minor deliverance that no one was badly injured or even killed. By kick-off time, a double line of spectators were on the running track, and rather more on the Bobbers Stand-Kenilworth Road corner, which caused reshuffling every time there was a flag-kick.

Luton were forced into two changes, with Tom Mackey suspended and Billy Thayne injured. Harry Reece and Hugh McGinnigle took their places.

Again Chelsea did not seem to have much stomach for a fight and their attempts to play 'first division football' were doomed to failure against a fired up Luton side. The game remained scoreless until 25 minutes from the end when a throw-in from Charlie Fraser saw Fred Roberts hook the ball into the goalmouth, where Chelsea goalkeeper Jackson parried it out to Jack Ball who shot into an empty net. The second goal was not long in coming. Bob MacAuley was dispossessed by Jack Ball, who played the ball inside to Fred Roberts who smashed it home.

With twenty minutes left, the injured Reece was reduced to a passenger on the wing, but even then Chelsea could not raise themselves. At the final whistle Luton supporters raced onto the pitch to chair off their heroes.

Sadly, the Town went out at Burnley in the next round, but the cup run had put a few more pennies into the pot. Remarkably, several honest supporters sent in postal orders to pay for their gate-crashing.

LUTON: Coen, Smith, Reece, Brown, McGinnigle, Fraser, Crompton, Bell, Ball, Roberts, Stephenson.

CHELSEA: Jackson, Barber, MacAuley, Russell, Craig, Miller, Spence, Argue, Bambrick, Gibson, Horton.

~~~~~~~~~~

After the new terracing was built on the Bobbers side at the end of 1933, three members of the Supporters Club sought to utilise the space underneath. One Saturday morning the intrepid trio dug their way in with borrowed implements to commence a project that would occupy their every weekend for the best part of eighteen months, by the end of which tons of soil had been removed. The fruits of their labour were revealed on 5th July 1935, when new club rooms were opened. They extended virtually the length of the pitch. Considering the time, the facilities were superb. They consisted of a games room and bar, a dining room, as well as a snack bar. These facilities were open seven days a week, with all profits being ploughed back into the football club.

The annual membership was 1s 2d (7p), with life membership of 21s (a guinea) and – in an age or little or no inflation – these fees remained unchanged for many years. The local population also exploited the bar facilities at the Bobbers Club, as most of Bury Park had been built on Quaker-owned land. Conditions imposed with the original sale meant that there would be no public houses allowed.

Luton's final position of fourth in 1934-35 was not good enough for Chairman Charles Jeyes, who had virtually demanded promotion. He made money available that summer to Harold Wightman, who spent it on Jock Finlayson and Billy Fellowes from Clapton Orient, and Jack Nelson from Wolves. All three were set to become firm favourites.

Everyone at the club was confident as the 1935-36 season started, perhaps more so than before any previous season. Whether or not this affected the players, the team got off to the worst start for a decade, losing the first three matches and then drawing the next two.

In these circumstances, the resignation of manager Harold Wightman, on 10th October, was not totally unexpected, but whether he was pushed has never been revealed. The words 'mutual agreement' were put out by the club to the local press. Wightman maintained that he did not need to resign but felt he ought to for the good of the club.

Wightman had assembled the nucleus of a side that was to go on to bigger and better things, but patience was not a virtue of the Board, and most particularly Jeyes, who now had the opportunity to assume a more hands-on approach to managing the team. Wightman, the ex-Notts County man, had turned down overtures from his old club during the summer. He eventually became manager of Mansfield before taking charge at Nottingham Forest until the outbreak of World War II. Wightman died in 1945 aged only fifty.

Whatever went on behind the scenes, the removal of Wightman seemed to work wonders, as the team embarked on a run of twelve wins and a draw from the next thirteen games. The club's league attendance record was broken during this run, when 18,100 turned up to see the 1-0 victory over Notts County on Boxing Day, as the team pushed themselves up from the bottom of the table into the promotion fight. Many supporters felt that the new players would have eventually found their feet anyway, and that the poor early-season form was just a bedding down period.

KENILWORTH ROAD CLASSICS: **Luton v West Ham** – 4-0

FA Cup, Round Three replay, 15th January 1936

For the third year running the Town were granted exemption in the FA Cup until the third round. The pairing with West Ham from Division Two at Upton Park created interest at both clubs, given that both were enjoying a winning run. Over 9,000 Luton supporters made the trip, paying a return train fare of three shillings (15p), and swelling the crowd to 42,000 which was not far short of Upton Park's record.

The Hammers took a quick lead through Dave Mangnall, only for Jack Ball to level. In the second period the Town surprised their opponents by taking control and it was no more than they deserved when Fred Roberts fired in with twenty minutes to go. The contest was not yet over, though, with Jimmy Ruffell earning the Hammers a replay with a late, fortunate equaliser.

The replay was scheduled for the following Wednesday afternoon. A crowd of 17,527, paying receipts of £2,099, turned up to see if the Town could finish the job and extend their unbeaten run which stretched back to 28th September. The game was goalless at the interval, but once Jack Ball bagged the opener after 51 minutes there was only going to be one winner. On a frosty pitch, the Luton players adapted better, and with winger George Stephenson running riot, further goals arrived at regular intervals. Wilf Crompton and then Roberts took advantage of Stephenson's trickery to increase the Hatters' lead, before the winger capped a marvellous performance by scoring the final goal to make it 4-0.

Fleet Street, the next day, glossed over the Luton performance to concentrate on the shortcomings of the West Ham forward line, as well as the state of the pitch. But the Luton fans did not mind, next stop Manchester and a clash with City.

At Maine Road, Wembley dreams ended as the Town lost 1-2, but some consolation was gained by the gate receipts generated by a massive crowd of 65,978, the largest to watch the Hatters in this country outside Wembley.

LUTON: *Coen, Mackey, Smith, Finlayson, Nelson, Fellowes, Crompton, Martin, Ball, Roberts, Stephenson.*

WEST HAM: *Conway, Chalkley, Walker, Fenton, Barrett, Cockcroft, Simpson, Marshall, Mangnall, Goulden, Ruffell.*

~~~~~~~~~~

Having fought their way to the top of the league by Christmas 1935, form in the New Year was patchy and as Easter approached the Town were clinging on to pole position by their finger tips. Draws at Bristol Rovers on Good Friday and at home to Millwall the following day finally meant that top spot had, temporarily one hoped, been relinquished.

KENILWORTH ROAD CLASSICS: **Luton v Bristol Rovers** – 12-0
Football League Division Three (South), 13th April 1936

In the lead up to the return game with Bristol Rovers on Easter Monday the Town faced a centre-forward crisis, with both Jack Ball and Bill Boyd on the injured list. Still without a manager since October, following the departure of Harold Wightman, directors and coaches were left to pick the team. Someone, and to this day no one is sure who, suggested that 22-year-old reserve half-back Joe Payne be given a chance up front.

Bolsover-born Payne, who had spent time as a coalminer as a teenager, had been recommended to the Town by an exiled Lutonian two years before, but his few league opportunities had either been at full-back or wing-half.

Few thought that Payne would make the grade as a professional footballer, and he had recently been loaned out to the club's nursery side Biggleswade Town, where he did not exactly pull up trees. Reporting for duty at Kenilworth Road for the Easter Monday clash with the Pirates, Payne was as surprised as anyone to be thrown the No 9 shirt. He immediately sensed that this was a make or break game, especially as the retained list was shortly to be announced.

A respectable crowd of 14,296 (although ten times this figure later professed to have been among them) turned out on an unseasonably cold day. With sleet lashing their faces the spectators probably had difficulty in recognising the 'new' centre-forward, especially as Boyd had been named in the programme.

Rovers were not going particularly well and the Town were expected to win comfortably, but in the first twenty minutes the two sides were evenly matched. Payne showed a willingness to get stuck in, as was to be expected, but little else. The breakthrough came on 23 minutes when he latched onto a long ball to beat John Ellis in the Rovers goal. Fred Roberts banged another shortly afterwards, getting the final touch when Ellis parried a George Stephenson effort. Payne was now beginning to enjoy himself and he scored twice more before half-time, taking advantage of further clever play from Roberts and Stephenson.

It is said that during the half-time banter someone jokingly suggested that Payne should strive to beat the record of Tranmere's Bunny Bell, who had scored nine goals in a 13-4 thrashing of Oldham the previous year. Sensing that Payne was having one of those days where nothing could go wrong, Stephenson, Roberts and George Martin made sure he saw plenty of the ball in the second half.

The ploy worked, with Payne scoring from a Stephenson centre after 49 minutes, from a Rich centre after 55 minutes, and then a contentious effort two minutes later. Payne had headed towards goal and Martin bundled the ball and the goalkeeper into the net. The referee had, however, ruled that the ball had already crossed the line and awarded the goal to Payne. (The writer's grandfather always maintained that Martin scored the goal but, there again, referees are always right!)

Stephenson set up further goals for Payne in 65, 76 and 84 minutes, before the stand-in No 9 – with the crowd baying for more – took his personal tally to ten. He took a wild swing at the ball whilst on his backside, and succeeded in deflecting it past a wrong-footed Ellis. Martin completed the scoring in the final minute to make it an improbable 12-0 win for the Town, a scoreline which surely will never be beaten.

Many years later, Payne recalled the game with difficulty. 'They told me to go out and get two or three goals if I could, but did not tell me what to do afterwards so I just carried on,' he said. 'Time blurs the memory but I recall the Rovers goalkeeper making as many good saves as the goals he let in. The chances kept on coming my way and after the first five, I had that much confidence I was beginning to think I could do it with my eyes shut, especially after that freak of them all, when I fell over on my backside to fool everybody – but the ball still went in.'

As a sign of the times, Payne picked up a win bonus of £2 to add to his £4 weekly pay, and in the days of the maximum wage the club had to apply to the Football League for a special dispensation to give him the match ball as a souvenir.

Just one representative from the London press was present that afternoon, but news of the amazing scoreline soon filtered through to the football world. One of the first of many telegrams of congratulation received by Payne was from Bunny Bell.

Finally, spare a thought for poor John Ellis who must have cursed the name of the Hatters. Not only had he conceded twelve goals that fateful day, but he had broken his collar-bone in the 2-6 defeat at Kenilworth Road the previous season.

LUTON: *Dolman, Mackey, Smith, Finlayson, Nelson, Godfrey, Rich, Martin, Payne, Roberts, Stephenson.*

BRISTOL ROVERS: *Ellis, Pickering, Preece, Wallington, Murray, Young, Barley, Hartill, Harris, Houghton, Crisp.*

~~~~~~~~~~

Naturally, Payne became an overnight sensation. Of more importance to Luton Town supporters was the fact that the win over Bristol Rovers had pushed the team back into second position, though don't forget that only the champions were promoted in those far-off days.

In top spot were Coventry City. The fixture list had decreed that two of the Town's final four games would be against the Bantams, as City were then called. The Hatters warmed up for the first clash with a 2-0 win at Newport, where the crowd was double its usual size, and where a certain Mr Payne netted both goals.

On 25th April 1936 the Kenilworth Road ground record was smashed yet again, when 23,559 squeezed in, partly to watch Payne and partly to see if the Town could overhaul Coventry at the top. The game itself was an anticlimax. An early Payne goal was cancelled out by City's Clarrie Bourton in the second half. The opening for Bourton's goal was made by ex-Hatter George McNestry. Two days later 42,809 – a record for Division Three

(South) and Coventry City at that time – were shoe-horned into Highfield Road for the re-match. This one ended 0-0, leaving City above Luton on goal-average. With Coventry set to play Torquay at home in their final game and the Town at QPR, City were the obvious favourites, needing only to equal Luton's result. McNestry tried to help his old pals by missing a penalty against Torquay, but two late goals saw City promoted. Town could only manage a scoreless draw. Despite Payne's fantastic late-season efforts, Coventry themselves scored over 100 goals that season.

Having done without a manager for most of the season, the Luton Board decided to advertise the position. From over fifty applicants they decided on West Ham scout Ned Liddell. The new man was a bit of an unexpected choice as, although his scouting abilities were unquestioned, he had not managed for four years and was also 59 years old.

Liddell did, though, inherit the nucleus of a good side. Promotion had essentially been missed the previous season by dropping silly home points, and supporters hoped that this weakness could be rectified and the championship won.

A crowd of 14,461 saw the first game of 1936-37, against Southend. They saw a win – albeit in a dull match – with the lone goal coming from Joe Payne. Liddell was dissatisfied with the performance and promptly dropped Wilf Crompton and Bill Godfrey – they were never to play for Luton again. The re-shuffled team played better in winning 1-0 at Walsall, courtesy of a George Stephenson goal, before a 0-3 reverse at Cardiff forced Liddell into more changes. This time old favourite George Martin was left out, together with Hugh Mills, a player Liddell had brought with him from West Ham.

Winning ways were soon restored. Walsall were seen off 2-0 at Kenilworth Road, followed by Crystal Palace 5-2 and then Reading by a thumping 4-0. The week before the Reading win the Town travelled to Exeter and quickly found themselves 0-2 down. They eventually won 4-2, including a pair of goals from Payne.

Payne's exploits were now attracting the attention of the national press. Those sceptics who thought that his previous season's feat of scoring ten against Bristol Rovers was 'just one of those days' were forced to think again. After all, he had now scored eleven goals in six games. He scored again the following week in a 1-2 defeat at QPR, but not in the next game, when Bristol City were hammered 4-0 at Ashton Gate.

Payne was back with a vengeance in the next game at Kenilworth Road, scoring a hat-trick in a 4-1 win over Watford. The Brewers, as they were then known, opened the scoring before Jack Ball equalised. Tempers became frayed and the Watford goalkeeper was spoken to by the referee for 'pushing Payne's face into the ground'. Luton skipper Jack Nelson took a blow on the head which prevented him from re-appearing for the second half. A groggy Nelson did eventually stagger back on, and somehow set up Payne to put the Town in front. Payne added another from a pass by John Hodge and completed his hat-trick, having been set up by Ball, to send the 20,569 crowd into raptures.

That game marked a temporary high spot. A couple of away defeats – at Brighton and Northampton – brought the team back to earth, but with the team still churning out home wins the Town were nevertheless bubbling around at the top of the table.

It was the away form that, for the time being, gave cause for concern. Yet at promotion rivals Millwall in late November a partisan crowd of almost 33,000 witnessed a surprisingly easy 2-0 victory for the Hatters.

The game was marred by an incident between Nelson and Millwall's Dave Mangnall. The pair had a stand-up fight unseen by the referee, who decided to book them in any case. The match had, however, been watched by Stanley Rous, recently appointed to the FA Council. His report of the incident was instrumental in Nelson receiving a suspension. The arguments raged for weeks as to whether a 'spectator' should have the power to influence the authorities in situations where the referee had not seen the offence.

Nelson had to endure a suspension. The game he missed was at home to Cardiff on 2nd January 1937 – the Town winning 8-1 to avenge their early-season defeat at Ninian Park. Veteran Hugh McGinnigle was summoned from semi-retirement in the reserves to take Nelson's place and must have enjoyed himself in what was to be his last first-team game in a Luton career that stretched back to 1930.

That win put the Town on top of the table. Christmas had started well with a home win over fellow challengers Notts County, but then turned sour with defeats at Southend and in the return game with the Magpies in Nottingham.

Liddell accepted that Joe Payne was best suited to the centre-forward position but that – despite his clever promptings – Jack Ball needed replacing. Crystal Palace's leading scorer, Albert Dawes, was brought in and he responded by scoring in the big win over Cardiff and again the following week in the 4-0 victory at, ironically, Crystal Palace. In that game Payne scored another two but missed a penalty in a contest made one sided by an early injury to a Palace forward who eventually had to hobble off with half an hour left.

The crowds were now flocking to watch Luton and the phenomenal Payne, with 17,193 paying to see the win at Bristol City, and then a ground record of 27,632 witnessing the 3-1 victory at Watford – Payne, inevitably, scoring in both games.

The next home match saw the visit of yet another challenger, Brighton. With the crowd swelled to 19,488 by three trainloads from the south coast, a classic was anticipated. Although the contest was played out on a quagmire, it was end to end stuff. The Town took a first-half lead from a header by Payne, which was cancelled out shortly after the interval. Payne then went off needing treatment for twenty minutes, but returned to inspire the forward line. Stephenson scored with two minutes to go but the thrills were not over. Brighton netted from the restart but the 'goal' was disallowed for offside. From Luton's resultant free-kick, Dawes was sent through and hit a post – all within the space of ninety seconds.

The Luton faithful were now beginning to believe this was going to be their year. Despite the team's 1-2 defeat at Bournemouth, Kenilworth Road welcomed 19,579 for the visit of Northampton. That match had the crowd shouting for different reasons. It descended into a brawl after Luton took a 2-0 lead through Payne and Fred Roberts. Luton full-back Tom Mackey was left a limping passenger on the wing after one particularly nasty challenge, and the referee had to continually lecture the players of both sides for 'persistent rough play'.

For Luton, disaster struck a minute from half-time when Billy Fellowes put through his own-goal. Worse followed when, six minutes after the break, Donal Tolland levelled. The Town reclaimed the lead when John Parris was upended in the box with Payne netting from the spot. The kick took several minutes to convert as the Northampton players argued so vehemently, but the boot was soon on the other foot when Nelson fouled Cobblers forward John Lauderdale, but this time the penalty was blasted wide. The referee had to summon the players to the centre-circle to administer another lecture, but when Roberts was shortly after fouled by ex-Town player and ex-boxer Billy Thayne, it was one offence too many and the big centre-half had to go.

Those precious two points meant the scene was now set for the run-in. Luton and Notts County were neck and neck at the top. A dismal 0-4 defeat at Bristol Rovers did the Hatters' chances no good at all, but in the players' defence, goalkeeper Humphrey Dolman had been incapacitated early on, which limited his movements and left him unable to stop shots he might normally have saved.

With eleven fit men, the Town won 2-0 at Clapton Orient the next week and followed up with a 5-0 thumping of Millwall on Easter Saturday before beating Clapton 2-0 in the return on Easter Monday. Home victories over Gillingham and Aldershot, both 5-2, came within three days in early April, with Payne scoring six, but stubborn County could not be shaken off, and when the Town lost 0-1 at Gillingham with County winning on the same day it looked likely that Luton would be pipped at the post again.

With three games left to play, the Magpies were two points ahead, but with an inferior goal-average. Swindon were seen off 5-1 at Luton, with Payne scoring another hat-trick, but County also won on the same day. Newport were then thrashed 5-0 seven days later, but this time the Magpies lost at home to Brighton. Level on points, all Luton now needed was to win their final home match against Torquay. To do so would earn the championship and promotion.

The players looked a bag of nerves on 1st May 1937, and the 20,755 crowd suffered many scares before Payne scored twice to calm everyone down. At the final whistle the spectators refused to depart until the players had re-appeared to take a bow. The biggest cheer was reserved for Payne, who had managed to bag an amazing 55 league goals over the season, a Town record never likely to be broken.

KENILWORTH ROAD CLASSICS: **Luton v Sunderland** – 2-2
FA Cup, Round Four, 30th January 1937
In view of all the excitement in the league programme during 1936-37, it is surprising to note that Luton also had a fair amount to shout about in the FA Cup. Paired at home to Blackpool of Division Two in round three, 13,892 turned up to see Ted Hancock injured in the opening minutes, limp for a while, then retire early. It was therefore no surprise when Blackpool's Bobby Finan scored after Hatters goalkeeper Humphrey Dolman had parried a hard shot from Dickie Watmough.

Five minutes later Payne equalised following a free-kick, but before the interval Blackpool went ahead again. Jack Nelson, who had a nightmare game, nearly put through his own goal, and John Middleton propelled himself and the ball into the net. When Watmough cut in from the wing to give the Seasiders a 3-1 lead it looked all over for the ten men, but Payne netted from a pass by George Martin, then in a frantic finale George Stephenson sliced the ball in after a ricochet from Martin's shot.

The replay four days later saw around 100 Luton supporters make the long trip, leaving the town by train at six in the morning. The players, meanwhile, enjoyed a couple of days at Cleveleys Hydro. On the eve of the game they trooped to the theatre, and afterwards tuned into the Lynch v Montana fight on the radio. An early defensive lapse allowed Finan to fire Blackpool into the lead but Frank Sloan, who had been forced off the field for attention to a head wound, returned to equalise after intricate play from Payne and Stephenson. From that point on the Town looked the better side. Fred Roberts latched onto a lobbed centre from Jack Hodge before luring the goalkeeper and netting.

Luton's reward was a home tie against champions Sunderland. By now, supporters were getting blasé regarding the procession of big sides arriving at Kenilworth Road. Even so, 20,134 gathered on a misty afternoon to see Roberts hammer two goals in five minutes midway through the first half. Sunderland's initial attempts at retaliation were thwarted by Jack Nelson – now back to his best – and the rest of the Luton defence, but Jimmy Connor reduced the deficit on the hour with a low shot and Len Duns equalised after Dolman pushed out a cross rather than catch or punch it. It was then backs to the wall stuff, but the Hatters held out.

A crowd of 53,235 filled Roker Park for the replay, an incredible figure for a midweek afternoon kick-off. Duns opened the scoring after four minutes when Dolman once more flapped at the ball. Two minutes later Payne netted from close range, but Connor restored Sunderland's advantage on seventeen minutes, despite the attentions of Dolman and Tom Mackey. The clinching goal came from Sunderland skipper Raich Carter. Only two minutes were left when he fired home from the edge of the box. Apart from their share of the gate money, the Town would be heartened to know that they had gone out to the eventual Cup winners.

LUTON: Dolman, Mackey, Smith, Finlayson, Nelson, Fellowes, Hodge, Sloan, Payne, Roberts, Stephenson. (Rich instead of Hodge at Roker Park)

SUNDERLAND: Mapson, Gorman, Hall, Thompson, Johnson, McNab, Duns, Carter, Gurney, Gallacher, Connor.

~~~~~~~~~~~

Luton celebrated promotion with a dinner at the George Hotel, where one of the guests of honour was Stanley Rous, presumably forgiven for the Millwall saga earlier in the season. Also present were members of Luton's redoubtable half-back line from the turn of the century – Fred and Bob Hawkes, plus Fred White. Sweetbreads were on the menu and the gathered throng was treated to Fred Yule, baritone, together with Haydn and his Novelty Quintette. The entertainment cost the club seven guineas (£7.35). Everyone present congratulated Joe Payne on winning an England call-up against Finland, the first Luton player to be capped while at the club since the days of Simms, Bookman and Mathieson in 1921.

The financial cost of promotion was an increase in the club's overdraft to £12,613, but Chairman Charles Jeyes was prepared to at least double that shortfall in his attempt to achieve First Division football.

Before approving ground improvements at Kenilworth Road the Board thought long and hard at relocation, with the Wardown Park Sports Ground being seriously considered. The area was not as built up as it is now, and adequate car parking was available nearby at the new swimming pool in Bath Road. Disapproval from locals, coupled with poor traffic access, was enough to kill off the idea.

In the event, some £30,000 was spent over the summer preparing the Kenilworth Road ground for Division Two football and the crowds it was hoped to attract. Houses were purchased in Kenilworth Road so that part of their gardens could be utilised to extend the terrace behind the goal, while some of the dwellings were refurbished as the club's new offices. The new Kenilworth Road terrace was regarded locally as one of the wonders of the modern world, as it was higher than the Clock end at Highbury. It was proudly announced that the Town's 75 steps with a four-inch rise dwarfed Arsenal's 72 steps with a 3.5 inch rise!

The Main Stand was extended down and over the Maple Road corner, which spelled the end for the standing terrace called Scotch Corner. The only part of the ground left undeveloped was therefore the Oak Road end, but houses adjacent to it were also bought in anticipation of further extension. The Board also attempted to buy twelve houses in Oak, Beech, Ivy and Kenilworth Roads, with the intention of demolishing them, diverting the Beech Hill Path, and thus allowing space for extending the Bobbers Stand. This latter idea did not, however, come to fruition.

It was touch and go whether the stand extension would be completed in time for the start of the new 1937-38 season. The uncertainly was partly caused by a world-wide steel shortage but, despite having to wait until the end of July for the necessary girders, much sweat and toil meant that the ground was just about ready for the big-kick off.

On the field, manager Liddell initially persevered with his promotion-winning side, but with Payne not fully recovered from illness and injury, Bill Redfern and Jack Vinall were signed as cover from Newry and Norwich respectively.

~~~~~~~~~~

KENILWORTH ROAD CLASSICS: **Luton v Aston Villa** – 3-2

Football League Division Two, 1st September 1937

The visit of sides such as Aston Villa truly brought home what promotion was all about, and throughout the summer supporters had ticked off the days since the fixture list had been published.

At the time, they did not come much bigger than Aston Villa, especially at Division Two level, and for this – the first home game of the season – supporters started arriving in the early afternoon for a 6.30pm kick-off. The gates were closed half an hour before the start with some 5,000 locked out. All roads leading to the ground were double-parked with motor cars, and even as far away as Biscot Road vehicles were causing an obstruction should a fire engine or ambulance need to get through. As had happened on occasions in the past, the site of the old Town Ground in Dunstable Road – still derelict because of planning objections – found use as an over-flow car-park.

The ground was by now reckoned to hold 34,000, with the new terrace accounting for almost half of that number. Commentators reckoned the previous attendance record had been smashed, but when the turnstiles had stopped clicking the crowd was recorded at a more modest 25,349. True, this constituted a new high, but many statistical histories – including that of Villa – recorded it as 29,372.

The game got off to a sensational start with the Town scoring almost from the kick-off, Albert Dawes capitalising on a poor Villa clearance. The visitors, looking quicker to the ball, levelled when Jack Maund netted from a breakaway. Payne was causing problems to the Villa defence and restored the Town's lead just before the interval, when he fended off two defenders before firing home.

In the second period Ted Hancock made it 3-1 when he drove home from 25 yards, but when Alex Massie reduced the deficit with a similar long-range effort it was all hands the pumps in the Luton defence. The final whistle sounded with every player, apart from Fred Biddlestone, the Villa goalkeeper, in the Luton penalty area.

LUTON: *Coen, King, Smith, Finlayson, Nelson, Fellowes, Hancock, Dawes, Payne, Roberts, Stephenson.*

ASTON VILLA: *Biddlestone, Callaghan, Cummings, Massie, Allen, Iverson, Phillips, Haycock, Broome, Starling, Maund.*

~~~~~~~~~~~

KENILWORTH ROAD CLASSICS: **Luton v Manchester City** – 1-3

FA Cup, Round Five, 12th February 1938

The Town were exempted from entry until the third round of the FA Cup by right, rather than invitation, following their promotion, but the draw pitted them at non-league Scarborough, which was a no-win contest as far as the Hatters were concerned. A record crowd of 11,162 somehow squeezed into the Seamer Road ground and while the Town enjoyed most of the play a Charlie Ferguson opener was cancelled out before the interval. The Hatters were probably relieved to have a second crack, this time at home, while Scarborough anticipated another pay-day from what would be their tenth FA Cup-tie of the season. This time the Town were far too strong, and with thick mud hindering play down the middle, the home side made full use of the wings, scoring at regular intervals to register a final 5-1 scoreline.

Next up were Swindon Town, old foes from the Third Division. A record crowd of 25,746 packed Kenilworth Road to see the Robins give the Luton defence an early chasing and go close on a number of occasions. The Town dug deep and scored against the run of play two minutes from the interval through Ferguson, who saw his shot deflected past the Swindon goalkeeper. Swindon levelled early in the second half but George Stephenson scored the Town's all-important second goal thirteen minutes from time. Even then the Robins refused to lie down and the Luton defence wobbled on several occasions before the referee finally put the crowd out of its misery.

Luton's reward was a plum home tie against reigning champions and 1934 FA Cup winners Manchester City. The Board, in its wisdom, decided to hike the prices. This generated much bad feeling, with the result that only 21,290 paid for admission. This time it was the Town who were a shade unfortunate, as full-back Tom King had to be carried off. City's first goal was considered to have been offside to everyone in the ground apart from the men who mattered, while their third was a gentle pass-back by Jack Nelson to his goalkeeper Joe Coen, who lost his footing and saw the ball bobble over the line. Payne's last-minute header was too little, too late.

LUTON: Coen, King, Smith, Finlayson, Nelson, Fellowes, Ferguson, Vinall, Payne, Roberts, Stephenson.

MANCHESTER CITY: Swift, Dale, Barkas, Percival, Marshall, Rogers, Toseland, Herd, Heale, Doherty, Brook.

~~~~~~~~~~

By February 1938 the Town were holding course in mid-table, preparing to wind down and reflect on a period of consolidation. As has so often happened with Luton Town Football Club over the years, the word 'consolidation' is not in their dictionary. Following the home match with Bradford on 26th February, it was announced that manager Ned Liddell would be leaving the club. Chairman Charles Jeyes presented Liddell with a silver tea service and an inscribed tray and spoke of the departing manager's integrity and loyalty. He then ominously added that they had not always seen eye to eye and that there were eight 'live' directors on the Board, which Liddell knew when he took on the job. Liddell, in turn, admitted that he could never hope to please all the directors, stopping short of blasting his employers for overwhelming interference, and said that he did not know where he was going next. Within days he had been appointed chief scout at Chelsea.

On the day Liddell's departure was made public, Joe Payne had been made captain for the afternoon, following his morning marriage at Luton Registry Office. His 'secret' wedding was attended by several hundred well-wishers as well as his best man – the provider of so many of his goals, George Stephenson. Despite the adoration with which he was held by Luton fans, less than two weeks later Payne was on his way – to Chelsea!

Whether Liddell had anything to do with the selling of Payne has never been revealed, but the fee of £2,000, one fifth of the sum being touted the previous summer, reflected Payne's susceptibility to ill-health and doubts as to his ability to withstand the rigours of top class football.

Tough full-back Tom Mackey had played over 200 games for the Town without scoring. In one of his final outings, against Burnley at Kenilworth

Road in February 1938, he broke this duck when he scored not once but twice in the 3-1 win. Having been crocked earlier in the game, Mackey was told to limp around on the wing for nuisance value. He took blind pot-shots at two passes, both of which flew into the net.

In March 1938, the ex-Watford manager Neil McBain was appointed as chief scout for the Town, and he was immediately instrumental in bringing Newcastle's Eddie Connelly to Kenilworth Road. This signing proved the spark the team needed to arrest the slide down the table following Joe Payne's departure, and Connelly was instrumental as the Hatters won their last three fixtures of the season to finish in a respectable twelfth place. This was not as healthy as it seems: Barnsley earned just four points fewer and were relegated.

As McBain's influence grew behind the scenes, the directors thought he might as well be given the manager's job, and he was officially appointed on 1st June 1938. McBain was a strong believer in youth, and quickly brought in youngsters such as Doug Gardiner, Horace Gager and, most importantly, Waterlows' marksman, Ampthill-born Hugh Billington. All three players would become major assets for the Hatters. Also arriving, this time for fees, were Tom Dunsmore from Hibernian and James Carroll from Leicester. Despite the club's massive overdraft, the Board were still chasing First Division football, come what may.

~~~~~~~~~~

KENILWORTH ROAD HEROES: **Joe Payne**

Although Payne was spotted playing as a centre-forward for Bolsover Colliery, it was soon decided by those at Kenilworth Road that wing-half was his best position. Payne began to learn his trade in the professional game in the Town's reserves and at the club's 'nursery' side, Biggleswade Town. It is now part of footballing folklore that, due to injuries, Payne was handed the centre-forward shirt on Easter Monday 1936 in a home game against Bristol Rovers and he went out and scored ten times in a 12-0 victory. Life was never likely to be the same for him again. That ten-goal haul was a Football League record, and he established another record the following season when bagging 55 goals as the Hatters won the championship of Division Three (South), and with it promotion.

A place with the England squad on a tour of Scandinavia in the summer of 1937 climaxed with Payne winning a full cap against Finland. With the Town now playing Division Two football, he found the net regularly. Inevitably the big clubs came sniffing around and it was no real surprise when he was transferred to Chelsea in March 1938 for a big fee. The war then took a large chunk out of his career. After a spell at West Ham when peace resumed, he retired at the age of 34, dogged by ill-health.

~~~~~~~~~~

One item for which the Board did not have to find money was ground improvements. Due to the generosity of the newly named Bobbers Stand and Supporters Club, cash was raised to put a roof over the Oak Road end and also replace the wooded terracing with concrete.

The 1938-39 season did not get off to a good start, as 24,377 watched the Town go down 0-3 at West Brom on the opening day. Matters had not greatly improved by late October, so out went goalkeeper Humphrey Dolman, defenders Tom Smith and Joe Loughran, together with striker Jack Vinall. They were replaced by Joe Coen, Tom King, Fred Roberts – who was moved from the forward line – and most controversially Hugh Billington.

Billington had netted fourteen goals in fifteen reserve-team appearances and manager McBain felt he was ready for the step up. He did not disappoint, scoring twice on his debut in a 3-2 win at Tranmere and followed up with another pair at Bury two weeks later. In that particular game the Town were two goals down at half-time but equalised within two minutes of the restart. The travelling Town directors missed both goals, but as Luton scored a further three they at least went into the boardroom at the end of the game with smiles on their faces. It is said that only then did they learn the correct score.

With Billington continuing to score regularly, including four in the 5-0 home thrashing of Chesterfield, the Hatters were climbing the table. Sadly, a week after the Chesterfield win skipper and centre-half Jack Nelson badly broke his nose at Millwall. Such was the subsequent form of his young replacement, Gordon Dreyer, that Nelson never played first-team football for the Town again.

With the Hatters scoring heavily, winning regularly, and playing particularly well away from home, bigger clubs started to take note. Large offers totalling £18,000 were made for Dunsmore, Billington and 'the cleverest inside-forwards in the land' Redfern and Connelly. To accept the offers would have meant a substantial reduction in the club's overdraft, but they were resisted in the hope of reaching Division One, which looked distinctly feasible as Easter approached. For once, the holiday period proved successful, with home wins over Southampton (6-2) and Fulham (2-1), and a 4-0 victory at the Dell. When the Town won 2-1 at fellow promotion aspirants Chesterfield the following week, a tremendous climax seemed in prospect.

Unlike in the divided Third Division, champions and runners-up from Division Two earned promotion. With three games to go, five points would have seen the Town up among the elite, but nerves set in and the 20,109 who witnessed a frustrating 0-0 home draw with Millwall, when the team did everything but score, feared the worst. A 0-2 defeat at Newcastle watched by only 10,341, meant the end of the promotion dream, and to cap a disappointing finish to the season, Coventry completed a double by winning 3-1 at Kenilworth Road on the final day.

On the plus side, Billington finished with 28 goals from only 27 games, to finish top scorer in Division Two. Moreover, he only scored in half the games he appeared in, which makes his record even more remarkable.

At the end of that final game, at home to Coventry, police had to draw truncheons to clear the pitch of around 1,000 spectators, many of whom were brawling. The crowd had been restive from the start, when they learned that three players would be 'rested' and reserves picked in their place. Rumours abounded that this was to prevent the Board from paying out bonuses. When a young lad was hauled from the Oak Road end by heavy-handed police for throwing a screwed up piece of paper onto the pitch, it was if the blue touch-paper was lit, for it sparked terrace anarchy which was most unusual for the time.

The major football talking point in Luton during the 1939 close season centred on the resignation of Neil McBain after only a year in charge. The explanation given was a difference of opinion with the board on policy, although it was also known that his wife had been ill and was anxious to return to Scotland. Again the parting of the ways was mutually agreed, with no bad words bandied about by either party.

The Luton Town Board was in no hurry to appoint a successor and left the team under the control of coach, and former Luton inside-forward, George Martin. Martin and the Board arranged the transfer of clever forward Bill Redfern to Derby in exchange for Reg Stockhill, plus a cash balance, and also engineered the departures of Tom Smith and Joe Loughran to Burnley. Smith and Loughran had both been dropped the previous November following a poor home showing against Sheffield Wednesday and were desperate for a move. The Town, in turn, needed to reduce the wage bill and also make room for some promising youngsters coming up through the ranks.

Most promising of all was young Hugh Billington, who scored twice as the Town started off the new season in emphatic style by beating Sheffield Wednesday 3-0 at Kenilworth Road. All the goals came in the first half and even when the Hatters were reduced to ten fit men, after local lad Horace Gager became a limping passenger, the Owls were unable to trouble the Luton defence.

The crowd that day was only 12,357 which was well down on the average for the previous season. Since the players had reported back for pre-season training, war with Germany had looked increasingly unavoidable, with Hitler massing his troops on the borders of Poland. Unsurprisingly, many people had more important things on their minds than football.

The players still had a job to do, however, and a 3-0 win at Bradford Park Avenue, with Billington again scoring twice, continued the perfect start to the season. By now, the evacuation of children from London had started and the police requested that the kick-off at Luton's third game of the season, at Fulham, be put back to 6.30pm to ease traffic congestion in the capital. With all other games having finished, the Luton players knew that one point would be sufficient to take them to the top of the table. Billington, inevitably, fired the Town ahead against the Cottagers. That lead was held until the second half, when Ronnie Rooke's equaliser turned out to be the last competitive goal scored for seven years. The following day, 3rd September, war was declared. The Hatters therefore remained top of Division Two throughout the hostilities.

Player contracts were immediately suspended and all competitions cancelled. This total ban was soon lifted, though. Some friendly games were arranged by the end of the month and regional competitions organised in October 1939.

During World War I, football was actively discouraged as an improper pastime for fit young men. This way of thinking had changed by 1939, especially as it was likely to be a different type of war, and sport was encouraged as a morale-booster. Restrictions were imposed as to the size of crowds, especially in the more 'at risk' areas of the country, but as the war stretched from months to years the major problems facing clubs were more prosaic – kit, footballs, and most importantly, players.

Every club in the country used 'guest' players. The Town were no different, and amongst the dozens who turned out in Luton colours were England international Eddie Hapgood and future Liverpool manager Bill Shankly. Teams such as Aldershot had the pick of the local Army barracks and for a long time could boast an England international half-back line, not to mention Tommy Lawton in attack.

Many wartime tales were told of spectators being hauled out of the crowd to make up the numbers, of referees not turning up, and games being started with less than eleven on each side. It was considered important, though, that the sport should continue through thick and thin.

Although Kenilworth Road emerged from the war unscathed, unlike grounds such as Old Trafford, St Andrews and Highfield Road, the Town did have more than their fair share of problems attracting decent players to turn out for them.

Organised wartime football was regionalised, for safety and travelling reasons. The Town were placed in a Midland Division in what remained of the 1939-40 season, and then in Southern Regional Leagues thereafter. During that first season the Town beat Coventry 7-0 at home but lost 2-10 away, and over the next few years suffered some horrendous beatings. They conceded eight goals on six occasions, nine goals four times, as well as a ten, two elevens, and a 3-12 hammering at Southampton. That 7-0 thrashing of Coventry was a certainly a one-off.

Full use was made of Kenilworth Road during the war years, with boxing and wrestling bouts a regular occurrence. There was even an exhibition baseball game between the Brooklyn Dodgers and the St Louis Cardinals in the final stages of the war, to cater for the many American servicemen in the area who needed entertaining.

Although peace resumed in 1945, there was far too much dislocation for the Football League to resume that year. So for the 1945-46 season, regional North and South leagues were put in place, allowing returning servicemen to be demobbed in time for the following season. Four Luton Town players never did return. Joe Coen, Charles Ladd, Charles Clark and James Gillespie were all killed during the hostilities.

In the interests of continuity, the Football League decided to replicate the 1939-40 fixture list for the coming 1946-47 season. This meant the Town once again kicked off against Sheffield Wednesday, with a much healthier crowd of 21,105 in attendance. Only two Luton players, Hugh Billington and Horace Gager, remained from the pre-war game, but the new-look side assembled by manager George Martin looked every bit as good as that of seven years before.

Martin had been upgraded from coach to manager in December 1944, and had lost no time in building a squad ready for the resumption of 'proper' league football. Amongst his signings were pre-war favourite Eddie Connelly, who had been at West Brom, and ex-England international Frank Soo, picked up from Leicester for a record £5,000.

The big crowd seemed impressed by the Town's performance against the Owls in the 4-1 win. Mel Daniel, another relative newcomer, netted a hat-trick, a feat matched by only one other player, future-Hatter Jesse Pye – then of Wolves – elsewhere on that opening day.

Martin's buying was not over: he went to Sheffield Wednesday to bring back Allen Driver, who was intended to complement Billington, for another record fee, and in a masterstroke that had far-reaching consequences, acquired veteran winger Dally Duncan from Derby as player-coach.

KENILWORTH ROAD CLASSICS: **Luton v Newcastle** – 4-3

Football League Division Two, 30th November 1946

As the first post-war season, 1946-47, wore on, lack of consistency, injury problems and dismal away form combined to ensure that the Town struggled to force their way above mid-table. The home record was the saving grace, however, with only one defeat suffered from the first seven games. The previous visitors, before Newcastle, saw the league attendance record broken yet again. Tottenham returned to north London following a 2-3 beating.

Newcastle were a different proposition, though, and sat proudly at the top of the division, having suffered only two reversals from the opening sixteen matches. They boasted a forward line that included Jackie Milburn, Roy Bentley, Charlie Wayman and Tom Pearson, all big stars of the day. As if that was not enough, they had recently added to their firepower by bringing Len Shackleton from Bradford Park Avenue. Shackleton, who had netted six goals on his Newcastle debut, as Newport went down 0-13, had signed for a post-war record fee £13,000 and threepence. Bradford had insisted on the threepence in order to beat the previous record set a couple of months previously, when Albert Stubbins went from Newcastle to Liverpool.

Naturally, this Geordie 'circus' attracted immense crowds wherever it went, and Luton was no exception, with 25,410 packing the terraces and all turnstiles locked well before the start. As older Luton Town supporters will confirm, the pitch used to slope slightly towards the Oak Road end. That meant that from about October onwards an area of the pitch extending from that goalmouth out to the Bobbers Stand was a muddy morass. Whichever side was defending that end was at a disadvantage. Against Newcastle, that was the Town's lot in the first half. Defenders had difficulty in turning and, when up against the Magpies' slick interpassing, the Hatters were always going to be up against it.

Goals from Bentley after twelve minutes, Wayman after 26 and a cracker from Shackleton on the half-hour put the Town in a seemingly impossible position. As the Luton players trudged off at half-time, the supporters must have wondered what the final Newcastle tally would be. Left-winger Dally Duncan, when interviewed some years later, shed light on the half-time team-talk given by George Martin. Red-faced with rage, Martin kicked over a bucket of water on entering the dressing room. Having calmed down a little, he stressed that the Town had not played badly, Billington had caused problems in the Newcastle defence as well as hitting a post, and they would now be attacking the swamp-like Oak Road end. Also, the undue reverence given to the Magpies had to stop forthwith!

Suitably chastised, the players set out to rectify matters, hoping that one goal could spark an avalanche. That goal was not long in coming. Billy Waugh converted a Duncan cross in the 54th minute, and when Mel Daniel headed in a Duncan corner two minutes later the crowd began to believe that anything was possible.

When Billington ploughed through the ooze to thunder home the equaliser on the hour the crowd was in uproar, and apart from a brief flurry from the Magpies when a penalty appeal for handball against Horace

Gager was turned down, there was only going to be one winner. There were only seven minutes remaining when Allen Driver slammed the ball home following further excellent play from Duncan, but Newcastle were dead on their feet by then.

Under a headline 'Town's most sensational win', Eric Pugh wrote in the *Luton News* that the second-half rally had to be seen to be believed and if there was one certain thing in an uncertain world, this game would be remembered and talked about for years to come.

LUTON: *Bywater, Cooke, Beach, Soo, Gager, Gardiner, Waugh, Daniel, Billington, Driver, Duncan.*

NEWCASTLE: *Swinburne, Craig, Graham, Harvey, Smith, Wright, Milburn, Bentley, Wayman, Shackleton, Pearson.*

~~~~~~~~~~~

Luton's FA Cup exploits in 1946-47 saw them beat Notts County 6-0, with Billington netting five, and Swansea, before going out in a replay to Burnley. All in all, this season was viewed as a little disappointing, considering the money that had been outlaid, but the future looked promising with the number of talented youngsters coming through.

During the summer of 1947 Newcastle – no doubt still shaken by the events at Kenilworth Road – sounded out George Martin to be their new manager. The lure of a big-city club was too good to turn down, and so the Town were left searching for yet another man to take over the hot seat. They received seventy applications, which were whittled down to a short-list of four. But in the end Luton plumped for the man on their doorstep, Dally Duncan, who was given the role of player-manager.

Duncan lost no time in strengthening the squad, and caused great excitement when a club record £11,000 was paid for Birmingham's Welsh international full-back Billy Hughes. Considered by many judges to be 'the most polished full-back in the country if not the world', it was a tremendous accomplishment for 'little' Luton to secure such a player. Not only did they beat off the approaches of three First Division clubs for his signature, but they doubled their previous highest outgoing fee in doing so.

In view of the hype, it came as a shock when the Hatters were hammered 1-4 at Coventry on the opening day of 1947-48, but this upset was rectified with a 3-0 win at Brentford four days later. Hugh Billington, now approaching the veteran stage, proved he still had some goals left in him by scoring all three, and followed up with a further hat-trick in the return against the Bees on 3rd September. From then on, the season became a bit of a struggle. Goals proved difficult to come by, although the defence looked settled, due in no small measure to a tall, gangly wing-half signed from Birmingham, with no fanfare, when Duncan became manager. Syd Owen would become one of the bargains of all time.

Goalless draws and 0-1 defeats were commonplace that season, and no fewer than thirteen different players were tried in the forward line in the period leading up to Christmas. One of those was player-manager Dally Duncan, who then decided to hang up his boots following the 0-0 home draw with Tottenham on 25th October. It was a fitting finale to a long and illustrious career to bow out before a new record crowd of 26,496. At 39 years and eleven days, Duncan remained the oldest player to take part in a league game for Luton for fifty years.

It seemed briefly that the Town's fortunes were on the upturn, as four wins out of five, including a Christmas double over Leeds, sent them surging up the table. This joy was short-lived. January saw the Town pointless after three straight defeats. The 1-4 reverse at St James' Park against promotion-chasing Newcastle was watched by a crowd of 64,931, a record league attendance for any Town match.

Hopes of a good cup run seemed fanciful, given the team's league form. The third round sent them to Home Park against a strong Plymouth side. With Horace Gager – a Luton lad who had become the side's kingpin at centre-half – injured, Les Hall, a promising but untried reserve, was drafted in. He played a blinder as the Town won 4-2. So well did Hall play that he kept his place, and Gager was subsequently sold to Nottingham Forest in March 1948 for a sizeable fee.

Two weeks after Gager's departure, Chelsea made a £20,000 bid for two Luton stars – leading scorer Billington and the full-back who had arrived at the start of the season, Billy Hughes. To the disgust of supporters, the offer – which in truth was good business for two players the wrong side of thirty – was accepted. The outrage was compounded when, with Easter approaching, relegation stared the Town in the face. The side was struggling to readjust with its new faces. Easter saw a disastrous 0-3 home defeat by Fulham followed by a 0-2 reverse at Chesterfield. The Town's directors were subject to vitriolic letters to the *Luton News*, blaming them for not spending some of the money received for Gager, Hughes and Billington. The directors sat tight, however. Les Lake, another local lad, gradually settled down at full-back, and Bobby Brennan – a £2,000 signing from Northern Ireland club Distillery earlier in the season – assumed a less restrictive position in the forward line, which enabled him to realise his full potential.

A glimmer of light was seen in the Town's 1-1 draw at Fulham on Easter Monday, which was followed by a battling scoreless home draw with West Ham the next Saturday. There then followed one of the longest 45 minutes Luton supporters have ever endured, as a 1-0 half-time lead at Tottenham was somehow kept intact, despite surviving a bombardment of siege proportions.

Fortune now started to smile on the Town. Other teams at the foot of the table, notably Doncaster and Millwall, couldn't pick up points, and when Luton rescued a draw at Bury after being 0-2 down, they were left needing two more points from their final four games to be safe. In the event, the Town won three of those four, ending up in a mid-table position which had seemed out of reach only a few weeks before.

With the Board pledging to strengthen the squad over the summer, they were now 'flavour of the month' in the eyes of supporters, but they would probably admit to a few beads of sweat before their gamble finally paid off. The most significant purchase in the summer of 1948 was a seventeen-acre field at Skimpot Farm, fronting on to Dunstable Road. It was the long-term aim that this might be the site of a new Luton Town football ground at some time in the future. Initially, though, it would be used for training and youth-team games.

On the field, 1948-49 proved to be another season of transition, with youngsters such as Bob Morton beginning to make a name for themselves and Bobby Brennan ensuring that the scouts flocked to Kenilworth Road. A final placing of tenth was an improvement on the previous season but nowhere near good enough for ultra-ambitious chairman Charles Jeyes.

KENILWORTH ROAD CLASSICS: **Luton v Leicester** – 5-5

FA Cup, Round Five, 12th February 1949

The FA Cup brought some respite in a mundane season, and the visit of fellow Division Two side West Ham in round three enticed 22,229 to Kenilworth Road. According to reports, the Town put on a five-star performance, winning 3-1. The prospect of a giant-killing, when Walsall of Division Three (South) visited next, saw 26,422 fill Kenilworth Road, but the Town were two goals up inside ten minutes. It ended 4-0 with Bobby Brennan claiming a hat-trick.

The fifth round pitted the Hatters at home once more, this time to Leicester of Division Two. Another near record crowd of 26,280 flocked to Kenilworth Road, paying record receipts of £4,678 to see a remarkable game that ended 5-5 after extra-time. Jack Lee scored for Leicester after six minutes but within another four minutes Peter Small and Brennan had shot the Town into the lead. By half-time, however, Lee had scored a further two goals. The Foxes' lead was wiped out when Tommy Kiernan netted from a Billy Waugh cross shortly after the break. Shots and chances were, according to the local scribe, far too numerous to detail. In extra-time, Mal Griffiths scored a soft goal for Leicester. Luton followers feared the worst as teams scoring in the first period of extra-time normally prevailed, but when Kiernan and then Charlie Watkins – with a twenty-yard rocket – put the Hatters ahead, a famous victory beckoned. With seconds remaining, however, City gained a corner. Griffiths' tired chip to the near post somehow allowed Lee to screw the ball home with his head as the referee blew the final whistle.

Several thousand Luton fans flocked to Filbert Street for the replay the following Saturday, swelling the crowd to 38,322. They were heartened when Brennan netted in the first minute, but saddened by a three-goal City salvo in fifteen minutes before half-time. With the Town pushing forward, gaps had appeared in defence, leading to Lee, Griffiths and Ken Chisholm setting up City's 3-1 interval lead. When Griffiths was felled by Les Hall just after the re-start, with Lee blasting home the penalty, the Hatters' cup run looked over, but eighteen minutes from the end Billy Arnison reduced the deficit. Brennan then hit a pile-driver – 4-3.

Leicester were now panic-stricken and when Brennan's header appeared 'in' with ten minutes left Luton seemed to have come back from the dead. The referee and linesman, however, did not think the ball had crossed the line. Play was waved on, and Griffiths swept to the other end to put the game finally out of the Town's reach. Ex-Town manager Ned Liddell, who was at the game scouting for Brentford – who were due to take on the winners – said 'The better team lost'.

LUTON: *Streten, Wilson, Cooke, Morton, Hall, Gardiner, Small, Kiernan, Brennan, Watkins, Waugh.*

LEICESTER: *McGraw, Frame (Jelly), Scott, Harrison, Plummer, King, Griffiths, Revie, Lee, Chisholm, Adam.* (replay in brackets)

LUTON (replay): *Streten, Mulvaney, Cooke, Watkins, Hall, Gardiner, Small, Kiernan, Arnison, Brennan, Waugh.*

~~~~~~~~~~~

The only news of note as the 1948-49 season drew to a close was that the original part of the Main Stand, dating back to 1922, would be re-roofed. The directors had finally bowed to complaints about rain water dripping down the necks of spectators. Although supporters accepted that this undertaking would not come cheap, they did not anticipate that the family jewels were about to be sold to cover the cost. Birmingham put in a £20,000 bid for Bobby Brennan, which the Board reluctantly accepted.

At the stroke of a pen Luton kissed goodbye to any hopes of promotion in the foreseeable future. Brennan was a natural predator and would be sorely missed. When his co-striker Billy Arnison was badly injured early in the following 1949-50 season, the goals dried up and the team struggled. Although George Stobbart was signed from Newcastle in an attempt to solve the problem, he only managed nine goals. That was enough to make him top scorer in a side that hit the net only 41 times over the campaign. Only a late run of draws and squeaky wins allowed the Hatters to avoid relegation, but it had been a close-run thing.

Only two points of interest stand out from that 1949-50 season. On 22nd October champions-elect Tottenham attracted a new record Town crowd of 27,319. The game ended 1-1. That same month goalkeeper Bernard Streten became the first Luton player picked for England since Joe Payne in 1937. Although England beat Northern Ireland 9-2, Streten was not selected again, despite not being at fault with either goal.

If supporters had breathed a sigh of relief thinking the worst was over, they could think again. The 1950-51 season proved even more depressing. After an opening day 2-0 home win over Brentford, it was to be another twelve games before victory was tasted again. The major problem was still the lack of firepower. A number of players were tried in the forward positions to accompany old warhorse George Stobbart, but with little joy. Another worrying trend was that the previously reliable defence was creaking, and terrible defeats such as a 1-6 hammering at Barnsley saw home crowds plummet.

Something had to be done and manager Dally Duncan, with his knowledge of Scotland, set his sights on St Mirren forward Willie Davie and Celtic utility player Pat McAuley. Paisley-born Davie was attracting scouts from many big clubs but Duncan felt he was one step ahead in the chase. McAuley was, however, an unusual target in that most clubs seemed to give him a wide berth. He was effectively on strike at Parkhead after holding out for more money or a transfer. Celtic did not wish to break their unofficial wage structure, nor did they wish the player to leave Parkhead, such was his enviable talent.

Hailed by some as the finest natural footballer to wear a Celtic shirt, the team had effectively been built around McAuley until his disagreements with the board. 'Snake-hipped, a football artist with delightful footwork and great intelligence and a true craftsman,' were some of the compliments paid by the Scottish press at the time. Luton supporters felt that Duncan was on a hiding to nothing in his attempts to entice such a player to Kenilworth Road.

On Wednesday, 13th December 1950 Duncan left Luton on the night train for Glasgow. The following morning he signed Davie for £7,500, with Tom Kiernan going to Paisley in part-exchange, and opened negotiations with McAuley. The talks broke down, so back came Duncan on the night train to Luton, from where he headed to Reading with the youth team. While at Elm Park, he learned that Celtic were prepared to re-open negotiations, so off he went to Glasgow again, signing McAuley on the Saturday morning for £4,500 and returning that evening, hearing on the way that the Hatters had lost 0-1 at Brentford.

These two signings transformed Luton. Two wins and two draws came from the next four games, among them a league double against struggling

Swansea over Christmas. Suddenly, the forthcoming plum FA Cup third tound tie with Portsmouth could not come quickly enough.

KENILWORTH ROAD CLASSICS: **Luton v Portsmouth** – 2-0

FA Cup, Round Three, 6th January 1951
Pompey, who had won the League Championship over the previous two seasons, were at the peak of their fame with a settled side that had played together, virtually unchanged, since the end of the war. They were expected to make short work of the Hatters but, such was the surge of optimism around Kenilworth Road in the short space of one month, that supporters felt that Portsmouth's perceived over-confidence might be punished. As it turned out, over-confidence did not come into it. Pompey were outplayed in a 2-0 defeat which to everyone, apart from the Luton faithful, was the shock of the day.

With rain falling on an already heavy pitch, the crowd of 21,631 saw the Town rip into Portsmouth, but had only one goal to show for their efforts at half-time – Willie Davie converted a through ball from George Stobbart in the 25th minute. The score assumed a more realistic look three minutes into the second period when South African Willie Havenga who, along with full-back Billy Cooke, was playing with a plaster cast to protect a broken wrist, smacked in a cross from Alec Glover. Thereafter skipper Syd Owen pocketed dangerman Duggie Reid, and goalkeeper Bernard Streten pulled off a couple of spectacular saves as the Town held on.

LUTON: *Streten, Cooke, Aherne, Morton, Owen, Watkins, Glover, Shanks, Stobbart, Davie, Havenga.*

PORTSMOUTH: *Leather, Stephen, Rookes, Scoular, Flewin, Dickinson, Harris, Ryder, Reid, Phillips, Froggatt.*

~~~~~~~~~~~

The round four visitors were Bristol Rovers of Division Three (South). This time the Hatters were favourites. Another near-record crowd rolled up, but this time the boot was on the other foot. Although Charlie Watkins gave Luton a thirteenth-minute lead against the run of play, shots from all ranges and angles were raining in on Streten. He was eventually beaten after half an hour, when he fisted out a shot to the feet of Vic Lambden, who was left with a gaping goal. The inevitable Rovers winner came early in the second half, when George Petherbridge dribbled past two Luton defenders and beat the advancing Streten.

The optimism that spread through Luton since before Christmas evaporated in the wake of the Bristol Rovers defeat, as supporters realised that a struggle against relegation was all they could look forward to. Luton went six league games before picking up a win bonus, but crucially won three in succession in late March, two of which were against fellow strugglers. The

Town eventually finished with just 32 points. In many seasons that total would have sent them down. On this occasion the three teams below them had suffered an even more woeful time. It had been close though.

Manager Dally Duncan was fortunate to retain his job, and only the casting vote of the chairman saved him. This was just as well, as 1951-52 saw some of his youngsters come to the fore, and some of his cannier buys finally show their worth. For once, the Town were in with a shout of promotion throughout the whole campaign. Aided by the signings of South African Roy Davies from Clyde and Bert Mitchell from Northampton, the team looked solid, and the transfer of Willie Davie to Huddersfield, for a handsome £23,000 in December 1951, was not felt as much as it might otherwise have done.

Youngsters such as Jack Taylor, signed from Stockton in 1949, finally came good, and future Kenilworth Road legends Bob Morton and Gordon Turner started to press for a permanent place in the side. The season was made even more exciting by the march to the FA Cup quarter-finals for only the second time in the club's history.

~~~~~~~~~~~

KENILWORTH ROAD CLASSICS: **Luton v Arsenal** – 2-3

FA Cup, Quarter-finals, 8th March 1952

The FA Cup run was sparked by Gordon Turner, in his first cup-tie, netting with a scorcher to see off First Division Charlton at Kenilworth Road. Brentford were the next visitors, and Turner scored after eighteen minutes. The Bees' veteran goalie Ted Gaskell kept out goalbound efforts from Bert Mitchell, George Stobbart and Jack Taylor before Taylor scored a second soon after the interval, but Brentford's Billy Sperrin, whose son would later play for the Town, turned the tie on its head, netting twice to force a replay. It was scheduled for 6th February, only for the death of King George VI that morning to threaten a late postponement. Frantic telephone calls to the FA confirmed that the match would go ahead. In the event, 31,143 turned up at Griffin Park, initially in sombre mood. With the interval approaching, Brentford's Billy Dare twice hit the woodwork. Extra-time could not separate the teams.

A second replay was necessary, on neutral territory. A Highbury crowd of 37,269 saw the Town take the lead after only thirty seconds, when Taylor's shot was deflected past Gaskell by full-back Kenny Horne. Dare levelled on the half-hour, but within five minutes Bernard Moore put the Hatters back in front. With seven minutes remaining, Dare levelled once more, which meant another period of extra-time. Seven minutes from the end, Bob Morton gathered the ball on halfway and with no one challenging him advanced to the edge of the area before unleashing a left-foot shot which deserved to win any game.

The reward was yet another home tie, this time against Swindon. The Robins had held the Kenilworth Road attendance record since 1938, when 27,546 were present for a fourth round Cup-tie, but that figure was now exceeded by seven. Swindon scored after six minutes, but Taylor levelled just before the interval and the Town ran out 3-1 victors.

The quarter-final draw pitched the Town against a team in red for the fourth time, with mighty Arsenal the visitors for an all-ticket tie. The ground record was raised again to 28,433, paying £6,159, another record. Moore headed in Mitchell's centre after nine minutes. The Gunners made little headway against a defence marshalled by Syd Owen. But just before the interval a crude challenge by Peter Goring left the Luton centre-half limping with a damaged ankle.

With Owen unable to kick with his right foot and unable to turn, Freddie Cox levelled on the hour. The Town were reduced to nine fit men when Roy Davies was carried off with a broken ankle, following a clash with Lionel Smith, and further goals from Cox and Milton seemed to put the game out of the Hatters' reach. With fifteen minutes left, Arsenal's Welsh international centre-half Ray Daniel handled, leaving Mitchell to net from the spot and spark a frantic finale. The final whistle left a sour taste, as witnessed by the hostile reception accorded the victors.

LUTON: *Streten, Cooke, Aherne, Morton, Owen, Watkins, Davies, Taylor, Moore, Stobbart, Mitchell.*

ARSENAL: *Swindin, Barnes, Smith, Shaw, Daniel, Mercer, Cox, Milton, Goring, Lishman, Roper.*

~~~~~~~~~~

In November 1951 the Town commenced investigations into the installation of floodlights. By that time, quite a few clubs were taking advantage of the new technology and inviting foreign clubs over for lucrative 'floodlight friendlies'. The Board was informed that the club would need to commission an electricity sub-station on site in order to provide sufficient power. It would be almost two years before a suitable site was found, in the back garden of one of the club-owned houses in Oak Road, whereupon the big 'switch-on' could take place.

In the 1952 close season two significant transfers took place. Luton supporters bowed to the inevitable when ace striker Jack Taylor was transferred to Wolverhampton, who were then one of the biggest sides in the land, for a massive £16,000. The sadness did not last long. A couple of weeks later, Jesse Pye made the reverse move for £8,000. Pye, a former England international and a consistent goalscorer in Division One, was still only 32, so not yet classed as over the hill. His signing was seen as a masterstroke by Dally Duncan as it immediately gave Hatters supporters a spring in their step.

After a slow start to 1952-53, the Town got into their stride. They challenged leaders Sheffield United and Huddersfield throughout the season but were tantalisingly unable to close the gap and finished a frustrating third, albeit the highest position in the club's history.

Although disappointed to have missed out on joining the big boys, few could complain at the entertainment served up. Pye was a revelation, showing silky skills for such a big man and netting 24 goals. He also acted as mentor to Gordon Turner and taught him the tricks of the trade, much as Bob Hatton would do to young Brian Stein 25 years later.

Goalkeeper Ron Baynham, signed from Worcester City in November 1951, replaced the out of sorts Bernard Streten midway through the season, after which the ex-England international could not get his place back. With an embarrassment of riches in the goalkeeping department, and with the aim of preventing a mutiny, the directors decided to pay each goalkeeper the maximum £15 per week. That sum was normally reserved for those that played. A dangerous precedent had been set.

KENILWORTH ROAD CLASSICS: **Luton v Manchester City** – 5-1
FA Cup, Round Four replay, 4th February 1953
The 1953 FA Cup run got off to a sensational start with young Irishman Arthur Taylor, on his debut, netting in the first minute at home to Blackburn. The Town were three goals up after seventeen minutes – Jesse Pye, and Taylor again, on the scoresheet – and another three goals (two from Pye) came towards the end. The final score, 6-1, was rather flattering to Luton, confirming Rovers' less than fond thoughts of Kenilworth Road as they had lost 0-6 in a league match two months earlier. Pye had netted a hat-trick in each game.

Next up were First Division Manchester City. Over 5,000 Luton supporters made the trip to Maine Road to swell the crowd to 38,411. On a blustery day, the Town played with the wind in the first half but conceded a goal after twenty minutes. Ivor Broadis fired in a left-foot shot after Bob Morton could only half-clear a Don Revie free-kick. Just before the interval Pye was sent sprawling outside the box and he hammered in the free-kick after Bernard Moore had dummied to take it. With Les Hall, deputising for the injured Syd Owen, in commanding form, Luton withstood City's attacks with relative ease.

The replay took place the following Wednesday afternoon, when 21,991 presumably reported sick for work and saw the Town repeat the blitz tactics employed against Blackburn in the opening minutes. This time Pye set up Gordon Turner – back in the reshuffled side following an injury inflicted on Wally Shanks at Maine Road – who fired home in the second minute. Shortly afterwards Bert Mitchell's cross was turned into his own goal by

Roy Little. City halved the deficit through Billy Spurdle after eleven minutes, but the next goal fell to the Town when Pye set up Turner to score from close range a minute before the interval. Four minutes after the break Mitchell took a pass from Pye and steered the ball past Bert Trautmann in the City goal. Ex-German prisoner-of-war Trautmann prevented a cricket score, but the Hatters did net a fifth just before the end. For once, Pye was not involved, leaving Bob Morton to set up Turner to complete his hat-trick.

Jesse Pye had been at his imperious best, but it was reported afterwards that he had felt unwell beforehand and was packed off to bed with suspected flu straight after.

The cup dream ended at the next stage, when Bolton won 1-0 in a tough contest on a Luton pitch that was a porridge of slush and mud. The Trotters reached the final, where they lost to Stanley Matthews' Blackpool.

LUTON: *Baynham, Jones, Aherne, Morton, Hall, Watkins, Cullen, Moore, Pye, Turner, Mitchell.*

MANCHESTER CITY: *Trautmann, Branagan, Little, Revie, Ewing, Paul, Meadows, Spurdle, Williamson, Broadis, Cunliffe.*

~~~~~~~~~~

At the end of the 1952-53 season the players, management, directors and wives set off on the club's first major foreign tour. The trip to Turkey and Greece took in eight games, among them Galatasaray, Olympiakos and Panathinaikos. Although the results were nothing to shout about, the exercise was judged a success and paved the way for more long-distance tours over the coming decade. The players were allowed £1 per day pocket money.

Back home, funds were allocated to a general tidying up of the ground. £400 went on a re-enforced concrete wall along the Bobbers Stand side of the pitch, replacing a fence that had been there since 1905. Also, for the first time, a ten-foot wire-mesh fence was installed above the Bobbers Stand to help catch stray balls.

On the playing side, the Town splashed out £9,500 on Johnny Downie from Manchester United and £12,000 to Everton for George Cummins. Both were inside-forwards and, on the face of it, players of similar style. Downie was the first to impress, scoring a hat-trick in the opening day 4-4 home draw with Oldham, although Cummins was to make the greater long-term impact.

The 1953-54 season got off to the, by now, typically slow start, but with Luton on a ten-game unbeaten run as Christmas approached, Pye broke an ankle at Oldham which kept him out for the rest of the season. This gave an opportunity for Turner to show that he had learned from the maestro, but it was too much to expect him to do it all on his own and the season petered out to an ultimately unsuccessful, but nevertheless respectable position of sixth.

The Town had finally switched on their £2,160 floodlights on 7th October 1953 for a friendly against Fenerbahce of Turkey, which was won 7-4 (the club had originally asked Arsenal and Chelsea to do them the honour but both declined). Due to the cramped and asymmetric lay-out of the ground, the Hatters were unable to erect traditional floodlight pylons in each corner, but had to make do with a row of lights along the Bobbers and Main stands, supplemented by ugly concrete posts at the Kenilworth Road end of the enclosure.

The summer of 1954 proved to be an awkward time for the club, for it brought the resignation of Chairman Charles Jeyes. The decision was sparked by the retirement of long-serving E. Hugh Woods from the Board, upon which it was proposed that, rather than replace him, the number of directors should be reduced to six. Jeyes felt that a change of this nature should be voted on by the shareholders. Other directors disagreed, knowing they could push it through on a poll vote in any case. According to Jeyes, this smacked of a dictatorship. He wanted none of it and resigned from his position on the Board, which he had held since 1927, and from the chair.

The Town's progressive Board had previously shown a united front to supporters, who regarded them as rock solid. This washing of dirty linen in public shocked the fans, who had been looking forward to another successful season in the knowledge that their club was in safe hands. At that moment they were not so sure.

As was to be expected, the matter was soon ironed out. Supporters were heartened to learn that old playing favourite, and now mine host at the Warden Tavern in New Bedford Road, Tom Hodgson, was invited onto the Board. Percy Mitchell stepped up to the chair.

One of the first tasks facing Hodgson was to sort out the Johnny Downie housing saga. The club had apparently promised Downie a new house to rent as part of the deal when he signed for Luton twelve months earlier. They then tried to fob him off with one of the established club houses dotted around the town. Downie stood his ground and demanded that the club honour its promise. For their part, the directors were not keen on further outlay and, in fact, were looking to sell some of their properties as they became vacant.

The Mexican stand-off ended with an unhappy Downie being transferred to Hull for £5,000, which represented a loss to the Hatters of £4,500, or two new houses, whichever way you look at it. At the time, houses were a major concern. Upon marrying, players looked to the Board for a club house to rent almost as a right. Trying to keep certain players happy was not easy, nor was ensuring that players transferred to other clubs vacated their homes as quickly as possible.

As well as the aforementioned properties, the club also owned those houses in Kenilworth Road that backed onto the ground, in addition to those on Oak Road. Entrances to each end of the ground had been drilled through the terraced houses. Although the club utilised the building on the, by now, oddly shaped 70-72 Kenilworth Road as offices, they had problems letting the butchered properties in Oak Road, particularly as the modern wonders of electricity seemed to have bypassed most of that row of houses even as late as 1954.

The Town opened the 1954-55 season wearing a 'Continental' style of strip (round-neck collar, tight-fitting shirt) not previously adopted by a British club. They also tried out a tactical idea pioneered by the powerful Hungarians – that of using a deep lying centre-forward.

With the fit Jesse Pye filling the role, the Hatters – after another stuttering start – won six games in a row and promotion talk soon filled the pubs and clubs of the town. But the first bombshell was dropped when Pye asked for a transfer and moved to Derby in early October. Although citing the health of his wife, he also had worries over pay. In common with most clubs, the Town paid a summer wage, a higher one during the playing season, plus an extra amount for playing in the first team. Pye had missed out on the first-team wage for most of the previous season on account of his broken ankle, had found it difficult to cope with the reduced weekly income and sought a guarantee of first-team football (and first-team money). The Town felt unable to oblige, presumably unlike Derby. Pye's departure meant the Hatters were now playing a deep lying centre-forward system with no deep lying centre-forward.

With no ready-made replacement to hand, a variety of experiments were tried, including Terry Kelly and Peter MacEwan, but after Luton's first (and last) home defeat of the season, against Swansea on 30th October, the drastic decision was taken to switch wing-half Bob Morton to centre-forward. Morton – who relished his new position – scored twice in his first game in the new role in a 3-3 draw at Notts County. With ace goalscorer Gordon Turner now given more freedom, the team at last began firing on all cylinders.

KENILWORTH ROAD CLASSICS: **Luton v Blackburn** – 7-3

Football League Division Two, 27th November 1954

The biggest test of the new-look team would come with the visit of runaway leaders Blackburn. Rovers were probably fearful of the prospect, having suffered some fearful thumpings in the recent past. True to form, the Town went three up in the first ten minutes. Gordon Turner opened the scoring on four minutes – reacting fastest when Rovers' goalkeeper failed to hold a Bob Morton shot – and Turner was on target again three minutes later, rounding off a sweeping move. Roy Davies bagged number three in the tenth minute, before Tommy Briggs, in a rare breakaway, pulled one back for the visitors. When Jim Adam and Davies scored again for Luton, the score was 5-1 with less than half an hour played.

The Blackburn defenders had trouble turning in the gluey mud, unlike the Hatters, who combined speed and accuracy of movement. It might have been ten by half-time, but more goals were not long delayed. Turner bagged his hat-trick four minutes after the turnaround. Jim Pemberton's long-range effort on seventy minutes was enough to break the Town's previous scoring record in Division Two. Blackburn pulled a couple of goals back, but does 3-7 sound that much more respectable than 1-7?

LUTON: *Baynham, Dunne, Aherne, Pemberton, Owen, Shanks, Davies, Turner, Morton, Cummins, Adam.*

BLACKBURN: *Elvy, Suart, Eckersley, Clayton, Kelly, Bell, Mooney, Crossan, Briggs, Quigley, Langton.*

~~~~~~~~~~

Taking confidence from the Blackburn performance, Luton embarked on a spell of ten games undefeated, which saw them take claim top spot and earn rave reviews with their wins at Nottingham Forest 5-1, Hull 4-0, and Rotherham in the FA Cup 5-1.

As the season neared its climax the Hatters had to face several of their chief rivals. They effectively pegged back Notts County, who had begun to appear a real threat, 3-1 at home, before earning a point at Liverpool in a 4-4 draw, after being 1-3 down at one stage.

Easter came, as did a crowd of 25,775 to Kenilworth Road on Good Friday. They witnessed a disappointing 0-0 draw with Leeds. Undeterred, a best of the season 27,148 turned up the following day to see West Ham beaten 2-0.

It was following this game that the season started to turn sour. In the return with Leeds on Easter Monday the Town were thrashed 0-4, with big John Charles hammering two from the penalty spot. The Hatters were suffering an epidemic of penalty-kicks awarded against them, but in the next game Blackburn's Bobby Langton shot wide as Luton luckily hung on to a point in a 0-0 draw at Ewood Park.

With hindsight, the crunch game was at Birmingham, where a crowd of 34,612 saw the Blues win 2-1, with the clinching goal coming after a dubious penalty award. That defeat left the Town with three games to play and needing to win them all to stand any real chance of promotion.

At a 'round table' conference the players agreed that experience was needed for the run-in. The outcome was that Charlie Watkins, about to emigrate to South Africa in the summer, was recalled to form a left-wing partnership with Jim Pemberton. Pemberton had been moved from the half-back line, leaving the way clear for Morton to return to probably his most effective position.

These unorthodox moves had 'gamble' written all over them, but they paid off as Port Vale were hammered 4-2 at Kenilworth Road, followed by Bristol Rovers beaten 2-0 in a game that saw Watkins score both in a fairy-tale end to his Luton career.

The final game took the Town to lowly Doncaster, where only a victory would do. A 3-0 win was the reward for a devastating team performance and it was then a case of hearing how their rivals had fared. Rotherham were the main danger, and had they won at Port Vale, one of the two promotion slots would have been theirs. At 1-1 the Millers were awarded a penalty which was saved by Vale's Ray King, later to become a Hatters coach. There was no further scoring, which meant the Town were promoted on goal-average ahead of Rotherham.

That combination of results actually sent Luton top, but while they and Rotherham had concluded their fixtures, Birmingham had one to play, the following week. City won it, climbing above Luton on goal-average in the process, the only time they had led the table all season.

So Luton Town had to be satisfied with runners-up instead of the championship. Never mind, they were now in Division One for the first time. An exciting but, at the same time, terrifying prospect.

Happy Luton players (Semple, Molyneux, Parker, Mathieson, Higginbotham and Hill) in front of the old main stand

Goalkeeper Harry Bailey poses in front of the main stand. It would appear that the Town had been ordered to post warning notices following crowd misbehaviour

A view across to the short-lived cover on the Beech Hill Path side of the ground

The rear of the old main stand

LUTON TOWN FOOTBALL TEAM, 1921-2.

The aftermath of the mysterious fire in 1922.
The club's directors do not appear to be too perturbed

Half-back Bob Millar (right) seems upset at the loss of his boots in the fire

After the fire in 1922, not much remained of the main stand

This photograph shows the bench seats which were situated in front of the main stand, plus the construction of the terracing

Chapter Three

The Third Quarter-Century

1955-1980

With promotion to the Promised Land secured, the directors of Luton Town FC now faced the worrying problem of how to accommodate the larger crowds that Division One football would attract. The players had embarked on an end-of-season tour to Denmark and shared out their promotion bonus of £440, Syd Owen had been appointed player-coach, taking over from the Bedford-bound Tim Kelly, unsettled George Cummins had been cajoled into signing a new contract, and the directors set to work planning ground improvements.

There were various possibilities. An extension to the Kenilworth Road terrace was considered, but as local by-laws insisted on a 15ft gap between the houses that backed onto the ground and the new structure, the costs outweighed the benefits, with only an extra 200 spectators able to be accommodated.

Building a double-decker stand on the Bobbers Stand side was also discussed, but again the costs – including the buying up of more property surrounding the ground – could not be justified. The Town had bought a strip of land at the rear of the Main Stand from British Railways several months earlier, with the intention of either replacing, extending or rebuilding the Main Stand. Mitcham Stadium in Surrey had stands available that were surplus to requirements. These were considered, along with various plans and costings for a brand new double-decker cantilever stand. If implemented, it would have increased the seating capacity by 1,000 and provided another 7,000 standing places.

In announcing the club's decision, Chairman Percy Mitchell stated: 'The present stand will be pulled down. It has served its purpose, most of it over a matter of 30 years. No longer is it big or good enough for the job in hand.' The new stand, which was estimated to cost £68,000, was to be set back 15ft beyond the rear of the old stand. It was soon discovered that, due to a mix-up between plans and estimates, the plan in question was more expensive – £101,000 – but the club decided to proceed, especially when it was discovered that, due to a chronic steel shortage, work could not commence for two years.

In view of the delay it was decided to press on with an extension to the Oak Road end, which would increase capacity in that part of the ground by 3,500. As the club owned all those houses in Oak Road that backed onto the ground, the directors thought they could push through an agreement with the tenants to seize half their back gardens in exchange for a small reduction in rent. The tenants, not surprisingly, were up in arms. When the club served them with notice to quit – intending to offer the properties back to them minus their gardens – they mobilised themselves into action and took legal advice. You could not get away with such bullying even in those days.

Following protracted negotiations the tenants were each awarded £63 compensation for loss of gardens and a substantial reduction in rent. The delay meant that the work could not start until the summer of 1956.

In view of the fight put up by the tenants in Oak Road, the club accepted that it would have to tone down plans for the new Main Stand. If, as hoped, it would extend to the Maple Road boundary, its height would have shrouded most of the houses in shadow. It was therefore decided to terminate the seated part of the stand 20ft from the boundary. This meant sacrificing around 400 seats.

All this became academic, as in February 1956 the proposed grandstand was quietly shelved. This was due to 'further restrictions imposed by the Government regarding loans, new buildings etc.' Out of all the talk, meetings and expensive consultations, only the extension to the Oak Road end was ever completed.

On the field the Town decided to stick by the players who had served the club so well in the promotion season as they embarked into new and uncharted territory. The first game in Division One took the Town to Charlton, where on a bone-hard pitch and under a blazing sun Gordon Turner scored the Town's first ever top-flight goal. A head injury left goalkeeper Ron Baynham concussed and the Robins took a 2-1 lead before South African Peter MacEwan stole in for an equaliser.

After losing at Preston in midweek, the eagerly awaited first home game arrived with old friends Tottenham the visitors. Spurs had regularly broken the league attendance record at Kenilworth Road in the late 1940s, but the crowd on this occasion was a disappointing 21,143, a figure attributed afterwards to poor 'packing' and the reluctance of spectators to move away from the entrances to allow more into the ground behind them. The game was a thriller which stood at 1-1 until the final minute, when Turner broke through and hit an unstoppable shot for Luton's winner.

The Town acclimatised to their new surroundings better and quicker than even their most myopic supporters could have imagined, and as autumn turned to winter some football commentators were talking of the Hatters making a bid for the championship.

Before the game at Birmingham in September 1955, the coach carrying the Luton team and directors was involved in an accident outside Warwick. The vehicle went off the road and landed in a field. Everyone on board was shaken and bruised, but mercifully no one was seriously injured. Talk of calling off the game was quickly dismissed, and the players performed bravely in a 0-0 draw which earned the plaudits of the national press the following day.

KENILWORTH ROAD CLASSICS: **Luton v Wolverhampton** – 5-1
Football League Division One, 5th November 1955

During the promotion year of 1954-55, when Dally Duncan felt the forwards were firing blanks, he had moved wing-half Bob Morton to centre-forward, where he proved inspirational. The trouble was that Morton was also needed in the half-back line, and it was a constant source of debate as to which was his best position.

Although the Town had performed better than he feared on their baptism in the top flight, Duncan was concerned by a couple of limp forward displays in October. His remedy was to move Morton back up front, and his re-introduction coincided with the visit of Wolves to Kenilworth Road on Fireworks Day.

Amongst the record league crowd of 27,911 – a figure never since exceeded – were England manager Walter Winterbottom and the Moscow Dynamo team which was due to play at Molineux the following week in the latest of the famous floodlight friendlies that made Wolves famous the world over in the 1950s.

Wolves deserved this acclaim as they had finished as League Champions in 1954, were runners-up the following season, and were making another bid for the title when they came to Kenilworth Road. Added to which, they boasted the England captain in Billy Wright, and every other member of their team was a household name, apart from Bobby Mason who was making his Wolves debut.

Morton's switch was vindicated when he finished off a slick movement involving the whole of the forward line in only the fourth minute. Wolves equalised in the eighteenth minute when tiny winger Johnny Hancocks crashed in a tremendous shot which Luton goalkeeper Ron Baynham had no chance of stopping. Gordon Turner put the Town back into the lead just before half-time when he turned in a George Cummins free-kick, but the real fireworks came in the second period when the Hatters scored three times without reply in eleven minutes. The first came when Morton anticipated a back-pass from Bill Shorthouse and whipped the ball into the net. That was quickly followed by another strike from Turner, who ran through to beat England goalkeeper Bert Williams, despite the Wolves' defenders shouts for offside. Right-winger Mike Cullen completed the rout with a header. Jim Adam on the left, who had the beating of Wolves full-back George Showell all afternoon, hit the woodwork.

The newspapers were full of the Town's achievements, and offered particularly glowing praise of Bob Morton, who had given Billy Wright the runaround. The *Daily Mail*'s comments were typical: 'Black-haired Bob Morton, with the build of a dreadnought and the speed and manoeuvrability of a corvette was on the fringes of the England squad as a wing-half. He should now be a contender to lead the attack!'

LUTON: Baynham, Dunne, Aherne, Pemberton, Owen, Shanks, Cullen, Turner, Morton, Cummins, Adam.

WOLVES: Williams, Showell, Shorthouse, Slater, Wright, Broadbent, Hancocks, Mason, Swinbourne, Wilshaw, Mullen.

~~~~~~~~~~

KENILWORTH ROAD CLASSICS: **Luton v Sunderland** – 8-2
Football League Division One, 19th November 1955
With Luton setting Division One on fire, the upstarts' biggest test would surely come when leaders Sunderland visited. Another large assembly, this time 25,802, was present, together with most of Fleet Street's football corps, to see the bubble burst.

Sunderland at that time in their history had never known life outside the top division. They boasted an expensive side which included Wales captain Ray Daniel, England's Len Shackleton and mercurial winger Billy Bingham, who was later to play for the Town. They had arrived after a run of six games without defeat.

Considering what was to transpire, the first half-hour passed without a goal, although it took a fine save from Town goalkeeper Ron Baynham to keep out a wicked shot from Shackleton. The breakthrough came in the 31st minute when Sunderland keeper Willie Fraser pulled down Mike Cullen from behind, and Gordon Turner scored from the spot. That was the turning point as by half-time the Town were 4-0 up. Cullen, normally a goal-provider rather than a scorer, drove in a 25-yard shot, and that was followed by close-range efforts from Jim Adam and Bob Morton. The Wearsiders' square defence was cut to ribbons by Luton's short through-passes on the ground.

The second period opened quietly, but then Daniel failed to find his goalkeeper with a back-pass, allowing Morton to nip in. Daniel then handled a corner for Turner to score from the spot. Sunderland replied through Ted Purdon before Cullen netted from an acute angle. Morton completed the Luton tally ten minutes from the end, running forty yards with the ball before beating Fraser to complete his first hat-trick. Purdon netted another consolation in the final minute.

As might be expected, the national press was full of it: 'The most attractive team in the land,' and 'The slaughter of Sunderland had to be seen to be believed', as well as 'Never was there a humiliation like this'.

Spare a thought for poor Willie Fraser who, apart from letting in eight, conceded six at Kenilworth Road the following season and seven in 1957-58. He made one other appearance, in the colours of Nottingham Forest, shortly before the 1959 Cup final, and picked the ball out of the net five times! One for the record books?

LUTON: *Baynham, Dunne, Aherne, Pemberton, Owen, Shanks, Cullen, Turner, Morton, Cummins, Adam.*

SUNDERLAND: *Fraser, Hedley, McDonald, Anderson, Daniel, Aitken, Bingham, Fleming, Purdon, Chisholm, Shackleton.*

~~~~~~~~~~~

Although the Town maintained their winning ways until Christmas and were full of confidence as the New Year dawned, things then began to go wrong. Inspirational leader Syd Owen was seriously injured during the 0-4 home defeat by Leicester in the FA Cup, and the Town did not relish the advent of heavy grounds, which did not suit their style of play. Also, of course, other clubs had had time to get wise to Luton's strengths and weaknesses. Newcomers to a higher division invariably do their damage in the first half of a season, not the second.

Six straight league defeats sent the Town plummeting. Unless arrested, the losing sequence raised fears that the Town's stay in Division One would be short. March proved to be the team's salvation. With pitches becoming harder, 2-1 wins at Sunderland and Wolves halted the slide. The victory at Wolves was particularly satisfying as the Town eleven was unrecognisable from that which had won at Luton four months earlier, yet the win was just as easy. This time it was Tony Gregory, in only his second league game, who gave Billy Wright a torrid time.

The season concluded with the Hatters safe in mid-table. In light of the injury problems that struck the club after Christmas – with Owen, Aherne, Turner and Cummins all sidelined for long periods – immense satisfaction was felt behind the scenes.

Once again there was little movement of players during the close season. The greatest thrill for this writer, then four years old, was watching a crane hoist slabs of concrete terracing over the top of the Bobbers Stand at the end of Ivy Road ready for the Oak Road extension. When everything was completed, the cost of the extension plus associated work, which included new stairways and an extra entrance being drilled through the adjacent houses – amounted to £12,425. The work was just about finished in time for the start of the new 1956-57 campaign.

The Town's mixture of youth and experience, plus an apparent 'no buy, no sell' policy, seemed eminently wise as the team once again ripped into the opposition. When the first league tables were published, after three games, the Hatters were top. Sunderland (6-2) and Wolves (1-0) had been defeated at Kenilworth Road, and a 2-1 win at Charlton had propelled the club to the highest position in its history.

After an epic performance, despite losing 4-5, in the return at Wolves – which older supporters still talk about – Luton were unable to hit the height again. By mid-winter the fans were becoming restless after a run of only two wins from fourteen games sent the team spiralling down.

Local employer SKF presented the club with a clock that was installed above the Bobber Stand. It became something of a landmark for a whole generation of Luton supporters, for it was undisturbed for almost thirty years. The clock was officially unveiled before the start of the game against Leeds on 29th September 1956.

But a new clock was no substitute for a struggling team. As is usually the case with football supporters, when things start to go wrong they blame the Board, especially if directors are not seen to be digging deep to spend money on the team. Chairman Percy Mitchell took the criticism personally and resigned, but was eventually talked into returning. This was followed by the resignation of vice-chairman Fred England, who again was talked round, but for a time the club was clearly in chaos behind the scenes.

At a stroke, the pressure was lifted. The directors 'scraped the bottom of the barrel' and spent £9,500 on Scottish international inside-forward Allan Brown from Blackpool. The signing of Brown re-ignited the team's spark. Aided by his clever promptings – which enabled the prolific Gordon Turner to end up with thirty goals in only 34 games – the team finished sixteenth, eight points clear of the drop.

Having forked out for Brown, the directors pleaded poverty once more, and so the summer of 1957 was uneventful. The youngsters introduced to the side were improving in leaps and bounds but Dally Duncan was aware that they could not carry the side on their own. In the foreseeable future the backbone of the side, which had stood the Hatters in good stead for so long, was ageing and could not go on for ever.

KENILWORTH ROAD HEROES: **Bud Aherne**

Although born in Limerick in southern Ireland, Thomas 'Bud' Aherne moved to the North in 1946, having left the British Army, to turn out for Belfast Celtic. The Windsor Park side at that time boasted players of the calibre of Jack Vernon and Charlie Tully, and Bud was enjoying his football when one afternoon in 1949 a riot erupted. Players were attacked by the crowd, with the result that Belfast Celtic were expelled from the Irish League. The club eventually folded.

'I decided to try for less dangerous duty in England and the first person to offer me terms was Luton chairman Charles Jeyes who convinced me that Kenilworth Road would be the place for me,' Aherne recalled.

For an outlay of £8,000, the Town picked up an established Irish international full-back who gave ten years' valuable service to the Hatters with many cultured and reliable displays.

'I thoroughly enjoyed my time at Luton and although we did not earn the money today's players get we were always a happy club and laughs were plentiful. I do not think we were unprofessional, but there seemed to be more humour in the game in those days.'

Aherne made his Luton debut on 19th March 1949 in a 1-2 defeat at Tottenham, and from then until 1957 he remained virtually ever present. He made 266 League appearances, but surprisingly never scored a goal: 'During my time at Luton I would rate Bob Morton as the best player I played alongside and I think he was desperately unlucky not to get the international recognition he deserved.

'The one game that sticks in the memory was the 4-5 defeat at Wolves early in the 1956-57 season. We had started off the season with three straight wins and then travelled to Molineux to play a team that could be regarded as the Arsenal of the day. The game had everything, with end to end football and a hat-trick from Gordon Turner, and it was unfortunate that there had to be a loser.

'On the international side of things I can well remember turning out for the South against England at Goodison Park in 1950 and being delighted in beating the so-called "masters" 2-1.'

Aherne was fortunate in avoiding major injuries and reckoned that he received more cuts and bruises from teammate Wally Shanks than from the opposition. It was ironic, therefore, that an injury should effectively end his career when he suffered a hairline fracture of the ankle.

'I was coming to the end of my playing days and I was slowing up, hence the injury. By the time I got back I was too old and with the shake up after the Cup final defeat I stepped down to look after the Youth Team.'

The playing did not stop, however, as Bud turned out for three or four years with Luton Celtic before hanging up his boots well into his forties.

~~~~~~~~~~

1957-58 saw the Town finish eighth, the highest in Division One so far. They might have done even better, but for a poor run of only two wins from the final twelve games. Long-term injuries to Bob Morton and Allan Brown in the spring confirmed that Duncan was right: the team could not rely too much on the younger players. Of these, though, local boy Dave Pacey had made his mark, making the mid-season sale of Reg Pearce to Sunderland for £17,500 easier for fans to swallow.

Talk of a move to a new ground reared its head once more during the season. A new stadium on club-owned land at Skimpot had been shelved several years earlier, with the club switching its resources to developing

Kenilworth Road. As the Skimpot area had by now been built up, and was a non-starter for stadium development, the club turned to the local council for help in finding a fresh site. A plot at Lewsey Farm was earmarked, with the council pledging to carry out all the necessary studies, but these seemed to drag on for months. As the Town were rarely getting near-capacity crowds at Kenilworth Road, the necessary urgency behind the move was probably absent.

The 1957-58 season was also the last occasion that the Town played on Christmas Day, a tradition that had been in existence for decades. It was long-accepted practice to play the same opponents home and away on Christmas Day and Boxing Day. In those pre-computer times it often happened that both teams would be sharing the same train from one town to another, often from one end of the country to the other, on Christmas night.

Upon entering the Football League Division Three in 1920, the Town had to face Southampton twice over the festivities. Luckily Boxing Day fell on a Sunday that year, so the players could travel at their leisure. As both games ended 1-1, the players probably wished they had agreed the results beforehand and therefore enjoyed an extended break.

The club's first 'double header' took place two years later when the Town played QPR on consecutive days. Luton lost the fixture in west London 0-4 on Christmas Day, then won the return 1-0 after making just one change to the side.

In 1930 probably the longest trip of the season was bizarrely saved for Christmas when the fixture planners, in their wisdom, paired the Town with Torquay. Having won 3-1 at Kenilworth Road on Christmas Day, Luton were just as jaded as their opponents 24 hours later in Devon, and 'fought' out a 1-1 draw.

For the remainder of that decade 'local Christmas derbies' were played at places such as Cardiff, Bournemouth, Brighton and Barnsley. From reading the match reports it would appear that few complained. Travelling long distances at an awkward time was accepted as a fact of life. The supporters obviously loved it, however, and turned out in their droves.

One surprising fact is that it took until 1935 before Luton either won or lost both their Christmas matches. The sequence was finally broken when they won 3-0 at Notts County on Christmas Day and followed up with a solitary Fred Roberts goal in front of a then record Kenilworth Road league attendance of 18,100. The Hatters repeated the Christmas 'double' over Nottingham Forest in 1938 and Leeds in 1947.

Christmas attendance records were broken all over the country in 1949, although in Luton's case, their two fixtures against Southampton were restricted by modest ground capacities. Although the attendances appear large by today's standards – 18,765 at Kenilworth Road and 26,878 at The Dell – they were no more than average at the time.

The Town then had a period of playing West Ham over Christmas, although 'local' games against Swansea and Leeds occasionally appeared, testing the resolve of would-be travelling supporters.

By the mid-1950s, crowds for the Christmas Day fixture were dwindling, due largely to a cut-back in public transportation. Bus and train drivers wanted to be with their families, too.

The Hatters' final Christmas Day fixture took place in 1957. The game holds poignant memories for many, as it was against the 'Busby Babes', a matter of weeks before the Munich air disaster. The Town travelled to Manchester to find United officials worried about the potential size of the crowd. The attendance of 39,444 was, however, still 10,000 higher than any other crowd that day. With first-teamers Bob Morton, Syd Owen and Gordon Turner absent through injury, Luton could have done without the fixture. But up stepped Dave Pacey, making his debut, and Terry Kelly and Tony Gregory, both for their first games of the season.

United, the defending champions, were awarded a penalty in the nineteenth minute when John Groves seemed to have won the ball fairly in a tussle with Bobby Charlton. The referee, though, thought otherwise and Duncan Edwards netted the resultant spot-kick. Just before the interval Tommy Taylor deflected a Charlton shot past a semi-incapacitated Ron Baynham. The scoring was completed on seventy minutes, when Charlton tapped the ball home from close range. Three-nil to United.

It seems quaint to hear that both sets of players and officials travelled back to Luton together by train that evening, ready for the return the following day. The game finished 2-2, thanks to a last-minute equaliser from Allan Brown. The goal came in front of a bumper crowd of 26,478 and saved the Town's proud record of never losing twice to the same opponents over Christmas.

KENILWORTH ROAD HEROES: **Bernard Streten**

A well-regarded amateur international goalkeeper plying his trade with Shrewsbury, Streten was enticed to Luton following the recommendations of his old teammate Frank Soo, who was by then on the books of the Hatters. Although not tall for a goalkeeper, Streten compensated with agility and bravery, not to mention a degree of showmanship. It was not long before he was a crowd favourite at Kenilworth Road and earning international recognition for England.

The Town were well-supplied with useful goalkeepers at the time, and Streten had to fend off the challenge of Iorwerth Hughes, a Welsh international, and Ron Baynham, a fellow England international, during his time at the club. It is to Streten's credit that he made over 300 first-team appearances for the Hatters during his ten years at the club, particularly when one considers the rivals to his position.

~~~~~~~~~~

KENILWORTH ROAD HEROES: **Wally Shanks**

Although born in Malta, Wally Shanks was raised in Scotland and was on the brink of joining Aberdeen when World War II broke out. After the war – during which he formed a friendship with Tommy Walker, the ex-Hearts player – Shanks toyed with offers from Blackpool and Spurs before following his old friend, now at Chelsea, to Stamford Bridge.

'With 65-70 professionals at Chelsea at the time and seemingly more arriving daily after de-mob, I was always going to have a job getting into the first team. Joe Payne, the ex-Luton player who was at Chelsea at the time, recommended me to Luton and so began a happy fourteen-year career at Kenilworth Road.'

Shanks debuted at Bury on 18th January 1947 and made a further seven appearances that season – all on the wing – and followed up with ten games in 1947-48, again in the No 7 shirt.

'I always regarded wing-half as my best position but Luton were well served in that department at that time. Frank Soo, Doug Gardiner, Ted Duggan and Billy Waugh were all the "governors", both on and off the pitch, but I was happy to bide my time and wait for a first team chance in my best position.'

The breakthrough eventually came in 1949-50 when Shanks made thirty appearances and bagged his first league goal – in a 1-0 victory at Preston. Wally then remained virtually ever present until 1957, when he joined the Town's coaching staff.

'I obviously remember the promotion season of 1954-55 as a highlight, especially the last game at Doncaster which we won 3-0. Despite winning we still did not know we were up until we got into the dressing room to find that Rotherham could only draw at Port Vale. My other main memory involves the home games against Sunderland in the mid-1950s when we beat them 8-2, 6-2 and 7-1 in consecutive seasons.'

Following Luton's relegation in 1960, Wally left the club amid the turmoil that followed and concentrated on his thriving sports business in partnership with Gordon Turner.

Shanks went on to run the 'Brown Owl' for many years but kept in touch with Bob Morton, Syd Owen and John Groves from that era when players played for the love of the game, not the money. Wally's wages when he joined Luton were £6 a week in the close season and £8 during the season – pocket-money compared to the money earned by today's players.

~~~~~~~~~~

The big news over the summer of 1958 was the signing of Northern Ireland international winger Billy Bingham from Sunderland for £15,000. Bingham was still at his peak and his signing was regarded as a major coup as far as little Luton were concerned. The Town had tried to sign Bingham from Glentoran in 1951, but he had preferred to join First Division Sunderland rather than Second Division Luton. Now that Sunderland had been relegated, the Hatters finally got their man.

Syd Owen was also talked into playing for another season, with the promise of an extension to his coaching duties at the end of it. He did not regret his decision, as the Town stormed to top spot after ten games.

KENILWORTH ROAD CLASSICS: **Luton v Preston** – 4-1

Football League Division One, 27th September 1958

A crowd of 24,425 saw new-boy Bingham make his debut at home to West Brom on the opening day of the season, and he did not disappoint, putting in a masterful performance in a 1-1 draw. Another 1-1 draw followed at Leeds, before the Town secured their first ever win at Birmingham, courtesy of a John Groves strike three minutes from the end.

Leeds drew 1-1 in the return at Kenilworth Road before early season leaders West Ham paid a visit. The Town and newly promoted Hammers were both unbeaten, a fact which encouraged 25,715 to force their way in. West Ham led at half-time through Vic Keeble, but when Luton replied with goals from Allan Brown, Dave Pacey and Gordon Turner (two), the Town's confidence knew no bounds.

A 1-1 draw at Manchester City, when an early City goal was pegged back by Groves, was followed by a 0-0 home draw with Bolton, in which the only event of interest was the referee being knocked out. Manchester City were beaten 5-1 at Kenilworth Road to send the Hatters briefly to the top of the table, whereupon the Hatters returned from one of their bogey grounds, Burnley, with a 2-2 draw. Despite stretching Luton's unbeaten run, Burnley only equalised two minutes from time when defender Bobby Seith scored with a thirty-yard 'hit and hope' shot that dipped under the bar at the last second.

The next game saw new leaders Preston visit Kenilworth Road. A win for Luton would put them top again, this time on a Saturday when league tables were published in all national newspapers (for some reason tables were not often produced after midweek games, so Luton supporters had been unable to see their side at the top of the table in print).

Preston had finished runners-up to Wolves the previous season, scoring 100 goals, of which Tom Finney and Tommy Thompson contributed sixty. In addition to the 23,056 inside Kenilworth Road, BBC television cameras were also in attendance, for their *Sports Special* programme.

The Town scored first, through George Cummins, but Dennis Hatsell equalised after Gordon Turner suffered his first ever penalty miss, seeing his spot-kick saved by Fred Else. During the second period Turner suffered an ankle injury which left him hobbling up and down the centre. It was left to the wingers to show the way. Bingham, repaying a chunk of his transfer fee, scored a fine goal, his first for the club, and left-winger Jim Adam hit home two in the last quarter. Town extended their unbeaten start to ten games and sat proudly at the top of the table.

LUTON: Baynham, Dunne, Hawkes, Morton, Owen, Pacey, Bingham, Turner, Brown, Cummins, Adam.

PRESTON: Else, Cunningham, Walton, Wylie, Dunn, O'Farrell, Mayers, Thompson, Hatsell, Lambert, Finney.

~~~~~~~~~~

Just as all seemed rosy in Luton's garden, the manager quit. There has never been a 'year of consolidation' as far as Luton Town Football Club is concerned. In early October promoted Blackburn made enquiries for Dally Duncan. The Board, in emergency session, decided that, in view of his eleven-year service, they were prepared to tempt Duncan to stay by raising his salary by £300 per annum to £1,500.

The ploy failed. A week later Duncan had gone, publicly stating that a change of scenery would do him good. Whether or not he felt he had taken the club as far as he could is open to question, but he left the club on good terms. His departure signified the end of an era, but beforehand, and unbeknown to anyone, the team was to have one final swansong.

Chairman Mitchell and directors England and Hodgson took control of the team selection, along with Syd Owen and trainer Frank King a month later. The new selectors did not preside over a winning team, and apart from a 6-3 thrashing of Arsenal on Boxing Day, the players went from winners to losers and were showing relegation form.

On the Saturday prior to the FA Cup third round, Luton plumbed the depths with a 0-1 home defeat by Birmingham, after which the selection committee took drastic action. For the home tie against Leeds, out went winger Jim Adam and – to the disgust of supporters – crowd favourite Gordon Turner. The pair were replaced by young Tony Gregory and Allan Brown. The upshot was that only 18,534 turned up on a cold day, a silent protest both against the Town's recent lack of form and the team changes.

Ninety minutes later, those present had changed their tune. A new-look side swept away their fellow Division One opponents. Billy Bingham skated over the icy surface to fire the Town into the lead on sixteen minutes, and after Leeds full-back Jim Ashall injured a wrist, which left him a passenger, it was one-way traffic. Tony Gregory increased the lead soon after the break, and although Leeds pulled one back, Bob Morton soon regained the two-goal advantage. Further strikes from Bingham and Gregory confirmed an emphatic victory.

The prize was a trip to Leicester, who were looked on as a bogey side at the time. The teams had met twice since the war in the FA Cup and on both occasions the Foxes had emerged victorious. Despite this, 3,000 Luton supporters made their way to Filbert Street to raise the crowd to 36,984 on another bitterly cold day. The pitch was a lottery, being partly frozen. The players were unable to turn and the game was liable to hinge on a mistake.

Leicester went ahead five minutes after the break. With Luton defenders slipping and sliding, Ian McNeill headed wide of Ron Baynham. There were just thirteen minutes left when Bingham repaid another slice of his transfer fee by chasing a seemingly lost cause and forcing the ball home for the equaliser. This meant that, for the first time, an FA Cup replay was staged under Kenilworth Road's floodlight and 27,277 turned up to see if the Town could finally lay the Leicester bogey to rest. After nine minutes, Bingham beat full-back Joe Baillie and his centre was headed in by Brown. Ten minutes later Bingham's corner was nodded down by Bob Morton to Gregory – 2-0.

It was ironic that the two controversial replacements should send the Town to a resounding victory. Brown slammed in goals in the 56th and 57th minutes to claim his hat-trick. Firstly, he chased a long ball down the middle, and from the restart Gregory's pinpoint cross was gobbled up by the ex-Scotland international. Although Leicester pulled one back through Ken Leek, new Foxes manager Matt Gillies had been confronted with a baptism he would rather forget.

Ipswich manager Alf Ramsey witnessed the carnage and probably shuddered at the prospect of what the rampant Hatters might do to his Second Division side in the next round. Ipswich made the game all-ticket with a capacity set at 26,700. The Town were allocated 6,000 tickets, which was initially regarded as generous, but Cup fever in Bedfordshire meant they quickly sold out. Ipswich's decision to increase prices did not go down well in Suffolk, which meant a further 1,000 spaces were found for Luton supporters, and even then some were disappointed.

The Town warmed up with a 6-2 home league win over Burnley. The tactics at Ipswich were to keep the game tight for the first twenty minutes, and then go searching for goals but, of course, things rarely go to plan in football. Almost at once Ray Crawford crossed from the right and the unmarked Derek Rees headed Ipswich in front. The Luton supporters found their voices a minute later when Dave Pacey was brought down on the edge of the area. Picking himself up, Pacey hammered the free-kick high past Ipswich's goalkeeper Roy Bailey.

Luton had all but won the game by the seventeenth minute. Neat inter-play between George Cummins and Billy Bingham saw Allan Brown's shot parried out to Morton. Bingham then climbed above Ken Malcolm to head a third into the top corner. And when Tony Gregory shot home just as two Ipswich defenders converged on him it was 4-1.

Ipswich's Jimmy Leadbetter headed onto the top of the bar before a poor ball from John Groves was intercepted by Crawford, allowing Rees to gallop through to score. Half an hour remained, but a late header by Morton from Bingham's cross made the game safe at 5-2.

The Town were now through to the quarter-finals for only the third time, with an unwanted long trip to Blackpool their reward. The Seasiders were arguably the strongest side left in the competition and the tie revived memories of a titanic struggle five years before, when the Town eventual-ly went out to Blackpool after three replays. This time the match was five minutes away from a replay when a long cross from Morton was headed home by Bingham on the blind side.

With the referee counting down the last seconds, Luton full-back Ken Hawkes played a weak back-pass to Baynham, and Ray Charnley nipped in to level. There was not enough time to restart the game and a devastated Hawkes said afterwards, 'I ought to be whipped.' Skipper Owen stood up for his inconsolable colleague and promised that the Hatters would win the replay.

KENILWORTH ROAD CLASSICS: **Luton v Blackpool** – 1-0

FA Cup, Quarter-final replay, 4th March 1959
After Blackpool's last-gasp equaliser the distraught Luton players had no choice but to prepare for the replay. Blackpool refused to play under the Kenilworth Road floodlights, apparently at the instigation of Stanley Matthews, which meant the tie had to go ahead on a Wednesday afternoon. The Town officials expected this to drastically curtail the gate, and were astonished to find a record crowd of 30,069 in attendance. Truancy was rife that afternoon, but as a good number of schoolteachers were also present there were few repercussions.

No quarter was given on a difficult pitch, few chances were created, and it was clear that one goal was likely to settle the outcome. It fell to inside-forward Allan Brown, who was playing against his old side. Six years pre-viously Brown had broken a leg as he scored Blackpool's quarter-final win-ner at Arsenal. This time he ran onto George Cummins' pass and swept the ball into the net, just as Seasiders' goalkeeper George Farm crashed into him.

Mercifully, Brown gingerly got to his feet and assisted the Town defence, marshalled by skipper Syd Owen, for the final sixteen minutes of this pulsating tie. At the final whistle the players were submerged under a sea of delirious supporters.

LUTON: Baynham, McNally, Hawkes, Groves, Owen, Pacey, Bingham, Brown, Morton, Cummins, Gregory.

BLACKPOOL: Farm, Armfield, Wright, Hauser, Gratrix, H Kelly, Matthews, Mudie, Charnley, J Kelly, Durie.

~~~~~~~~~~

The Hatters were now through to the FA Cup semi-finals for the first time in their 74-year history, where their opponents would be Norwich City of Division Three. This was the kindest of draws, as the alternatives were Nottingham Forest or Aston Villa. The Canaries, however, commanded respect as they had already 'giant-killed' Manchester United, Tottenham, Sheffield United, and Cardiff on their epic journey.

The semi-final was scheduled for Stamford Bridge, but Norwich objected, as Luton had a league game there the week before. It was then switched, amid some confusion, to White Hart Lane. When tickets were finally made available, just six days before the tie, the vast queue at Kenilworth Road was headed by a couple of coachloads of Norwich supporters!

The first half at White Hart Lane was one-sided, but Luton only had an Allan Brown header to show for their dominance. The Canaries threw caution to the wind in the second period and were rewarded when ex-Hatter Bobby Brennan, celebrating his 34th birthday, volleyed right-footed past Ron Baynham. The Town rallied but could not find a way past reserve goalkeeper Sandy Kennon, whose last-minute save from Billy Bingham was breathtaking.

The replay took place at St Andrews, Birmingham, and this time the Canaries had more of the play. Were it not for Jimmy Hill – the little Norwich inside-forward – missing a sitter on the stroke of half-time, Luton would have been up against it. In the second half, a back-heel from Bob Morton set up Bingham who hammered the ball high into the net.

Back on the ground where he started his career, 36-year-old Syd Owen, playing his final season in football, was the rock upon which the wave upon wave of Norwich attacks foundered. This was perhaps his finest moment in a Luton shirt. As for Norwich, their dazed players were applauded off by their fans, who had seen hopes of becoming the first Division Three side to reach Wembley dashed at the final hurdle.

The last words were left to Owen: 'This is a great day for me. In my last season as a professional footballer I have achieved one of football's most coveted honours – to captain a side at Wembley.' No one, not even Norwich manager Archie Macaulay, could begrudge him that.

During the six weeks that elapsed before the final, neither the Town nor their Wembley opponents, Nottingham Forest, distinguished themselves.

Each side won only three of their fourteen league games played. The Town, however, had seized what they hoped was a psychological advantage by beating Forest 5-1 at Kenilworth Road on 9th April, when Allan Brown netted four. Unfortunately, that 'advantage' was tempered by the fact that Forest put out a phoney side that bore no resemblance to their 'Cup eleven'.

Luton's 'selection committee' had kept the same side throughout the Cup run – omitting goalscoring ace Gordon Turner and winger Jim Adam. Despite the results, these omissions had not gone down well with everyone. Even more provocative was the distribution of tickets for the big day. With an allocation of only 16,000, the Board – in an attempt to squeeze a quart out of a pint pot – decreed that all non-season ticket holders should be subjected to a postal ballot. This obviously produced winners and losers. The local press was inundated with irate letters from the unlucky, and resentment from some lingers to this day. On the day before the final, cruel rumours spread that spare tickets were on sale at the club. A queue swiftly formed which club office staff frantically attempted to disband but 'sharp suited London spivs' were soon on the scene offering 3s 6d (17.5p) tickets for £4.

No real preparations were made for the big day. The only concessions Luton made to the fact that they were about to experience Wembley's lush turf were training sessions on the hockey pitch at Cedars School at Leighton Buzzard. That surface was supposed to mirror Wembley's but the players were soon exhausted after training on such heavy ground. Nor were they given any special team talks: the Cup final was almost regarded as just another game.

Forest, on the other hand, were secreted away during the week prior to the showpiece. This meant their nervous tension was presumably building, while the Town players were theoretically more relaxed. Only time would tell which was the best approach.

On the Thursday Syd Owen was presented with the Footballer of the Year award by the Football Writers' Association, a fitting finale to a playing career which was due to end at 4.40pm on Saturday, 2nd May 1959. By now, anyone patrolling the streets of Luton could not fail but know that the Hatters were Wembley-bound. Black and white ribbon and straw boaters adorned every shop in the town centre and along Dunstable Road. A special floral display had been carefully laid out on the Moor, and Dudley's wet fish shop had dressed up a skate in Luton colours and straw hat with the legend, 'May you skate to victory!'

Britain's oldest woman, 108-year-old Mrs Hannah Taylor of Norman Road professed that she would be unable to sleep. After all, the pubs were allowed to extend their opening hours until 10.30pm, and with the cost of a pint having been reduced to 1s 1d (5p), following the reduction in duty in the recent Budget, it looked like being a long night. Full-back Ken Hawkes, who lived in a house in Kenilworth Road, was seen answering his door at midnight to desperate supporters seeking tickets.

The big day finally arrived. At 8.30am, 56-year-old Bill Wright set off on the 29-mile run to Wembley Stadium, closely followed by a 1909 vintage Commer bus bedecked in black and white on its 20mph crawl to the stadium.

As was normal on match-days, wing-half John Groves caught a bus from Sundon Park to meet up with his playing colleagues at Kenilworth Road. Now, after a few photo calls with teammates bashfully sporting boaters, it was off on the short drive to north-west London. As a departure from normal custom, the players were treated to a pre-match lunch at the Hendon Hall Hotel and later arrived at the stadium in good time to inspect the lush, green turf.

Meanwhile, back in Luton, every coach for miles around was mobilised to take the fans to Wembley, while several special trains were laid on to ship supporters direct to Wembley Park station. Although the local Chamber of Commerce had advised all shops to stay open, Luton was like a ghost town. Those not lucky enough to secure a ticket gathered around the latest 14in television sets to watch the game on BBC in black and white. These armchair supporters endured Eileen Fowler's 'Keep Fit' demonstration and then listened to half an hour of community singing.

As the two teams lined up in the tunnel, the Luton players did indeed look more relaxed and confident than their tense opponents. The Forest players became even more apprehensive when they learned that their counterparts had not been holed up in a hotel. They assumed that this was a ruse, designed to hide something special up their sleeves.

Director Tom Hodgson – in the absence of a manager – led out the Luton team. After both sets of players had been introduced to the Duke of Edinburgh, the captains exchanged banners – a first in Wembley history. Battle then commenced.

Much was expected of the Hatters, so much so that the opening fourteen minutes came as an unpleasant shock. Forest ripped into the Town and pinged the ball around on the true surface with the result that the Hatters were left chasing shadows. With ten minutes gone, Forest's Roy Dwight raced onto a pull-back from Stuart Imlach and flashed the ball into the net. Four minutes later Billy Gray's diagonal centre was headed back into the far corner of the net by Tom Wilson.

Two goals down, the Town were given a lifeline on 32 minutes when Dwight and Luton full-back Brendan McNally went up for a high ball. Dwight's studs caught McNally's chest and as both players went down it was clear that the Forest player was badly injured. After attempting to carry on he collapsed with what was later diagnosed as a fractured shinbone.

The introduction of substitutes was still six years away and the so-called 'Wembley Hoodoo' had struck again, leaving Forest to battle on with ten men. The pitch was often blamed for the many injuries seen at Wembley and this game was no exception. The trainers were summoned into action eleven times in total, and McNally's cartilage problem – a legacy of his clash with Dwight – left him limping on the fringes.

Maybe the Town were not aware that a ten-man side had yet to win a Wembley final, but hopes were raised in the 62nd minute when Dave Pacey, eight yards out, drove in a Ken Hawkes cross. Allan Brown almost forced extra-time against a tiring Forest when he launched himself at a Billy Bingham cross, but his header flashed narrowly wide. In truth, an equaliser would have been an injustice and when the final whistle sounded everyone agreed that Forest were deserving winners.

The 1959 FA Cup final does not rank as one of the best to grace the Twin Towers as far as the neutral spectator was concerned. This was illustrated when, at the end of the game, Sir Stanley Rous from the Football Association asked the Queen, 'Who do you think played best, Ma'am?' 'The band' was her reply!

The Luton players have since maintained to a man that the preparation was all wrong. They were far too relaxed and casual and were not keyed up enough, unlike the Forest team who were as taut as guitar strings, seeing the game as a welcome release. Either way, the defeated Hatters trooped up to receive their runners-up medals. The moment was particularly poignant for Syd Owen, who was now hanging up his boots. A muted 'celebration' dinner was held at the Piccadilly Hotel and the players probably thought that the following day's open-top bus ride through Luton was going to be akin to a wake.

They were therefore shocked and delighted to see thousands line the streets as the bus made its way to the Town Hall on a wet, miserable day. All Syd Owen could say to the massed crowds from the Town Hall balcony was 'See you at Wembley in 1960'. Owen already knew that if the Town were to return a year later, he would be in charge. His appointment as team manager – on a three-year contract – was confirmed by the Board on 29th April 1959, to take effect from 4th May.

Owen was aware that the forward line needed strengthening and that someone to fill his own vacated position was also required. His first job, though, was to transfer the unsettled Jim Adam to Aston Villa for £7,250, thus creating another hole in the side.

The 1959-60 season started poorly and steadily got worse as the ageing team split at the seams. Youngsters introduced to the side, promising though they might have been (although not as promising as Dally Duncan's protégés of ten years before) were unable to turn things around on their own as the team plummeted down the table.

The Board was accused of allowing half the profits from the previous season's Cup run to be frittered on various taxes rather than spent on vitally needed new players. The directors responded belatedly, buying forward Joe McBride from Wolves for £12,500. The signing was against the wishes of Owen, but it was too little, too late and the Town ended up bottom with only 32 points, suffering relegation in the Football League for the first time in their history.

Undermined, disappointed and disillusioned, Owen handed in his resignation a week before the end of the season, with the board citing 'a fundamental disagreement on policy' to the press. Out, too, went Owen's right-hand men – ex-players Wally Shanks and Bud Aherne – with more of Dally Duncan's 'team of the 1950s' soon to follow.

The Annual General Meeting, as the season drew to a close, was the longest since the war, with the directors under fire for the parlous state of the Hatters. Chairman Percy Mitchell sought to defend himself and his colleagues by confirming that funds had to be held back to pay for the proposed new Lewsey Farm ground, that the tax position had to be 'regularised' at some stage, and that Syd Owen had sole control of the playing side, and only had to ask for money for it to be provided.

Owen, who had not been invited to the AGM, disputed the chairman's version of events, pointing out that meddling and unjustified criticism by members of the Board were the main reasons behind his resignation. He added that he wished to buy Denis Law from Huddersfield but was told he was too expensive, and then centre-forward John McCole from Bradford City, but could not find a director with the authority to sanction the required fee of £10,000. McCole was sold to Leeds while Luton dithered. The signing of Joe McBride behind the manager's back was probably the final straw as far as Owen was concerned. It also did the directors no favours as the purchase smacked of desperation at the end of a depressing campaign.

Mention of the Lewsey Farm ground raised eyebrows, as most supporters had given up hope of moving from Kenilworth Road. The long-awaited results of an almost forgotten public enquiry were suddenly announced, and the directors were confident that they could overcome the published objections put forward by the Minister of Housing and Local Government. These objections included inadequate car parking for a 50,000 capacity stadium, inadequate access, and unacceptable traffic congestion, as far as the nearby Luton and Dunstable Hospital and M1 motorway were concerned.

Renewed discussion of a possible new ground prompted a fair amount of newspaper talk. The local press guessed that although the Luton Corporation favoured the Lewsey site, the County Council would rather keep a 'green wedge' between Luton and Dunstable. They were fighting a losing battle, however, as pressure was mounting to release land for building purposes. On the one hand, a new football ground could be seen as preserving an open space, while on the other it could be seen as creating a precedent.

The local press proposed Stockwood Park, which they sensed would be favoured by the County Council as it was not on green belt land. Luton Corporation, however, wanted to keep Stockwood as a park, hence the reason for favouring Lewsey Farm. This argument was likely to go on and on. There were compelling arguments for a new stadium at Stockwood rather than Lewsey Farm, not least for logistical reasons. The new M1 motorway, with its slip road only yards from Stockwood, would enjoy greater and easier access than Lewsey Farm ever would, especially with a new eastern bypass mooted (now built) which would link up with the site.

Stockwood Park was a 265-acre white elephant which was hardly ever used. The Corporation, for reasons best known to itself – but probably stemming from agreements made when it purchased the land in 1946 – did not wish to part with the land, even though it was 'as well known to Lutonians as is the middle of Africa'.

The club, doubtless influenced by Luton Corporation, backed the Lewsey Farm option, even though the land was sited above a badly drained, seven-foot thick band of clay. They also felt that Lewsey, being situated midway between Luton and Dunstable, was in a better spot for attracting spectators than Stockwood, which was out on a limb.

Looking at it dispassionately, the football club was being asked to solve the traffic issue at M1 Junction 11, Dunstable Road, the Luton and Dunstable Hospital, Lewsey Road and Leagrave High Street, caused by siting the ground at Lewsey Farm, upon which they, on their own, could have no influence. It was now a matter for the Ministry of Transport. Decisions had to be made about spending taxpayers' money on widening roads and improving junctions for Saturday football matches and the occasional midweek game.

The alternative was a perfectly good site at Stockwood, which was cursed by few of the Lewsey traffic problems. It is also likely that if the club had a choice of Stockwood or nothing, it would have accepted the sensible site without any reservations, despite what the directors had stated publicly in the local press.

Although the Kenilworth Road stadium was hardly perfect, and the pitch with its slope and poor drainage was not conducive to good football in mid-season, the supporters' first priority was a team to be proud of. As such, interest was now mainly focused on the new man to take over the hot seat at the club and, it was hoped, a quick return to Division One.

KENILWORTH ROAD HEROES: **Syd Owen**

Born in Birmingham in 1922, Owen left school at fourteen and, although playing local football, the outbreak of war put a halt to any thoughts he might have had about playing professionally. 'I joined the RAF and saw service in Italy but while I was there I managed to play a fair amount of representative football,' Owen said. 'It was while I was in Italy that I met up with several professional footballers, including Bill Nicholson who was at Tottenham and we became firm friends, and I must say I learned a lot from him.'

While home on leave from Italy in 1945, Owen was invited for trials at Birmingham City and on de-mob signed for the St Andrews side. Due to the large number of professionals on the books at St Andrews, Syd only managed five appearances in 1945-46, when the Blues won the Football League (South) competition, and another five in the following campaign – the first year of normal league competition:

'You have to remember that I was 25 and needed first team football,' said Owen. 'Manager Harry Storer made it fairly obvious that he did not rate me and placed me on the transfer list with a price tag of £1,500. I was desperate to prove him wrong and jumped at the chance to come to Kenilworth Road.'

Luton chairman Charles Jeyes negotiated the transfer that brought Owen to Luton in June 1947, but his arrival was overshadowed when the Town signed Welsh international full-back Billy Hughes, coincidentally from Birmingham, for £11,000 the following month. Hughes lasted less than a season, despite all the hype, while Owen gave twelve years' solid service to the Town rearguard.

Owen did not have to wait long before getting his chance. Following a 1-4 defeat at Coventry on the opening day of 1947-48, he found himself picked instead of Doug Gardiner at left-half in the following game, at Brentford. The Town won 3-0, courtesy of a Hugh Billington hat-trick, and that was the start of a career that ran to 388 league appearances in the black and white of the Town.

After almost two years with the Hatters, Owen was switched to centre-half, a position he had played as a schoolboy. Initially reluctant to forego his wing-half position, it soon became apparent that his ability in the air meant that he was made for central defence – although it put paid to his prodigious long throw, which was used by the Town to good effect in the late 1940s.

Owen's displays at centre-half, with his dominance in the air, cool distribution and long legs, that seemed to snake out to dispossess opposition forwards, earned him the captaincy at Kenilworth Road and the honour of travelling with the FA party to Australia.

Further honours followed – for the Football League against Denmark and Scotland, and trips to the West Indies and South Africa with the FA. It seemed only a matter of time before he would win a full England cap. England had lost 3-6 to Hungary at Wembley in 1953, the first time they had been beaten by a foreign side on their own soil, and for the return in 1954, Owen was given his chance at centre-half. Sadly, the Hungarians ran riot and ended up 7-1 winners. As if to prove that it was not Syd's fault, he earned two more caps and took part in the 1954 World Cup finals. He would have probably earned more caps had Billy Wright not been an almost automatic selection at centre-half at the time.

Owen licked his wounds, knuckled down at Kenilworth Road, and in 1954-55 captained the side to promotion to Division One. Such was Syd's influence that season, it is worth noting that of the six games he missed through injury, four were lost.

In Division One, Owen, by now 33, was given the extra responsibility of coaching the youngsters, but this did not detract from his performances on the pitch, as the Town took to their new higher status like ducks to water and saw off some of the best teams in the land. Syd was injured in mid-season, in the FA Cup-tie against Leicester, and only came back for the last few games. During his absence the team went off the boil. It is conjecture to think what might have happened had he been ever present, as many Town fans felt that this was one of the best Hatters sides in the club's history.

Owen did battle against the greatest forwards in the country, but by the summer of 1958, despite being super fit, he decided to call it a day. He wanted to concentrate on coaching, having been appointed chief coach: 'I had told the club I wanted to finish but it was not as easy as it sounds and the board and manager Dally Duncan talked me round,' he remembered. 'For that I shall always be grateful.' The reason for this show of appreciation? The Town reached the FA Cup final twelve months later!

Manager Dally Duncan, of course, had resigned in October 1958 and for the remainder of the season the team was picked by a consortium which included Owen, trainer Frank King and the Board. The loss of Duncan affected the side for a while and, by the time of the third round FA Cup home clash with Leeds, performances were at a low ebb. Changes had to be made, including axing record goalscorer Gordon Turner. On an icy pitch, the Town thrashed their Yorkshire opponents 5-1 to set up a fourth round tie at Leicester. On another icy pitch, the Hatters scraped a

draw, but in the replay Luton went through, with Turner's replacement –
Allan Brown – scoring a hat trick.

'I honestly can't remember whose idea it was to effectively keep the
same side going through the Cup competition, despite the call of fans to
include Turner, but it certainly was not myself,' said Owen. 'After we had
beaten Ipswich away 5-2 and then managed to scrape through against
Blackpool after a replay in round six, perhaps we thought our name was on
the trophy.

'Reaching Wembley was my proudest moment. But the hurdle we
cleared to get there brought me one of the most satisfying moments of my
life when we beat Norwich, with Billy Bingham's replay winner in the semi-
final at St Andrews, Birmingham. That day I was to take Luton, as captain,
to the Cup final, the complete fulfilment of an ambition in every footballer's heart. But to win such an honour on a ground from which I had
been effectively sacked twelve years earlier put that little extra spice into the
achievement.'

Owen's last appearance in a white shirt was not a happy one. Although
he had been named 'Footballer of the Year' in midweek, and had the proud
honour to be the first Luton player to skipper a Town side at Wembley, the
team were second best on the day and it was a sad Owen who picked up a
losers medal from the Queen.

It was common knowledge that Owen would assume the manager's job
after the Cup final, but the new season opened badly and got worse. The
team had grown old together and new blood was needed. As had been well
chronicled, there seemed to be a reluctance on the part of the Board to
spend the money that had been accumulated during the Cup run. Owen
explained: 'The directors believed we had some very talented youngsters on
the books whom we could develop and play in place of the older players
in the First Division. The jump from local youth football was too much to
be made in a short space of time and we left it too late to find top-quality
replacements. The directors did not give me any power to conduct transfers and, instead, went against my advice and signed Joe McBride from
Wolves for £12,500 when it was too late anyway.'

Owen resigned a week before the season's end, with the club already relegated. The official explanation for his departure was 'a fundamental disagreement on policy'. He reflected on the offers open to him and decided
to accept a coaching post with Leeds, taking with him trainer Les Cocker
from Kenilworth Road. A year later Don Revie was handed the player-
manager's position at Elland Road and the stage was set for the growth of
the great Leeds side of the 1960s and '70s.

'I had played against Don during his days at Leicester and had attended FA coaching courses with him. We shared the same beliefs and spoke

the same language and I was therefore more than pleased to see him get the manager's job. We had a brilliant side at Leeds and it must be remembered that most of the players came up through the youth side that I was responsible for. That side won League Championships in 1969 and 1974, the FA Cup in 1972, the League Cup in 1968 and the Fairs Cup in 1971. But many remember them for what they could have won. So many times Leeds came second in the race for the championship, and in the 1965, '70, and '73 FA Cup finals.'

Following Revie's departure from Elland Road to manage England, Owen also left and took on the assistant manager's job at Birmingham City under Willie Bell, one of his old players at Leeds, before taking up coaching positions at Hull and Manchester United.

~~~~~~~~~~~

After first offering the top job to ex-Hatters coach Jack Crompton, who decided to stay at Manchester United, and then interviewing several other applicants, the Board plumped for ex-York City boss Sam Bartram. The new man had enjoyed a long and loyal playing career with Charlton Athletic and was regarded by many as the best uncapped keeper of his generation before folding up his gloves in 1956. His managerial career at Bootham Crescent had seen him win promotion for the Minstermen, but then fail to consolidate the club's position at its higher level.

One of Bartram's first tasks was to convince the Board that Luton should enter the inaugural Football League Cup, because not to do so was unfair on the players. The Town therefore ceased being among the six clubs set to boycott the new competition. They entered the draw for the first round, and received a bye.

With regard to the players he inherited, Bartram had no worries over his goalkeepers until a pre-season injury to reserve Alan Collier left Ron Baynham as the only experienced man. Baynham's skull fracture early in the season during the visit of Sheffield United left Bartram with no option but to blood sixteen-year-old Mike O'Hara, who remains the Town's youngest ever league debutant.

Although O'Hara was not ready for the first team, Bartram needed time before landing a suitable replacement. With unsettled winger Billy Bingham yearning to be back in the First Division, Bartram cannily set up an auction. Arsenal offered Danny Clapton, Ted Magill plus £7,500; Everton were prepared to part with Alec Ashworth, John Bramwell and £10,000; while West Brom offered £25,000 cash.

Bartram felt that Everton's offer best suited the Hatters' interests. In one fell swoop he recruited a really useful full-back in the shape of Bramwell, who would be talked about as a possible England international before the season was out, a goalscorer to take the weight off Gordon

Turner's shoulders, and enough surplus cash to buy experienced goalkeeper Jim Standen from Arsenal.

KENILWORTH ROAD CLASSICS: **Luton v Manchester City** – 3-1

FA Cup, Fourth Round, 1st February 1961

By Christmas 1960 it was obvious the Hatters were not going to leap straight back to Division One, and in order to stimulate some excitement a good run in the FA Cup was necessary. The third round draw saw the Town pitted against neighbours Northampton for the first time since 1937. The tie created the necessary excitement and, after deliberation, was made all-ticket.

It is curious to observe how the ticket allocation was divided for what was the first all-ticket game since the visit of Arsenal in 1952. It also shows how the ground capacity was calculated. After allowing for 3,632 seats in the Main Stand, 5,000 tickets were allocated for the enclosure, 10,500 for the Kenilworth Road terrace, and 11,000 for the Oak Road end and Bobbers Stand, which totalled 30,132.

Match-day saw a local bus strike, but as 26,000 tickets had already been sold the Town's directors were not too bothered by the prospect of a low gate. Most ticket-holders got to the ground somehow or other, even though there were the normal stories of supporters taking hours to arrive in time for kick-off.

The Town ran out 4-0 winners and rubbed their hands at the prospect of another all-ticket home draw against Manchester City, who boasted Denis Law amongst their ranks. The day dawned with heavy rain, which persisted into the afternoon. Despite the obvious threat to the match, 23,727 turned up to find much of the pitch under water. The referee, Ken Tuck, decided to start the game and Luton supporters were glad he did as Alec Ashworth put the ball in the City net twice in the first eighteen minutes. Then Law notched a hat-trick.

In the second half Law was just as unstoppable, gliding over the surface to score another three. But now the rain had turned into a deluge, and after 69 minutes, with the score at 2-6, the referee had little option but to take both teams off.

Legend has it that the referee intended to keep the teams in their dressing rooms until the downpour had eased before attempting a restart. The Luton players, however, showing admirable speed of thought, immediately jumped in the bath. When the referee decided to try again, a visit to the Luton dressing room gave him little alternative but to abandon the match, leaving a shocked Law to moan about the unfairness of it all.

The game had to be replayed on the following Wednesday afternoon, as City's German goalkeeper Bert Trautmann complained that the Kenilworth

Road floodlights were not up to scratch. Although Manchester City sent out an unchanged team, the Hatters bolstered their defence in a bid to curtail Denis Law.

Bob Morton had been omitted on the Saturday, and on Monday he turned down a move to Preston. He was now brought back to shadow Law, while John Groves was given a similar marking job on City's playmaker George Hannah.

Looking more solid, the Hatters again went two goals up – through Ashworth and Jim Fleming – and although Law reduced the deficit on half-time the Luton players were in no mood to let the lead slip. A second goal from Ashworth sealed an unlikely victory.

In truth, the conditions were worse for the second game than for the first, with a waterlogged but even pitch giving way to thick, cloying mud which prevented the ball from running clean and true.

Denis Law was now set to become the subject of that most popular of sports quiz questions, 'Who scored seven goals in an FA Cup-tie but still finished on the losing side?'

The Town went out in the next round like a damp squib, losing 0-1 at Barnsley of Division Three.

LUTON: Standen, Dunne, Bramwell, Morton, Kelly, Groves, Noake, Ashworth, Turner, McGuffie, Fleming.

MANCHESTER C: Trautmann, Leivers, Betts, Barnes, Plenderleith, Shawcross, Barlow, Hannah, Baker, Law, Hayes.

~~~~~~~~~~~

That season – 1960-61 – earned a final position of thirteenth. Bartram had overseen the dismantling of the squad he inherited, with six of the team which reached the FA Cup final having left Kenilworth Road.

KENILWORTH ROAD HEROES: **Seamus Dunne**

Seamus Dunne is regarded as one of the all-time great players to have worn the black and white of Luton Town. His love affair with the Hatters began in 1950 when he came over from the Republic of Ireland.

Born in Wicklow in 1930, Seamus made a name for himself with his local team, before transferring to Shelbourne in the League of Ireland. He had a glittering youth career, obtaining six international caps and captaining his country in the World Youth Tournament of 1948. Clubs in England took note and the Town sent over chief scout Hubert Day to try and entice Dunne to Kenilworth Road.

'I was not particularly keen to leave as I had a good pensionable job as a Local Government Officer in the County Council offices, but as the opportunity presented itself, I decided to give it a go, which turned out to be a decision I never regretted.'

Dunne signed for the Hatters in July 1950, joining up with compatriot Bud Aherne, and embarked on a Luton career that was to embrace 301 games. After one season in the reserves, his league debut came on Boxing Day 1951 in a 6-1 home win over West Ham, a game which also saw a hat-trick from Gordon Turner – his first goals for the club.

'In my first full season in the league side at Luton, Jesse Pye was signed from Wolverhampton and he had a remarkable effect on the team,' added Dunne. 'He was the mentor for Gordon Turner and created so many goals for him, as well as netting a fair share himself. It was a tragedy when he broke his ankle in an accidental clash with Oldham's England centre-half George Hardwick but, by then, Gordon was the finished article.'

By this time, the Town were building their promotion-winning side. Dunne, by now an Eire international, was part of a solid defence that included Bud Aherne, Syd Owen, Charlie Watkins and international goal-keepers Bernard Streten and Ron Baynham.

'The promotion-winning season of 1954-55 remains vivid in the memory,' continued Seamus, 'but I can remember being up all night before our important home game with promotion rivals Blackburn when my eldest son was born. We went out and won 7-3! I also remember floating over a cross in the first minute at Doncaster in our final game, for Peter MacEwan to score, thus settling the nerves and setting us up for the win that earned us the runner's-up spot.

'During my time at Luton, in the days before substitutes, I was regard-ed as the emergency goalkeeper, and I was instrumental in relegating Portsmouth from Division One in 1959. In the game at Kenilworth Road at the end of the season, Portsmouth had to win to avoid the drop, and with the game finely balanced, Ron Baynham pulled down a Pompey for-ward in the box, something for which he would have been sent off today. He was injured in the challenge and had to go off, and so it was left to me to face the penalty. The penalty taker was Peter Harris, who was deadly from the spot, so I just decided to dive to the right and hope for the best. The ball cannoned off my body and went out for a corner and we went on to win 3-1 against a demoralised side.

'To add insult to injury, in the game at Fratton Park earlier in the sea-son, Portsmouth winger Jackie Henderson cut inside me to shoot home a great goal. Ron Baynham called the referee over and pointed to a split in the side netting which he maintained the ball had passed through. The ref disallowed the goal, much to the annoyance of the crowd, and we went on to take a point in the 2-2 draw. I still remain convinced that the goal should have stood!'

Although Dunne's biggest regret in his time with the Hatters was fail-ing to get a place in the side that carried the Town to Wembley in 1959, it also rankles that he never managed to score a single goal in 301 league appearances.

After the Town were relegated to Division Two in 1960, the side began to split up and Seamus played his last game in a 1-4 defeat at Bristol Rovers in February 1961. He went to non-league Yiewsley, managed by Jackie Milburn, for three years and then took over as player-manager at Dunstable while working at Vauxhall Motors in the engineering section. The chance of an assisted move back to Ireland to work at a chemical plant was too good to turn down, despite the wrench of leaving his adopted town, and so in 1970 he said farewell to these shores and settled in Bray.

~~~~~~~~~~

The Lewsey Farm saga dragged on but, such was the optimism amongst the Board members, that Chairman Percy Mitchell publicly confirmed his confidence that the new ground would be completed by 1965 – in good time for the World Cup. He apparently had been assured by Sir Stanley Rous that Luton stood a good chance of staging some of the matches in the forthcoming tournament, should their new stadium be operational in time.

With the Board distracted by thoughts of a new ground, the existing one at Kenilworth Road fell into disrepair. Complaints about the floodlights, the toilets, the lights under the Main Stand, and the pitch all fell on deaf ears, as it was felt that any money spent was dead money. It must have provoked much wringing of hands when the club was ordered to spend the considerable sum of £3,128 on nine steel columns to re-enforce the rear of the Kenilworth Road terrace, which was cracking.

On the pitch, the major signing was Ron Cope from Manchester United, as Bartram sought to solve the centre-half problem that had existed since the retirement of Syd Owen. Unfortunately, Cope did not hit the heights in 1961-62. The Town stuttered through another frustrating season, finishing in an identical position (13th) and with the same number of points (39) as in the previous season.

The season did have one oddity. In the Easter Monday game against promotion-chasing Orient, the Town played goalkeeper Ron Baynham in attack in place of the injured Gordon Turner. Predictably, Baynham looked like a fish out of water in the 1-3 defeat.

In June 1962 it was announced that manager Sam Bartram would be leaving the club 'by mutual consent', although privately the Board had felt for some time that he was not 'fulfilling his duties in the manner hoped'. Bartram felt aggrieved, and in the new spirit of the age told all to a Sunday newspaper. Football, after all, was changing. The maximum wage had gone, the retain and transfer system was under pressure, and celebrities were being encouraged to 'kiss and tell' on the sports pages of the popular press.

The Town's directors maintained a dignified silence as they searched for a replacement, and the furore soon passed over. Approaches were made, for a second time, to ex-coach Jack Crompton. This time he accepted, but just seven days after signing a three-year contract he resigned on medical grounds. Apparently a stomach ulcer had flared up, following his decision to take charge at Kenilworth Road, and a specialist advised against taking up the position.

Next in the Town's sights were Roy Bentley and Ted Drake. Both said no, whereupon the search fell on the Bristol City coach Bill Harvey. Highly regarded in the coaching world, Harvey came personally recommended by England manager Walter Winterbottom and was seen as one of the new breed of all-action, tracksuited managers becoming more and more popular in the game.

Harvey started as he meant to go on, transfer-listing Jim Standen who he would not tolerate combining professional cricket with Worcestershire with a career at Kenilworth Road, especially as the football and cricket seasons overlapped more and more. Standen was in time transferred to West Ham, where he combined both careers quite successfully.

The 1962-63 season started miserably and the Hatters were soon down among the dead men. Sensing the club was now in free-fall, attempts were made to bring in desperately needed new blood. Bids of £14,000 and £16,000 were made to West Brom and Preston for David Burnside and Alfie Biggs respectively. Both players turned down Luton, ostensibly for domestic reasons, before Harvey finally signed highly rated Ron Davies from Chester for £10,200.

They say it never rains but it pours, and this was certainly true for the Town that season. In the early hours of Sunday, 2nd December 1962 a fire broke out in the Main Stand. Mercifully, the fire was spotted by nineteen-year-old David Weedon of Wimborne Road who, having returned from a dance, had needed to enter his house through the back door as he had forgotten his front door key. From his vantage point he could see across the railway line to the rear of the Main Stand and saw a bright red glow. He rushed to the telephone box at the end of the road to call the Fire Brigade and by the time he returned home the stand had burst into flames. Twenty firemen in four engines took an hour to bring the flames under control, having arrived just in time to prevent them spreading sideways.

The fire had started under the directors box and a smouldering cigarette end discarded a few hours before, during the home game against Grimsby, was the likely cause. The directors box was destroyed, 200 seats and the main electricity control room went up in flames, a section of the stand roof was burnt through, and the floodlights were put out of action. The final bill came to £5,000. But it could have been a lot worse.

Soon after the fire came another stormy AGM, with many of the share-holders giving vent to their frustration at how the club was being run. A 'ginger' group attempted to force the resignation of chairman Percy Mitchell, and to raise the number of directors from six to eight in an effort to bring in fresh ideas. As before, both motions failed on a poll vote.

The Town played only one league game and one FA Cup-tie between Boxing Day 1962 and 9th March 1963. This was due to the dreadful winter weather, but the enforced rest did not help the team, which sank to the bottom of the table with relegation the inevitable conclusion to a disastrous period in the club's history.

Luton faced a return to Division Three for the first time since 1937. Needing to cut wages, several players were offered minimum terms of £13 per week. Knowing they would be unable to accept, the club effectively placed them on the transfer list, while retaining the right to dictate transfer fees. This was in accordance with Football League rules, which aimed at preventing non-League clubs from poaching players for nothing.

Unfortunately for the Town, three players – Terry Kelly, Brendan McNally and Ron Cope – took their cases to the Football Association, who ruled that they were free to join non-League clubs if they wished and fees would only be payable should they be signed by a League club. The players, particularly Kelly and Cope, became 'cause célèbres' on the back pages of the tabloids, and the Town's directors were miffed to think that they should become scapegoats when they were merely following prescribed regulations.

The only glimmer of hope arising from relegation was the form of young Welshman Ron Davies, who had netted 21 goals in only 29 games. He now signed a new, improved, contract, but only on condition that if a suitable bid consistent with the Town's valuation of him came along he could go. The 'suitable bid consistent with the Town's valuation' was not long in coming, and in September 1963 Davies was sold to Norwich for £35,000. The Canaries had been trailing Davies ever since he scored six goals against them for Luton the previous season.

Elsewhere, all was gloom – literally. Concerned by comments from referees and visiting clubs about the twilight feebleness of the Town's flood-lights, the directors had to dig deep and order a fresh set, at a cost of £7,606. The work was completed in a rush, after a further complaint by the referee of a League Cup-tie against Coventry City provoked a letter of ultimatum from League Secretary Alan Hardaker.

As there was no room to mount standard floodlight pylons in the corners, the Town had to settle for eight 65ft towers situated along the side of the pitch. The new floodlights were officially switched on before the game against Port Vale on 9th October 1963.

Behind the scenes, the 'ginger' group was mobilising for another tilt at the Board during the forthcoming AGM. Although the motions were again defeated by a poll vote, this time the directors could no longer shrug off increasing public disquiet. Controversial chairman Percy Mitchell stepped down, to be replaced by Tom Hodgson, while two extra directors of the Board's choosing were co-opted. By resorting to the co-opting option, under club's rules it would be almost twelve months before they would come up for formal election. Presumably the merry-go-round of poll voting would start again should the 'ginger' group wish to continue its war of attrition, which it was never likely to win.

Against this background, the team continued to drop like a stone and by the turn of the year relegation to the football basement looked likely, thus completing a disastrous plunge through the divisions. Just before Christmas 1963, the Town had introduced their new free-transfer signing from Chelsea, nineteen-year-old ex-England youth international John O'Rourke. The new boy starred in the 2-1 home win over Reading and was unlucky not to bag a hat-trick. It soon became evident that a forward line with O'Rourke assisting veteran Gordon Turner could conjure up enough goals, provided the gaps were plugged at the other end. Luton had conceded three in each of four consecutive games after the Reading win.

Slowly results began to improve, culminating in an improbable 6-2 win at Brentford with O'Rourke scoring four. This was the first Luton away win in 27 attempts in a sorry record dating back sixteen months. Sadly, three defeats in the next six games sent the Town plummeting back to the foot of the table. With only nine games to go, the situation looked beyond redemption.

The start of an improbable revival began at Notts County on 26th March, where a crowd of 4,406 witnessed a 1-1 draw, with Tom McKechnie scoring the Town's goal. Two days later, at home to promotion-chasing Bristol Rovers, the Hatters got off to a flying start with O'Rourke scoring twice in the first four minutes. He went on to complete a hat-trick in a 4-2 victory.

The crowds were now returning to Kenilworth Road, and 8,387 saw O'Rourke on target again with both goals in the 2-0 return win over Notts County, and 7,094 for the 3-1 home win over Wrexham the following week – O'Rourke scoring the second goal. With three successive away fixtures to follow, it was anticipated that the bubble would surely burst, but the pessimists were made to eat their words as five points were picked up from the six on offer. O'Rourke was on the mark yet again, scoring both goals in the 2-0 win at Bristol Rovers, and followed those with the Town's goal in the 1-1 draw at Colchester, where the Hatters were making their first ever visit. At Oldham, O'Rourke, for once, failed to score, but Mark Lownds did, thereby setting up a nail-biting climax with two points needed from the final two games to ensure survival. The visitors for the last home game were Watford, who needed to win themselves to retain hopes of promotion to Division Two.

The biggest home crowd since the visit of Norwich in September 1960 – 19,799 – were heartened by an all-action first-half display by the Town, with O'Rourke and Turner going close and Watford's Ken Nicholas surviving a penalty appeal when he brought down O'Rourke. Disaster struck ten minutes after the interval, however, when Watford left-winger George Harris put the Hornets ahead. Yet with nine minutes left O'Rourke latched onto a loose ball to slip it past Pat Jennings in the Watford goal. With barely two minutes to go, O'Rourke capped a marvellous display to beat Jennings at the second attempt to send the crowd delirious.

After the game Chairman Tom Hodgson cracked open the champagne to toast the amazing run of fourteen points out of sixteen, and the goalscoring prowess of O'Rourke, who had notched 21 goals in only 22 appearances. Churlish Watford boss Ron McGarry, meanwhile, refused to accept the champagne sent to the visitors' changing room.

O'Rourke also scored the Town's equaliser in the final game of the campaign – 1-1 at QPR. Some 500 Town supporters made the trip for what was a meaningless fixture to prove the upsurge of support and the hope of better things. The celebrations were akin to winning promotion, for the Luton party was treated to a 'slap-up' meal at Stanmore on its way back from Loftus Road.

The summer of 1964 saw the departure of loyal servants Bob Morton and Gordon Turner, who both joined non-league clubs. Only Ron Baynham remained from the glory days. The new-look side hoped to continue the winning ways from the spring, but disaster struck when John O'Rourke was crocked during the opening-day draw at Brentford. With O'Rourke having netted four goals at Griffin Park in February, the Bees defenders buzzed around him – particularly after he scored in the opening minute. A ghastly tackle inflicted ankle ligament damage which took months to heal properly.

The signing of speedy winger David Pleat – another ex-England youth international – from Nottingham Forest was intended to provide the ammunition for O'Rourke to fire the team to promotion. In the event, although Pleat was a revelation, his clever play was wasted with no one to stick the ball in the net.

KENILWORTH ROAD HEROES: **Gordon Turner**

Football-mad Gordon Turner was seeing out his National Service in the Royal Navy when two of his Chief Petty Officers, who lived in Luton, put the word in to Hatters manager Dally Duncan. It transpired that Duncan had played in the same pre-war Hull City side as Turner's father, and it was not long before the nineteen-year-old was on the books at Kenilworth Road.

Turner had to wait until the 1950-51 season before making his debut as a right-half. His first two games were spent marking Ken Chisholm of Coventry and Don Revie of Hull. In the 1951-52 season he was given his chance up front. After scoring a hat-trick against West Ham in his fourth game, and the only goal in an FA Cup-tie against First Division Charlton, a legend was born.

Still finding his feet, Turner was always full of praise for Jesse Pye who was brought to Kenilworth Road in 1952 and who guided, mentored and taught him all he knew. Turner banged in 32 goals as the Town clinched promotion to the top flight in 1955 and regularly topped thirty goals each season during the club's time in Division One. It was puzzling and frustrating that he was never picked for England. The closest he came to international honours was as a travelling reserve for the 'B' team and a representative appearance for the Football League.

Deadly shooting, ice cool in front of goal, and a brilliant tactical awareness made Turner the idol of Kenilworth Road. Most supporters shared his disgust when he was dropped for the FA Cup side in January 1959. With the selection committee keeping an unchanged team throughout the Cup run, it meant no place for Turner in the final at Wembley. Who knows what might have happened had he played.

Despite his disappointment he played on for the Hatters until the end of the 1963-64 campaign, by which time he had amassed 243 league goals for the club – a record never likely to be beaten.

On retiring from league football, Turner enjoyed a spell at Wisbech under his old pal Jesse Pye before turning out for Kettering and netting 37 goals in his final season.

This writer remembers Gordon Turner as being happy to pump up a young boy's football at the sports shop he owned with another Hatter, Wally Shanks.

Gordon Turner died in 1976 at the young age of 46 after suffering from motor neurone disease for five years.

~~~~~~~~~~

KENILWORTH ROAD HEROES: **Bob Morton**

Born in Aston Clinton, Bob Morton stayed loyal to his roots throughout his life. He showed the same loyalty to his only Football League team, Luton Town, with whom he spent nearly twenty years.

Whilst playing locally for Waterlows, Bob was spotted by Hubert Day and asked to sign amateur forms as the war drew to a close: 'Luton did not seem in too much of a hurry to sign me full-time and after a County representative game at Bishops Stortford – which we won 5-4 after being 1-4 down at half-time – Jimmy Seed and Jimmy Trotter asked me to go to Charlton. Luton got wind of this and on my return home a telegram arrived asking me to report to Kenilworth Road. I signed the following day on 50 shillings a week to play for the Colts.'

Morton served his time as a toolmaker while working his way up through the ranks. He eventually made his Football League debut at West Ham on 30th October 1948 in a game which the Town won 1-0. This marked the start of a league career spanning 495 games which is a record for the club.

Although starting with the Hatters as a centre-forward, Morton played equally well at centre-half or wing-half, and it is for this reason that international honours at senior level – seemingly a certainty – never came his way. The selectors did not know where to play him!

Regarded as the best wing-half at Luton, it was at centre-forward where he enjoyed the greatest headlines, partnering prolific goalscorer Gordon Turner: 'I used to play as a deep lying centre-forward, in a similar role to the one perfected by Don Revie, and draw the opposing centre-half, leaving a gap for Gordon to go in. If the defenders got wise we would simply play wall passes off each other. I scored a fair number of goals when playing up front and can remember my only hat-trick in an 8-2 home win over Sunderland in 1955.'

Obviously, the high point in Morton's career was the FA Cup final in 1959 which saw the Town – having beaten Forest 5-1 in the league just weeks before – lose 1-2: 'Looking back we were frankly over-confident. It never entered our heads that we might lose. The greatest and saddest day of my life.'

Following the Cup final defeat, the fortunes of the club took a dive but Morton remained loyal – despite a transfer bid from Preston – all the way through the divisions before leaving at the age of 38 in 1964 to become manager of Bletchley Town for three years. 'The Club always treated me fairly and generously and, in fact, granted me a testimonial against West Ham in 1964. I never regretted one moment of my career.'

After leaving Bletchley, Morton enjoyed sixteen years with *Luton Sports Press* which involved him travelling the length and breadth of the country visiting just about every League club en route, and meeting up with many old and new friends in the football world.

~~~~~~~~~~

In 1964-65 Luton Town appeared to be in terminal decline. Looking back, it can be seen that several senior players did not have the heart for the battle and lacked self-discipline. This in turn affected younger players who needed role models to look up to and learn from. Last but not least, the ground was falling apart.

After a dismal autumn which brought some heavy away defeats – culminating in a 1-7 drubbing at QPR, trainer Frank King was sacked. His departure was quickly followed by the resignation of manager Bill Harvey. The Board asked ex-player Charlie Watkins, now back from South Africa, to take charge on a caretaker basis, but Watkins quickly realised that the situation was impossible as the team lurched from defeat to defeat.

In desperation, chief scout George Martin was asked to return to football management. Martin had left Luton for Newcastle in 1947. Following a spell at Aston Villa he had not been in management since 1953. Now 64 years old, he was reluctant to return to the cut and thrust, but Hatters chairman Tom Hodgson was persuasive.

Martin accepted, but was in a no-win situation. Although the signing of ex-Ipswich sharpshooter Ted Phillips signalled a mini-revival – four straight wins – the team was soon back to its losing ways and a 1-8 defeat at Scunthorpe confirmed relegation and the final fall from grace.

As if to confirm the depths of the malaise, ex-England international goalkeeper Ron Baynham had been forced to play on when not fully fit. He made a fuss and was admitted to hospital, where it was confirmed that he had been playing with part of his pelvic structure pulled away by torn muscles and tendons. His career was obviously over but he was lucky not to be left invalided for life.

With only one senior goalkeeper left on the books, Martin acquired Tony Read from Peterborough. But no sooner had the new man arrived than his foot was placed in plaster. He had, in fact, broken it.

As this woeful season drew to a close, only 2,915 hardy souls turned up for the final game, a 0-0 draw with Workington. By this time a lady supporter was suing the club after a toilet cistern fell on her head. Things were as bad as that.

KENILWORTH ROAD HEROES: **Ron Baynham**

For most Luton supporters of a certain age, memories of Kenilworth Road in the 1950s conjure up the likes of Stanley Matthews, Nat Lofthouse and Tom Finney bearing down on the Luton goal, where a tall, strong and athletic goalkeeper was there to repulse their efforts. Ron Baynham was the goalkeeper in question, forming the last line of defence behind an accomplished side that more than held its own in Division One.

Yet Birmingham-born Baynham may not have enjoyed a long career between the sticks if he had followed his first instincts, which were to play cricket. 'I was cricket daft and until I left school had probably not kicked a "competitive" football more than twice,' recalled Baynham. 'My brother organised a local side and I was dumped in goal, which was thought of as the best place for someone who had never played.'

Baynham stayed in goal. Whilst in the Army he was spotted by a Wolves scout who offered him a trial at Molineux. 'I turned it down because I did not think I was good enough and on leaving the Army joined Worcester City in the Southern League.'

Two years later he was offered another trial, this time at Kenilworth Road, and was now more confident in his abilities and ready for the step-up. He signed in November 1951 in exchange for £1,000. Until the previous summer the Hatters had the luxury of two international goalkeepers on their books – Bernard Streten, who had earned an England cap in 1949, and Iorwerth Hughes, who won four Welsh caps in 1950-51. As a Division Two side at the time, the Town could not keep both happy, so reluctantly allowed Hughes to move on. Baynham was therefore seen as Streten's understudy.

Baynham was content to patiently learn his trade, but within a year was contesting the No 1 spot with Streten, although it was not until 1957 that the pupil made the position his own.

The Hatters won promotion to the old Division One in 1955 and the following autumn Baynham was capped when England thrashed Denmark 5-1 in Copenhagen. Two more caps swiftly followed as England beat Northern Ireland 3-0 and Spain 4-1 at Wembley, whereupon he was inexplicably overlooked in favour of Reg Matthews of Third Division Coventry City.

Asked in later life which he considered his biggest achievement, winning England caps or playing in the 1959 Cup final, Baynham replied: 'Both were tremendous highlights, but I rated Wembley for the Cup final, even though it brought me the biggest disappointment of my career when we lost to Nottingham Forest. Sadly the team that day did not play like the team I knew.'

The Cup final was the pinnacle of the playing careers of Baynham and many others from the 1959 squad. They had all ripened and grown old together and within twelve months they had to face up to the slippery slope that would eventually lead to Division Four.

Baynham stayed on, but he should have quit in September 1960 when he fractured his skull during a home game against Sheffield United. He returned five months later, but by this time the Town had signed Jim Standen and Ron had to share the goalkeeping duties with the ex-Arsenal man. Baynham even resorted to playing one game at centre-forward, which was not his fondest memory.

As the Town slipped through the divisions, Standen was transferred to West Ham, leaving the way open to Baynham once more. In 1965 he pulled on a goalkeeper's jersey for the last time after being forced to play in a reserve game while suffering from torn stomach muscles.

Baynham worked as a painter and decorator, then at Luton Airport for some years, and is now happily enjoying his retirement. He was a welcome guest of the Hatters in 1999 for the FA Cup final fortieth anniversary, where he proved to be the life and soul of a memorable party.

~~~~~~~~~~~

It had taken Luton Town just five years to drop from Divisions One to Four, and a weary George Martin set about trying to take the club back to its former glories. He instilled some badly needed discipline, and the new, tougher regime was immediately apparent when four players were suspended due to their reluctance to live in the Luton area. Three eventually bowed to the pressure, but Ted Phillips decided to leave the club rather than uproot. Experienced players Matt Woods and Bobby Thomson were brought in, but on the debit side David Pleat broke a leg in training just as the season started.

Woods was seen as the centre-half that the Town had missed since the retirement of Syd Owen, while at the other end John O'Rourke was back to his best and banging in the goals. As the season commenced, self-confessed 'bad-boy' Graham French was signed from Wellington Town to take Pleat's place on the wing.

KENILWORTH ROAD CLASSICS: **Luton v Notts County** – 5-1

Football League Division Four, 20th November 1965
O'Rourke was not the only successful Luton forward. He was developing a good understanding with probably the most unlikely looking attacker in the whole of the club's history.

Tony Read had been signed from Peterborough as a goalkeeper, but manager George Martin obviously saw something in him during pre-season training. With the campaign only a few days old, Martin slung him into the forward line. By the time of the visit of Notts County, the partnership with O'Rourke was beginning to prosper and the Town were looking pretty impregnable at home. In the eight previous home games, seven had been won, with 24 goals being scored, most of them by the Read-O'Rourke strikeforce.

The Hatters had endured a gruelling FA Cup home replay against Romford on the Thursday evening, winning 1-0 in front of 11,061, so it was disappointing when only 6,486 turned up see a match between fifth (Luton) and fourth (County). In the third minute, winger Ray Whittaker exploited a quickly taken free-kick, sprinted thirty yards and shot hard and low into the Magpies net. Derek Shiels levelled five minutes later, when he reacted quickest to a loose ball in the Luton penalty area.

County, who had made five changes following their FA Cup defeat at Southend, were on the back foot on the sodden surface, and their spoiling tactics against the fast and clever Luton forwards aggravated the Kenilworth Road faithful.

After sixteen minutes Graham French was hacked down on the edge of the area, leaving Read to hammer in the free-kick with all the power of an ex-goalkeeper. County, having to respond, then stretched Luton's defence on several occasions before the interval. The Hatters appeared to be losing their grip, but two minutes from the break O'Rourke eluded full-back Ivan Hampton on the goal-line and shot home from a narrow angle to give the Hatters a slightly flattering 3-1 interval lead.

Conditions were deteriorating, with water standing on the surface in places. Whenever Luton's attackers approached the Oak Road end, which in those days was always the muddiest part of the pitch, the ball stuck fast, making it easy for the Notts County defenders. Nevertheless a fourth goal followed on 69 minutes, when an interchange involving Graham French and O'Rourke left Read with time and space to pick his spot. Three minutes later Read completed his hat-trick when he dived full length to head a Whittaker corner into the net. By the end, Whittaker had also hit a post and Read had a goal-bound shot stopped on the line.

Read finished the season with twelve goals to his name, but found them harder to score as the campaign wore on. Over the next two seasons he combined goalkeeping duties with occasional outfield appearances, before becoming the acknowledged No 1 stopper.

'Beryl', as he was affectionately known, ended his Luton career in 1972 after amassing 229 first-team appearances, not to mention twelve goals.

LUTON: *Tinsley, Thomson, Edwards, Reid, Woods, Moore, Harber, Read, O'Rourke, French, Whittaker.*

NOTTS CO: *Butler, Hampton, Bircumshaw, Coates, Gibson, Sheridan, Bates, Moulden, Shiels, Still, Flower.*

~~~~~~~~~~

Christmas 1965 came and went with the Town still in a threatening position. Crunch games came thick and fast. Chester, who lost both their regular full-backs to broken legs the week before, were victims of a Graham French-inspired Luton, who won 5-2. The next three home games saw wins over Aldershot, Hartlepool and Torquay, with the Devon men playing their part in the match of the season.

KENILWORTH ROAD CLASSICS: **Luton v Torquay** – 3-2
Football League Division Four, 26th February 1966
By the time of the clash with the Gulls, the Hatters were up to sixth place. Torquay were second, but they had played more games than the Town.

The new stand rises from the ashes. And what wonderful men built it

An aerial view of Kenilworth Road taken in 1927

Messrs Black, Clark, Fraser and Fulton standing in front of 'Scotch Corner' in 1929

A pre-season 'Whites v Stripes' practice game in 1927

A 1927 aerial photograph showing the Dunstable Road ground (north-west),
Dallow Road (centre), and Dallow Road Recreation Ground (south-east)

Tom Hodgson clears the ball at the Oak Road end in 1929

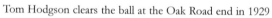

A 1933 team group sitting in front of the 11-year-old main stand

Spectators perch on top of the newly erected Bobbers Stand before
the Chelsea FA Cup replay in 1935

A female spectator is bodily lifted onto the pitch to escape the crush before
the Chelsea FA Cup replay of 1935

Fans take any vantage point they can find at the Kenilworth Road end.
(FA Cup replay with Chelsea 1935)

Another lady is helped to safety, this time in the Bobbers Stand.
(FA Cup replay with Chelsea 1935)

An altogether happier set of supporters at the opening of
the extended Kenilworth Road terrace in 1937. Aston Villa were the visitors

Eyes front! Another view of the extended Kenilworth Road terrace in 1937.
The game was against Aston Villa

The visit of Aston Villa in 1937 also showed a more 'up-market' crowd
in the main stand and enclosure

Action from a Second World War game at Kenilworth Road

A 1945 photograph showing the main stand extension carried out in 1937

The 1940s squad set off for training from the top of Kenilworth Road

The Town players about to leave by coach for their 1-4 defeat at Coventry in 1947

Spectators queue to stand on the Kenilworth Road terrace. It is 1947 and they will see
Hugh Billington score a hat-trick in the 3-0 win over Brentford

An icy match against Chesterfield in the 1940s

A shirt-sleeved crowd watch the Kenilworth Road action in the 1940s

A packed Kenilworth Road terrace watches the game against
West Ham on the opening day of the 1949-50 season

The main stand being re-roofed in 1949

Leicester's Jack Lee beats the despairing dive of Bernard Streten
during the 5-5 FA Cup draw in 1949

West Ham attack the Oak Road goal during this clash in 1949

The Preston defence is on the rack in September 1949

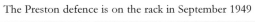

Roy Davies is thwarted by some unconventional Everton defending in October 1951

Young Gordon Turner scores the only goal of the FA Cup-tie against Charlton in 1952

The visit of Arsenal attracted a record crowd in 1952. Bernard Moore is shown opening the scoring in this FA Cup quarter-final

Bernard Moore is congratulated, but the spectators in the Bobbers Stand can barely raise their arms in the crush. (Arsenal Cup-tie 1952)

George Stobbart is forced wide by Arsenal defenders during Luton's 2-3 defeat.
(Arsenal Cup-tie 1952)

Arsenal goalkeeper George Swindin is beaten by Bert Mitchell's penalty. Whether those
spectators in the Oak Road/Bobbers Stand corner can see anything is debatable.
(Arsenal Cup-tie 1952)

The Town wear dark (blue) shirts against Bolton on an ice-rink of a pitch.
(FA Cup fifth round 1953)

Kenilworth Road and its surroundings in 1954. Note that there was only one exit into Oak Road prior to the raising of the terrace behind that goal two years later

Another Kenilworth Road
lottery of a pitch. This time
the visitors are Blackpool
in the FA Cup in 1954

The Town take on Manchester United six weeks before the Munich disaster.
The new floodlights sit rather uncomfortably on the Bobbers Stand roof

Bernard Streten shows safe handling as the Hatters beat mighty Wolves in August 1956.
The floodlight pylons on the main stand side of the pitch look rather clumsy

Training on concrete, 1950s style

Ron Baynham clutches the ball during the FA Cup quarter-final replay with Blackpool in 1959. The crowd of 30,069 remains a record at Kenilworth Road

Luton supporters queuing in the rain for FA Cup semi-final tickets in 1959

The same queue for FA Cup semi-final tickets, snaking past the Odeon cinema,
on which the former Dunstable Road ground once stood

Skipper Terry Branston in the thick of the action during the Town's Division Four
championship season of 1967-68

Another promotion season as Matt Tees rises against Bradford City in December 1969

Action from the 3-3 draw with Portsmouth in the 1973-74 promotion campaign.
The seats have yet to be installed in the wooden section of the Bobbers Stand

Looking out towards the Kenilworth Road terrace in the mid-1970s

The main stand in the mid-1970s

Looking across from the Bobbers Stand in 1974

Another general view of Kenilworth Road in the 1970s

The view from the main stand

The car park at the top of Kenilworth Road in 1974

The club's offices were once situated in the houses behind the Kenilworth Road end

Another view of Kenilworth Road in the 1970s

The waste ground behind the Kenilworth Road end, where this author played countless hours of football as a child. The rags to riches story ends there!

Brian Stein nets from the spot during the 3-2 win over Newcastle in 1982

Brian Stein celebrates with the fans in the Bobbers Stand after scoring against Barnsley at the end of the promotion-winning season of 1981-82

Brave or foolhardy persons risk life and limb to watch the FA Cup clash with Ipswich in 1982

Part of the Bobbers Stand after the infamous visit of Millwall in 1985

Luton Town's main entrance disappeared after the building of the A505 relief road

A snowy scene in the early 1980s

The houses at the top of Kenilworth Road are demolished in readiness for the many changes to take place at the ground

The artificial pitch is laid during the summer of 1985

The original Oak Road entrance, source of bewilderment and hilarity
amongst away supporters over the years

The roof goes on the Kenilworth Road terrace in 1986

The executive boxes are installed on the Bobbers Stand side in the summer of 1986

A crowd of 9,271 including four coachloads from Torquay, filled the Kenilworth Road terraces to see if the Hatters could make it four wins in a row. In the opening stages it seemed that only inspired goalkeeping from Torquay's Gary McGuire was keeping Luton at bay. McGuire, who had won an Amateur Cup-winners medal with Walthamstow Avenue, had written begging letters to many league clubs, including the Town, for a trial. Torquay took him on, and after starting the current campaign as third choice, a mixture of injuries and the poor form of others had catapulted him into the first team.

As often happens in these instances, a team under the cosh somehow manufactures a soft goal from a breakaway. Torquay did just that when Robin Stubbs hit a long-range, wind-assisted drive into the top corner after 23 minutes. Luckily the crowd were not silenced for long as, only a minute later, O'Rourke gathered a pass from Tommy McKechnie and at last beat McGuire. On the hour, eighteen-year-old Bruce Rioch netted what was to become a trademark twenty-yard pile-driver, and eight minutes later O'Rourke appeared to make the game safe when he brushed off the challenge of the veteran Torquay centre-half, Reg Wyatt, and slammed in a third.

McGuire, who had single-handedly prevented the Town from registering a cricket score, was hurt in a goalmouth clash, but bravely continued to thwart the Luton forwards. A goal from Ron Barnes with ten minutes to go, following a disputed free-kick, gave the scoreline an unrealistic look, but when the final whistle sounded the limping McGuire left the field to a standing ovation.

LUTON: *Tinsley, Riddick, Jardine, Reid, Woods, Moore, French, McKechnie, O'Rourke, Rioch, Whittaker.*

TORQUAY: *McGuire, Smith, Bond, Benson, Wyatt, Wolstenholme, Barnes, Kirkman, Stubbs, Spratt, Clarke.*

~~~~~~~~~~~

The 1965-66 season also saw the introduction of substitutes for league games. Bruce Rioch became the Town's first No 12, coming on for the injured Ray Whittaker during the 1-3 defeat at Aldershot on 29th August. The Town's directors agonised over what to pay substitutes, especially if they played, say, 45 minutes. Eventually, and very reluctantly, they agreed to grant full appearance money to substitutes, but only if they actually entered the field of play.

Luton's quest for promotion gathered momentum. After losing at Hartlepool, three straight wins were recorded as Easter approached. The home win over Tranmere was the most important. Rovers typified a Division Four promotion-seeking side of the time, nobody under six foot tall, the turning circle of a wardrobe, but resolute when behind the ball, especially at a ground like Kenilworth Road where it was simple to boot the ball into back gardens.

Easter saw the Town play Colchester Unitd twice and Darlington at home, each of them a promotion four-pointer. In the Good Friday fixture at Layer Road, a best of the season crowd of 10,200 witnessed a 2-2 draw. The second Colchester equaliser looked to many observers to be offside. Darlington, another team in the Tranmere mould, were defeated 2-0 in a bruising encounter. The return against Colchester on Easter Monday saw the Town grab a late equaliser, courtesy of Gordon Riddick, in a below-par display. The attendance was 15,309, the best at Kenilworth Road for two seasons.

Behind the scenes, the Lewsey Farm saga was still rumbling along, and the Council finally gave public notice of the club's application for outline planning permission. The Town were confident that the traffic problem had been sorted with the dualling of the A505 near the hospital. The club anticipated building a sports stadium with gymnasium, bowling alley and masses of parking. But in the meantime the Lewsey Farm housing estate, with its additional traffic, had been developed adjacent to the site, which meant the scheme looked increasingly likely to be doomed. The Town's Board eventually heard that schools were to be built on the land earmarked for the stadium and an expensive and long-drawn out saga was finally put to bed.

In the league, however, Luton still had their fate in their own hands, and wins at Barrow and at home to Stockport convinced the doubters that promotion was still on the cards. Then came a game that appeared to carry little significance at the time. On 11th May 1966, the Hatters were 2-0 up at Chester when a cloudburst forced an abandonment. The following week the Town experimented by playing on FA Cup final day, in the evening. They beat Port Vale 5-0, all the goals coming in the first twenty minutes, O'Rourke missed a second-half penalty which would have given him five hat-tricks for the season.

After beating Barrow at home, two points were needed from the final two games, away at Newport and in the rearranged game at Chester, to virtually seal promotion. When the team bus stopped at Chepstow en route to the Newport game, manager George Martin informed the players that they would each receive a £60 bonus for gaining promotion. This sparked an almighty row. Chairman Tom Hodgson had to enter the dressing room before kick-off in an attempt to stem a mutiny. The senior professionals, led by Matt Woods, demanded £300 for each player, having heard on the grapevine that another promotion-chasing club had offered that figure to its players. Hodgson would not budge, insisting that Luton could not afford such a sum. It appears that a few of the more disgruntled players were content to go through the motions at Somerton Park, and Luton duly lost 1-3.

For the final game, the rearranged fixture at Chester, several players were axed following the Newport fracas. A makeshift side could only draw 1-1, which meant Luton missed out on promotion on goal-average.

Now that the club was staying at Kenilworth Road, the Board feared changes to parking provisions in the streets surrounding the ground. They feared that supporters were hesitating in renewing their season tickets, as they might no longer be able to park within easy reach of the ground. Gone were the days of being able to park right outside. Fans were now expected to walk the two minutes from Warwick and Hampton Roads, or from the roads leading off Dallow Road.

With the Town having to accept another season in the football basement, much to-ing and fro-ing took place among the playing staff in the close season. John O'Rourke was sold to Middlesbrough for £18,500, while John Reid and Matt Woods were shown the door following the promotion bonus rumpus. With hindsight, the quality of players brought in over the summer of 1966 was poor, and it was always destined to be a season of struggle.

1966-67 opened well enough with a 2-0 home win over Halifax but three successive away defeats confirmed that the inexperienced Town youngsters were not about to make much impression against the cynical old pros that graced most Division Four sides.

By the end of October, the Town were in the re-election zone (the bottom four clubs had to go cap-in-hand to seek re-election each year) and, following a 2-2 home draw with Bradford Park Avenue, George Martin finally threw in the towel. Several players had complained to the Board that he had been too hard on them!

The Town turned to ex-Hatter Allan Brown, then the successful player-manager of Wigan Athletic of the Cheshire League. He accepted the challenge, but following his baptism – a dismal 0-1 defeat at Port Vale – he conceded 'There is much to do'.

A home win over high-flying Crewe followed, but this proved to be a flash in the pan. Three more rapid away defeats followed, culminating with a 1-8 thrashing at Lincoln, who were bottom of the whole Football League.

Luton experimented with playing midweek home games on Thursdays rather than their traditional Wednesdays. The original idea behind playing on Wednesdays was because it was half-day closing in the town. Before the advent of floodlights, midweek games were played on Wednesday afternoons, and switching to Wednesday evenings seemed a sensible option. Thursdays were now proposed because it was 'pay-night', and also because there was less competition from television. Modern readers perhaps have little idea, for example, how popular was the police series *Z-Cars,* which was broadcast on Wednesday evenings.

The problem with Thursdays, however, was that players did not have sufficient time to recover from knocks before turning out again on a Saturday. This was brought home when, having survived a bruising FA Cup replay against Exeter on the Thursday before the Lincoln mauling, the Town had to field a team of walking wounded at Sincil Bank.

'A centre-forward and centre-half must be my priorities', said Brown, realising what the supporters had known all season. He promptly went out to secure Max Dougan from Leicester and the much-travelled ex-England striker Derek Kevan from Peterborough. Dougan made an immediate impact in a 3-2 home win over Chesterfield, while Kevan made a scoring debut the following week in a 1-1 draw at Halifax, which gave the Town their second away point of the season from twelve starts.

Such was the sense of euphoria, that air-headed supporters asked the local press if any other clubs had won promotion after being near the bottom at Christmas. The optimism spread to the terraces, and a crowd of 9,123 came to Kenilworth Road on 27th December 1966 to witness the new boys star again in a 2-0 win over Tranmere.

With youngsters Bruce Rioch and Alan Slough now realising their potential, the Hatters got into the welcome habit of winning. Although Kevan did not stay long, he waited until the first away win of the season – a 2-1 victory at Notts County on 4th March – before agreeing to an exchange deal that brought Keith Allen to Luton from Stockport.

Despite the relative upsurge in fortunes, the loss of so many early-season points, and the indifferent away form, left the Town too close for comfort to the re-election zone. It was not until the penultimate home game of the season, when Lincoln were beaten 2-1, that supporters could sleep soundly at night.

With the pressure off, the most depressing season in the club's history ended with a flourish as York were walloped 5-1 at Kenilworth Road, but by that time Allan Brown was already making plans for the following year.

If ever a season dawned full of optimism it was 1967-68. An encouraging end to the previous campaign, plus a squad strengthened with some experienced names, meant that much was expected for success-starved Luton Town. This writer believes 1967-68 to mark the start of 'the modern era' of the club, which is the title given to his detailed statistical recent history of the Hatters.

Encouraged by wealthy new Board members Tony Hunt and Reggie Burr – from insurance giant Vehicle and General – the players were offered a £5,000 bonus to be shared out between them should they win promotion. The first match was at Wrexham, who had gone through the whole of the previous season unbeaten at home. The Town fell behind after Brian Johnson, a half-time substitute for Alan Slough, was carried off injured. Luton were reduced still further when Graham French was sent off along with Wrexham's Terry Bradbury for fisticuffs, but secured a draw when debutant Rodney Green netted two minutes from time. Luton's travelling supporters, who had seen the Hatters pick up only six points on the road the previous season, were heartened by the fact that the players had not rolled over in the face of an attacking onslaught. This squad was made of stern stuff.

Luton looked competent in their opening home games, which saw the crowds steadily increase, but the public responded in even greater numbers when Allan Brown, in order to fill the striker vacancy caused by Green's cartilage operation, paid Derby £11,000 for Ian Buxton. The new man made his debut at home to Southend when a crowd of 13,332 turned up to see a 3-1 Town win.

The long-awaited first away win arrived on 7th October, 3-1 at Chester. In their first seven away games they had equalled their tally for the whole of the previous season. All told, eight consecutive wins were rattled up, including 5-0 at Exeter, 5-3 at home to Doncaster, and 4-0 home wins over Workington and Swansea – when the Town scored all four in the space of six minutes near the end.

A loss at high-flying Bradford City halted the run, but with Christmas approaching Luton still boasted a 100 per cent home record. A crowd of 16,599, the best for three years, saw Luton's eleventh straight home win when Bradford Park Avenue were seen off 2-0 on Boxing Day.

The Town faltered slightly, losing in quick succession at Bradford Park Avenue in the return and at snowy Hartlepool, both by 1-2. There followed the first dropped home point when Newport hung on for a 1-1 draw.

The winning ways returned when Rochdale were thrashed 4-1 at Kenilworth Road, all the goals coming in the first half. The power play of Bruce Rioch, the wing wizardry of Graham French, and the sound captaincy of ex-Northampton centre-half Terry Branston combined to devastating effect. Due reward was gained the following week when the Town won 2-0 at Brentford and went top of the league for the first time — an achievement which would surely have come earlier had they played as many matches as their rivals.

The toughest game of the season was the visit to Chesterfield. Luton's benefactors Hunt and Burr, who had made a £100,000 loan available on joining the Board, packed the team off to Blackpool for a few days rest and relaxation. The bonding trip presumably did its job, and the 14,075 crowd at Saltergate were silenced when the Town held out for a 0-0 draw. Not long after came a 1-0 win at Aldershot, courtesy of Ian Buxton, in a game supporters feared might would never be played as it had previously been called off twice.

Easter arrived. Although no defeats were suffered, a flattering 2-0 home win over Notts County, a 0-0 home stalemate with Chester, followed by a 2-2 draw in the return at Meadow Lane – after the Town had led 2-0 – was less than the fans expected.

All was forgiven the following week when a goal from Bruce Rioch gave the Town a 1-0 win at Halifax to secure promotion with four games left to play. For a generation of Luton supporters this was a memorable day as it was the first time they had seen their heroes win something. Nine years of torment, starting with the 1959 FA Cup final, were finally over.

KENILWORTH ROAD CLASSICS: **Luton v Crewe** – 4-0

Football League Division Four, 24th April 1968

The first objective had been accomplished. Luton were promoted. Now for the Fourth Division championship. As a bonus, there was the record points score for the division to aim at. One more point was needed for the title, with Crewe the visitors. Crewe arrived in second place, seven points behind the Town, needing the points for their own promotion bid. A vast crowd of 18,904, the best for four years, turned up on a warm evening to make it a carnival atmosphere.

Crewe's Gordon Wallace put the ball in the Luton net in the fourth minute, but the effort was ruled out for offside. The Town then proceeded to put on a display that would possibly have seen off most sides in the country at the time. A foul on Keith Allen brought about the first Luton goal. Alan Slough tapped the free-kick to Rioch, who blasted the ball straight at Willie Mailey in the Crewe goal. John Moore put away the rebound. The Hatters were two up after twenty minutes: a short free-kick routine ended with another thumping shot by Rioch. Eight minutes later Slough netted a third after a corner-kick provoked a goalmouth scramble. A minute from the interval Rioch scored the goal of the night. Racing through the middle he took Buxton's pass to hammer the ball into the roof of the net. 'Rioch for England' chanted the supporters behind the Oak Road goal, little realising that the sharpshooter would eventually opt for the land of his father and turn out for Scotland.

Crewe, despite realising they were going home with nothing, never resorted to spoiling tactics and continued to try to play football. At the final whistle the crowd was encouraged to stay off the pitch with the players performing a promised lap of honour. Skipper Terry Branston was carried shoulder high around the ground, but it took much persuasion before manager Brown came out. When he did, he received the biggest cheer of the night: He said: 'We've done it. What a triumph. All the players have given me 100 per cent effort. Now we want to break the record for the number of points scored for promotion. We want 67, then I'll be satisfied.'

LUTON: Read, Dougan, Jardine, Slough (McDerment), Branston, Moore, French, Buxton, Allen, Rioch, Whittaker.

CREWE: Mailey, Lowry, Ratcliffe, Stott, Barnes, Gannon, McHale, Curley, Regan, Wallace, Dearden.

~~~~~~~~~~

The champagne celebrations probably went on too long, because three days later Luton surrendered their unbeaten home record to promotion-chasing Bradford City.

The championship trophy was presented prior to the last game of the season, when Brentford were the visitors. Television cameras were there to record highlights of a game that the Town won 2-1 to equal the points record (66) for the Fourth Division.

The ambitious Tony Hunt put himself about that summer, which was one of the busiest on record, both on and off the pitch. 'A period of consolidation' did not enter the former Battle of Britain pilot's thoughts. His infectious enthusiasm spread throughout the club as he attempted to return the Hatters to their former glories. Hunt also showed his ruthless side when he rid the Board of two directors, confirming that he would brook no argument in his determination to take the club through Division Three at the first attempt.

Hunt oversaw in a massive spending spree – at least by Luton Town standards – over the summer months. Mike Harrison arrived from Plymouth for £7,000, Brian Lewis from Coventry for £18,000, and Laurie Sheffield from Oldham for £10,000. Added to this, the club spent £55,000 on new changing rooms and a gym behind the Main Stand. A new luxury coach was purchased to carry the players to away games, and no longer would the club have to economise on hotel accommodation. The supporters responded to this show of commitment by buying season tickets in numbers never seen before.

KENILWORTH ROAD CLASSICS: **Luton v Oldham** – 4-0

Football League Division Three, 10th August 1968
1968-69's opening-day visitors were Oldham. On a hot summer's day 14,747 converged to see if the Town could steamroller their way straight through to Division Two. The three new signings were all on show, which meant no places for last season's heroes – Ian Buxton, Ray Whittaker and John Moore – even though Buxton was otherwise engaged playing county cricket for Derbyshire.

But for Oldham goalkeeper David Best, Luton could have been three up in the opening ten minutes. The breakthrough came in the seventeenth-minute when Oldham defender Walter Joyce tripped Brian Lewis, leaving Mike Harrison to score from the spot.

The Hatters hit the woodwork three times before Keith Allen put away a shot from Laurie Sheffield that had cannoned off the bar.

Winger Graham French was incapacitated early in the second period and limped off, before full-back Fred Jardine smacked in a 25-yard shot on the hour, his first goal for more than a year. The biggest cheer of the afternoon, however, was reserved for Lewis, who netted the fourth goal from close range in the dying seconds, following an all-action display in an unfamiliar forward position.

Afterwards it was announced that the Hatters' newest supporter, Eric Morecambe, had already booked his ticket for the next game. Oldham, by the way, would finish bottom.

L*UTON*: *Read, Dougan, Allen, Branston, Jardine, Slough, Rioch, French (Moore), Lewis, Sheffield, Harrison.*

O*LDHAM*: *Best, Doyle, Hunter, Joyce (Bowie), Wood, Blair, Philpott, Magee, Chapman, Johnston, Aitken.*

~~~~~~~~~~

The sun continued to shine as far as Luton were concerned. Rotherham were defeated 3-1 at Kenilworth Road in a game where Bruce Rioch scored twice and led Rotherham centre-half Dave Watson a merry dance. The opposition manager that afternoon, Tommy Docherty, was making a note about Rioch and would later sign him. Barnsley were beaten 5-1, and a 3-1 victory at Gillingham followed, with Tony Read saving a penalty.

K*ENILWORTH* R*OAD* C*LASSICS*: **Luton v Mansfield** – 4-2

Football League Division Three, 18th September 1968

With seven matches gone, the Town were three points clear at the top. Next up were third-placed Stags. An attendance of 19,315 saw 'golden boy' Rioch immediately sent off for allegedly striking an opponent. The local evening paper carried a series of photographs in its next edition in an attempt to vindicate Rioch, but reference to the 5,000 behind the Oak Road goal would have saved all the bother.

Luton would play a man short for 87 minutes. The game continued in an unreal atmosphere which bordered on the belligerent. As so often happens in these cases, the ten men fought like twelve. Their persistence was rewarded by a doubtful penalty tucked away by Mike Harrison.

In the second period Doug Jones equalised. With the Town down to nine men for periods, when John Moore and Terry Branston had to leave the field for running repairs, they began to look a sorry sight, but they were thrown a lifeline by the referee. Mansfield's Phil Waller was sent off for a nothing tackle on Brian Lewis, and it seemed the official was attempting to level up the numbers. Four minutes later Laurie Sheffield headed in Harrison's cross. Then Lewis added a solo effort to make it 3-1.

The best was yet to come. French collected the ball in his own penalty area, loped up the pitch and beat three players and the goalkeeper before firing home. A fantastic goal on a fantastic evening.

Many who were there to see it still claim it to be the finest goal ever scored at Kenilworth Road, and that if cameras had been present they would still be replaying it today. Certainly I have never seen a better goal, but credit should be given to Brian Lewis who carried defenders with him on a mazy decoy run.

LUTON: Read, Dougan, Jardine, Slough, Branston (McDerment), Moore, French, Lewis, Sheffield, Rioch, Harrison.

MANSFIELD: Hollins, Roberts, Hopkinson, Quigley, Boam, Waller, Frude, Partridge, Ledger, Goodfellow, Jones.

~~~~~~~~~~

The cost of defeating Mansfield was high. Moore, French and Branston all took knocks, and it was no real surprise when the unbeaten record went at Brighton (0-1) in the next game. The team kept winning at home, but less and less convincingly, and a string of away defeats meant that leadership of the division was passed to Swindon and Watford.

In late October, Brown bought full-back Jack Bannister from Crystal Palace and goalkeeper Sandy Davie from Dundee United. Both starred in a 2-0 home win over Swindon – the eventual League Cup winners – but were unable to halt the run of poor away performances.

Benefactor Tony Hunt was ambitious and expected hard work, honesty and loyalty from the staff and players. Allan Brown was interviewed for the vacant Leicester City job, just before Christmas 1968, and although he was not successful he was immediately sacked by Luton for 'disloyalty'. The decision was not, of course, taken by Hunt alone, but it was endorsed by the Board, who realised that Luton's success made it inevitable that more approaches would keep coming in for Brown.

Within hours of dismissing Brown, the club unveiled ex-QPR manager Alec Stock to the waiting media. Stock had been dismissed by the west London club in controversial circumstances the previous summer and was desperate for a return to football.

The players responded with a 2-0 home win over Plymouth in front of TV cameras, and then recorded a rare away win – 2-0 at Northampton – in a game played on a sheet of ice.

Away performances continued to improve – as typified by a 0-0 draw at pacesetters Swindon – but in late January Rioch was injured during the home victory over Walsall. The first of many cartilage operations was the outcome.

Aided by the signing of Mike Keen from QPR, Luton continued to string together good results, but they had a fair amount of leeway to make up on account of their failings before Christmas. A 1-0 win at Oldham, courtesy of an own-goal after thirty seconds, a 1-1 draw at foggy Reading, and a 2-2 draw at Rotherham put the Hatters third, but they remained five points adrift of the promotion places.

Three home wins and a draw from four home games, and draws at Bristol Rovers and Torquay lifted the Town level on points with Swindon, only for 'Easter-itis' to strike with a vengeance. Over 3,500 fans journeyed to Mansfield to see if Luton's twelve-match unbeaten run could be extended. Instead they endured a 0-1 defeat.

Thoughts of promotion were effectively ended the following Tuesday when Southport's ten-man defence held out for a 0-0 draw at Kenilworth Road. Brian Lewis had a game he would not forget, for he started at inside-forward, dropped back when Fred Jardine went off injured, and finished up in goal (in a jersey several sizes too big) after Sandy Davie was hurt saving at the feet of George Andrews, who had been on the Town's books as a youngster.

With the pressure off, the Town went unbeaten through the final five matches and at one stage were again within a whisker of Swindon. The final match attracted a season's best 25,523 to see if the Town could upset the champions-elect Watford. Luton won 2-1 with goals from Ian Buxton, in his last game for the club, and Keith Allen, but with over 100 injured in crowd disturbances, three players sent off, and frequent pitch invasions the match is best forgotten. What must be remembered, however, in a season where only the top two were promoted, is that the Town finished ten points clear of the fourth-placed club while remaining unbeaten at Kenilworth Road.

KENILWORTH ROAD HEROES: **Tom Hodgson**

Born in Hetton-Le Hole, County Durham in 1902, Tommy Hodgson was a coal miner as a youth. His footballing talents saw him snapped up by West Ham from Hetton Colliery in 1921. A tough full-back, Hodgson remained at Upton Park until 1930 and would have made more than his 87 league appearances in this time but for illness and injury.

He came to Kenilworth Road in 1930 at the behest of manager George Kay, who had been a teammate at West Ham. But after just 67 league appearances at Luton his football career was cut short by a serious knee injury.

After quitting the game, he joined the licensed trade and was mine host at the Old Bell in Harpenden and the Warden Tavern in Luton. He joined the Board at Kenilworth Road in 1954 and his football knowledge came to the fore five years later, when he became a team selector following the departure of manager Dally Duncan. Hodgson was also the natural choice to lead the team out at Wembley for the 1959 FA Cup final. He succeeded Percy Mitchell to the chair in 1964 and his most significant act was to encourage Allan Brown to return to Kenilworth Road in 1966 to take over the hot seat. Relinquishing the chair to Tony Hunt in 1969, Tom Hodgson became President. He therefore holds a unique position in English football, by being a player, captain, director, chairman and president of the same club.

~~~~~~~~~~~

Disappointment at failing to win promotion in 1969 was followed by the shock of seeing top scorer Bruce Rioch sold to Tommy Docherty's Aston Villa for £100,000. The fee represented a record sale for a Division Three club, as well as a record purchase for a Division Two club, and was a figure that not even recently appointed chairman Tony Hunt could afford to turn down.

Supporters were unsure whether the sale of the club's gem would affect another attempt at promotion. They were no more confident after hearing of the club's summer signings. The fans had at least heard of John Collins (from Reading) and John Ryan (from Fulham), but spending £17,500 on a nineteen-year-old full-back from Fulham by the name of Malcolm Macdonald seemed madness. On a lighter note, excuse the pun, winger Graham French was fined £25 for returning to pre-season training 12lb overweight.

The Town's go-ahead Board recognised the need to pamper the paying spectators, and another large sum was spent on building the Hatters Club – now the Eric Morecambe Suite. A new enlarged club shop was opened at the bottom of Oak Road, and talks were entered into with British Rail to charter trains to take supporters to away games at 25 shillings (£1.25) return wherever the destination.

In view of a glut of injuries during pre-season friendlies, Stock was forced to play Macdonald initially on the wing, and then up front, where the manager soon realised that the club might have uncovered another young diamond.

Macdonald was in the forward line for the opening-day 3-0 home win over Barrow, and was on the scoresheet for the first time in the 1-0 victory at Bournemouth the following week. The execution of that goal was to become a Macdonald speciality – sprinting clear of the defence to be first to a through ball, drifting round the goalkeeper, and placing the ball into the net with his left foot.

Stock had been keeping his purse dry. It was full of gold from selling Rioch, but he wanted to wait for the right moment to buy. In need of a

centre-half – plus a forward to replace the ageing Terry Branston and
Laurie Sheffield – the manager liked what he saw in Halifax stopper Chris
Nicholl, especially as he had just blotted out Macdonald in a 1-1 draw at
Kenilworth Road. Stock parted with £35,000 for a player who, according
to his manager, Alan Ball senior, 'would play for England one day,' and then
paid Charlton £25,000 for Matt Tees, who it was hoped would provide the
stealth and guile to go alongside Macdonald's blood and thunder.

Tees and Nicholl made their debuts in a 2-0 win at Gillingham to consolidate Luton's position at the top of the table. The Hatters, in fact, went
undefeated in the first thirteen games, only to lose their fourteenth 0-2 at
Doncaster. A few games later Rochdale were beaten 2-0 at Kenilworth
Road in a cracking contest that was a fitting choice for the Town's home
debut on BBC's *Match of the Day*.

Following the 5-0 home demolition of Bradford City in mid-December,
the Town's fortunes took a dive with four straight defeats. Among them
were the first at Kenilworth Road for eighteen months, when Gillingham
won 2-1 on 27th December, and Plymouth 2-0 on 17th January. The Argyle
defeat was captured by the BBC cameras.

Luton's subsequent 3-1 win at Bury saw Graham French play a blinder,
partying the night before and arriving for the team's train – unbeknown to
Alec Stock – somewhat the worse for wear.

In late January 1970 John Eric Bartholomew was voted onto the Board.
Better known as the comedian Eric Morecambe, his route to the Hatters'
boardroom started when Luton secretary Bob Readhead received a request
from Harpenden resident Morecambe for a pair of season tickets for himself and his son. Cannily, Readhead placed him close to the directors box
and it was not long before he was invited into the boardroom at the end of
games. The rest is history.

The Morecambe and Wise Show was a national institution, with Luton supporters always wondering in which ingenious way Morecambe would plug
the club. He was a marvellous ambassador for Luton Town Football Club
but although a natural joker he took his boardroom duties seriously and
was not frightened to get his view across.

A run of generally poor results meant that Luton travelled to Reading
in early March for a 'four pointer'. A crowd of 18,783, which would have
been much higher but for torrential rain, were enthralled by a game settled
by a last-minute Malcolm Macdonald effort.

More topsy-turvy results followed. With five games left it seemed likely that Orient and Bristol Rovers would claim the two promotion spots,
with Fulham best-placed to disturb them. By coincidence, the Town now
travelled to Fulham, where Macdonald scoring the only goal against his old
side to stun the crowd of 18,987.

Home wins over Walsall (on the evening of the FA Cup final) and Southport (thanks to Viv Busby's spectacular dipper), coupled with Bristol Rovers' home defeat by Gillingham, transformed the situation, leaving the Town wanting just one point from their final two away games to clinch promotion back to Division Two. Numerous Luton supporters trekked to Mansfield to see the Hatters shamelessly hang on to the point they started with. Winning at Rochdale in the last game was not enough to overhaul champions Orient.

Again there was feverish activity at Kenilworth Road over the close season. Chairman Tony Hunt sought planning permission to extend the Main Stand, to cantilever it over the railway line, and also construct a double-decker stand over the Kenilworth Road terrace, much as had been proposed in the 1950s. The council refused and suggested the club move away from Kenilworth Road.

That brought an angry response from Hunt. Building a new ground would cost around £2.5 million, which the club did not possess, and an out-of-town site would prevent supporters' wives shopping in the town centre while their menfolk watched the match. Parking, he stressed, would no longer be a major problem once the railway company had freed up land adjacent to Kenilworth Road, and even without it the Town had more car parking than many of the London clubs. What the club needed was an increased capacity from around 27,500 to 40,000. The council remained unimpressed by Hunt's rant, with traffic congestion their major concern. This argument was likely to roll on and on.

For his part, Alec Stock was busy recruiting for the new season. He raided Old Trafford for four players, including Don Givens and Jim Ryan, as well as buying midfielders David Court from Arsenal and Roger Hoy from Crystal Palace. Before Stock had time to sit back and admire his new-look squad, he was dealt a blow when bad-boy Graham French, living up to his reputation, was arrested and subsequently imprisoned following a shooting incident.

KENILWORTH ROAD CLASSICS: **Luton v Oxford** – 4-0

Football League Division Two, 1st September 1970

All the new signings, with the exception of Court, made their debuts on the opening day of the 1970-71 season at Bolton. For this, the Town's first game in Division Two since 1963, Viv Busby, Alan Starling and Terry Branston were preferred to Court, Tony Read and Chris Nicholl, which seemed strange to the many supporters who made the trip to Burnden Park on two special trains. The supporters' fears were vindicated as the Town went down 2-4 to a team that would finish rock bottom. With tiny wingers Gordon Taylor and Terry Wharton running rings around the Luton defence, it was a shell-shocked Alec Stock who faced the press: 'I didn't feel very good about that one. The goals we gave away were scandalous.'

It was, therefore, back to the drawing board in preparation for the visit of Norwich the following Saturday. The three players missing were reinstated, but Ron Saunders' Canaries, fearing a newly promoted side, shut up shop. Another draw followed, this time at fancied Birmingham, Macdonald netting the equaliser with a penalty.

Oxford arrived on the following Tuesday unbeaten, having won both of their away games at Middlesbrough and Millwall. The crowd of 16,173 was treated to bold, attacking football played at speed, with the Town two up early on and three up by the interval. Oxford had declared beforehand that they were set to attack, but when they fell behind they were unable to alter their formation, giving the Hatters ample opportunity to rattle in more goals had they set their minds to it. Matt Tees, recalled at Birmingham to replace the injured Jim Ryan, had probably his best game in a Luton shirt, thumping in two headers from crosses from Court and John Ryan. The other goals in the 4-0 victory came from the trusty left peg of Macdonald, who was now showing he was fully capable of scoring at this level and would soon bring the scouts flocking to Kenilworth Road.

'Radiant Luton come to boil', screamed the headline in the *Evening Post* with the reporter saying, 'With one of the most entertaining displays of powerful, high speed football that I have ever seen them give, Luton demolished Oxford. They pounded them into the turf with as good a performance as you are ever likely to see.'

The reporter's only criticism was the size of the crowd!

LUTON: *Read, John Ryan, Slough, Hoy (Jim Ryan), Nicholl, Moore, Macdonald, Court, Tees, Keen, Givens.*

OXFORD: *Kearns, Lucas, Shuker, Smithson, Clarke, Thompson, Sloan, Graham Atkinson, Skeen, Clayton, Ron Atkinson.*

~~~~~~~~~~~

A sequence of home wins followed, stretching through September and October. The psychologically important first away win came at QPR at the end of September, in what was a happy return to Loftus Road for skipper Mike Keen and manager Alec Stock, who had both left Rangers two years previously in acrimonious circumstances. It was Keen, in fact, who scored the only goal of the game, in the first minute, direct from a thirty-yard free-kick.

27,023 were inside Kenilworth Road to see Arsenal – on their way to the league and FA Cup 'double' – win 1-0 in a League Cup-tie via a flukey goal against the run of play. This was the last time Kenilworth Road would see a crowd of that size, given subsequent ground alterations and safety concerns, but it is interesting to note the attendance breakdown.

The Main Stand was filled to its new reduced (because of widening of the gangways) 3,350 capacity, while the Oak Road end saw 5,392 gain admission against a stated capacity of 5,500. The Bobbers Stand at 3,480 and the Kenilworth Road terrace at 6,123 were both well below capacity, which were given at the time as 4,500 and 10,000 respectively. The enclosure, however, was massively overcrowded at 8,678 against a maximum safety limit of 6,500. It was reckoned that many who paid for admission to the enclosure 'escaped' to other parts of the ground.

In the autumn of 1970 the Hatters were playing with pace and power and looked ready to make an assault on the two promotion places. The game that probably turned the season came in early October when Luton won 5-1 at relegated Sheffield Wednesday. Malcolm Macdonald scored a stunning hat-trick with the unsung Don Givens weighing in with the others. The problem was that the TV cameras were there, to share South Bedfordshire's secret with the whole country. Macdonald was dynamite and the newspapers couldn't get enough of him.

At first, the Town seemed to relish the extra media attention and the team were up to second as Christmas approached. After briefly claiming the leadership in early January, a combination of postponements and an inexplicable loss of form saw the Town drop off the pace. Macdonald even went on a run of five games without scoring.

KENILWORTH ROAD CLASSICS: **Luton v Hull** – 3-1
Football League Division Two, 20th March 1971

After losing at fellow promotion aspirants Carlisle the previous week, manager Alec Stock was desperate to get the promotion show back on the road. Hull, who had never played in the top division, lay third, three places above the Town, having played two games more. Hull had strengthened their position on transfer deadline day by splashing out £60,000 on Blackburn's Ken Knighton and £13,000 on Billy Baxter of Ipswich.

Both players were in a Tigers side greeted by a Kenilworth Road crowd of 19,566. Like the earlier clash at Boothferry Park, which Luton won 2-0, this was also transmitted by the *Match of the Day* cameras, although commentator David Coleman was heard to sneer at the size of the crowd for a Division Two promotion clash!

Viv Busby, out of favour for much of the season, raced at a ponderous Hull defence on a boggy pitch. The Tigers, though, were also slick in attack which made for good viewing. The deadlock was broken by John Moore, whose shot took a deflection off Hull player-manager Terry Neill before cannoning in off a post.

Early in the second period Busby was up-ended by Ian McKechnie in the Hull goal. For the second week running Macdonald wasted the spot-kick. Reprieved, Hull equalised when Ken Houghton headed in a cross from Ken Wagstaff. Luton regained the lead when Busby took advantage of a short back-pass to slot to ball home. The points were made safe with ten minutes to go. McKechnie could not hold Busby's shot, leaving Macdonald with a simple task to end his goal drought.

LUTON: Read, John Ryan, Slough, Givens, Nicholl, Moore, Jim Ryan, Busby, Macdonald, Keen, Anderson.

HULL: McKechnie, Baxter, Beardsley, Wilkinson, Neill, Simpkin, Houghton, Knighton, Lord, Wagstaff, Butler.

~~~~~~~~~~

As has so often happens in the life of the Hatters, when everything appears rosy, something always brings them back to earth with a bump. Now, that 'something' was the collapse of Vehicle & General Insurance, which entered into a voluntary arrangement with its creditors after over-extending itself. The news made national headlines for days as frightened policy holders besieged the switchboard at Kenilworth Road. It was well known that Tony Hunt and Reggie Burr were on the Board and that answers would be easier to obtain at the club rather than via the company's headquarters in Bushey. The shares of V & G underpinned the debts of the football club. As those shares were now rendered virtually worthless, there was the fear that creditors would come chasing the soft option, which was the football ground.

Tony Hunt did the decent thing by resigning his chairmanship. Auditor Robert Keens – from the club's long-standing accountants, Keens, Shay, Keens, – stepped into the breach.

At the suggestion of Eric Morecambe, Keens became chairman. It was hoped that Keen's unique knowledge of the club's finances, together with his high standing in the town, would help to protect the club's interests. There was, however, no magic wand. As the club harboured debts of £167,000, it was agreed that the Town should enter into unofficial receiver-ship pending the raising of funds. To raise those funds obviously meant the sale of more of the club's crown jewels, with Macdonald and Nicholl top of the list.

KENILWORTH ROAD CLASSICS: **Luton v Birmingham** – 3-2

Football League Division Two, 3rd April 1971

The players, aware of the disruption behind the scenes, had to concentrate on forcing themselves back into promotion contention. Since beating Hull, the Hatters had lost at Middlesbrough and drawn at home to Millwall, and now faced the division's form team, Birmingham. From being near the foot of the table at Christmas, they had gone fourteen games without defeat and were now just one point behind the Town.

Leading Birmingham's surge was sixteen-year-old Trevor Francis, scorer of fifteen goals in only sixteen appearances. The Town were expecting their biggest home gate of the season, with 8,000 travelling from the Midlands. By 12.30 the queue of City supporters stretched the length of Oak Road and by kick-off the crowd had soared to 25,172, which has not been bettered in the league since.

Birmingham claimed a two-goal lead inside twenty minutes. A half-fit Chris Nicholl failed to clear a through ball, leaving Bob Latchford with an easy chance. When Phil Summerill was then granted a free header, the Town's season seemed in tatters. But after 36 minutes the in-and-out Viv Busby headed a Macdonald pass between two defenders before slotting the ball home. Busby then deflected an off-target Macdonald shot past Mike Kelly in the Blues goal to make it 2-2. The fight-back was completed shortly after the break when Alan Slough hammered in a thirty-yard free-kick with the Birmingham defenders still setting up a wall.

LUTON: Read, John Ryan, Slough, Givens, Nicholl, Moore, Jim Ryan, Busby, Macdonald, Keen, Anderson.

BIRMINGHAM: Kelly, Martin, Page, Smith, Hynd, Robinson, Campbell, Francis, Latchford, Summerill, Taylor.

~~~~~~~~~~

Whether the off-field saga had anything to do with the team's disintegration over Easter 1971 is difficult to say, although Alec Stock always maintained that, but for the V & G collapse, the Town would have won promotion back to Division One that season.

The downfall was spectacular. Two goals up at Bristol City, the Hatters lost 2-3, and then sank 0-4 at Millwall the following day. The grim holiday was completed when champions-elect Leicester won 3-1 at Kenilworth Road on Easter Monday in front of a crowd of 24,405.

After four years of heady excitement, the Hatters and their supporters had to face up to an uncertain future. The fag end of the season was played out in an almost funereal atmosphere. The vultures were circling over the club and Alec Stock had to fetch the best price for Macdonald. He handed the task to chief scout Harry Haslam, who soon had Manchester United, Chelsea and Newcastle engaged in a bidding war.

The final game was at home to Cardiff, who had missed out on promotion by a whisker. The occasion was given a little spice as, should the Hatters win by three clear goals, they would qualify for the following season's Watney Cup, which was open to the two clubs in each division who scored most goals without winning anything or gaining promotion.

In the crowd was Joe Harvey, manager of Newcastle, who had emerged as the front runner in the chase for Macdonald As if on cue, the striker bagged all three goals in a 3-0 win. It is said that the hat-trick raised the fee to the recorded £160,000, but it mattered little to Luton supporters who wondered what might have been as they watched Macdonald destined to become the new superstar of Tyneside.

Those same supporters probably cared little when, out of the blue, the local council granted permission, in principle, to carry out the £600,000 works at Kenilworth Road. The news was welcomed by the Board, but they were no longer in a position financially to pursue the matter. Events finally overtook them with the announcement of a planned A505 relief road from Luton to Dunstable which was to follow the line of the railway track past the ground. Coupled with this proposal was an edict from the Ministry of Transport that no supports could be placed along the road. This effectively ruled out any chance of moving the Main Stand backwards.

The subject of 'Milton Keynes' – which would occupy the minds of successive Luton Town boards over the years – first came to the fore in 1971, when director John Bain and manager Alec Stock met with 'consultants of the Milton Keynes project'. What size stadium did Luton Town require, and what rent could be afforded? The answer was a 40,000-50,000 all-seater stadium with a maximum annual rental of £20,000.

The fans had enjoyed the four year roller-coaster while it lasted, but at least they knew what to expect with the club now short of money, which is the way it always was. Alec Stock was a realist and knew why Macdonald had to be sold, but he also knew that to replace a thirty-goal-a-season man, with no funds, was going to be no easy task.

As expected, the 1971-72 season was much ado about nothing. The defence was hard to breach, but there was precious little excitement at the other end. There were eighteen league draws, half of them goalless, which did little to arrest the slide of attendances, which dropped to their lowest level for four years. Don Givens was tried up front with a succession of partners, including early season signing Vic Halom, and Viv Busby – who had a frustrating loan spell at Newcastle, where he was supposed to team up with his old friend Macdonald.

The fallout from the V & G crash meant supporters merely shrugged their shoulders when Chris Nicholl, the rock of the Hatters defence, was sold to Aston Villa for a ludicrously low £90,000 to keep the creditors at bay. For once, everyone was glad when the Town limped over the finishing line, with five points to spare from being relegated.

Once the curtain came down, a wearied Alec Stock resigned, citing the daily travel from his Epsom home as injurious to his health, although he must have despaired over the chain of events at Kenilworth Road. His assistant, Jimmy Andrews, left too, in his case to become manager at Cardiff. The Town's Board responded to this double loss by appointing Harry Haslam to the Luton hot seat.

Haslam had originally arrived at Luton on the coat-tails of Alec Stock, in 1969, when he served as 'entertainments manager'. He had latterly been operating as chief scout. With such a scratchy background, elevating Haslam to the manager's chair seemed crazy. Haslam was regarded by supporters almost as a favourite uncle, but he was a canny character, and after he had installed Roy McCrohan as his assistant he set about wheeling and dealing and stamping his own personality on the club.

Overseen by new directors Denis Mortimer and Roger Smith, Haslam agreed to the departures of record signing David Court, skipper Mike Keen, and Don Givens. Haslam's first intake included Leicester's Rodney Fern, who had ripped Luton's defence to shreds over Easter 1971, ex-England international full-back Bobby Thomson from Birmingham, and – a signing that shocked and delighted everyone – Manchester United winger John Aston.

Haslam, an ex-United player and friend of Old Trafford coach John Aston senior, had to use all his persuasive powers to entice Aston junior to Kenilworth Road, but this single signing was enough to virtually double season ticket sales. John Aston, voted 'Man of the Match' after the 1968 European Cup final, when Manchester United beat Benfica, was pure class and the supporters knew it.

The Board sanctioned new floodlight gantries costing £14,000, with the new bulbs six times stronger than the old ones. Football had moved into the colour television age. With this in mind, Haslam proposed that the club's second strip be changed from red – which it had been since time immemorial – to orange and black, which would show better for the cameras as well as assist the spectators in identification.

The 1972-73 campaign also introduced a new playing formation, which involved a lone striker and five floating midfield players. Despite losing the first game, at Cardiff, the new tactics proved to be effective away from home, but seemed to play into the hands of their opponents at Kenilworth Road. Away wins were common, and if the home form had kept pace the Town would have been up among the front runners. That they were not, frustrated Haslam no end. In an effort to inject greater threat at home, he acquired Derby's reserve striker Barry Butlin for £50,000.

KENILWORTH ROAD CLASSICS: **Luton v Millwall** – 2-2
                    Football League Division Two, 16th December 1972
Back in 1965, George Martin had signed a winger from Wellington Town by the name of Graham French who soon became a crowd favourite at Kenilworth Road. He was deceptively quick for a biggish man, with neat ball control and the ability to cross and shoot with either foot. Luton supporters wondered why he was with them, in the depths of Division Four,

and not playing at the highest level. Stories then started emerging of his liking for wine, women and song. His frequent brushes with the football authorities meant that his chances of playing for England had died with his youth caps, and his dream move to Chelsea had been scuppered. On his day, French was truly spell-binding, but on his off-days he would let the ball slide under his foot for a throw-in. Perversely, he often appeared to play better when he had been out partying the night before. Teammates would pass the ball to him at every opportunity, hangover or not, and from then on let his football brain take over. Truly a poor man's George Best.

French, due to his lifestyle, inevitably became involved with the wrong sort of person and in July 1970 he was arrested following a shooting incident at a local pub. At his subsequent trial he was convicted, but fortunately served most of his time at 'football friendly' Stafford Prison.

Although the Town cancelled his registration, they left the door ajar for French to return, and in September 1972, following his parole, he came back determined to make up for lost time.

Training like a demon (which he he never did before), French got himself fit and, following some reserve-team appearances, his form persuaded Haslam to give him a second debut. A crop of injuries sustained during a home game with QPR meant that Haslam had to re-shuffle the pack for the following week's match with Millwall, leaving the way clear for French to make a welcome return.

The Lions, who had narrowly missed promotion in May, had a strong following in the crowd of 11,550. Luton goalkeeper Keith Barber did not have a direct shot to save in the first half, with French responding to the encouragement of the crowd to torment the opposition. After six minutes Millwall keeper Bryan King fumbled a shot from Peter Anderson and Barry Butlin pounced from close range. Shortly after the break French took the ball through midfield, drew King out, and then shot past him into the empty net. Over two years of pent-up emotion meant that this goal was greeted by one of the biggest cheers ever heard at Kenilworth Road and even French was seen to smile.

Unfortunately, that was the end of the fairy-tale. Almost immediately Derek Possee headed home for Millwall, and when Doug Allder was up-ended in the box by Barber, Gordon Bolland equalised from the spot. The disappointment of letting slip a two-goal lead was tempered by the thought that 'Frenchie was back'.

LUTON: *Barber, Shanks, Thomson, Anderson, Garner, John Ryan, Jim Ryan, French, Butlin, Halom, Aston.*

MILLWALL: *King, Bolland, Cripps, Dorney, Kitchener, Burnett, Brown, Possee, Wood, Dunphy, Allder.*

~~~~~~~~~~

As a postscript, it is sad to note that French never did recover his old self. He was probably running on adrenalin against Millwall. The years lost in prison had taken their toll and he made only seven more appearances for the Town before moving to Reading in November 1973 where he turned out on a handful of occasions. His last comeback was in 1976 when he played twice for Southport, for his old boss Allan Brown, under the assumed name of 'Lafite'. French could have gone to the very top, and his was a terrible waste of a supreme, natural talent.

When the third round FA Cup draw was announced, the visit of Crewe from Division Four was seen as a passport to round four for the first time in twelve years. A crowd of 9,411 assembled at Kenilworth Road on a bitterly cold day to see Luton make hard work of disposing of opponents who were ably prompted by ex-Town player Gerry Jones. Goals from Jim Ryan and Barry Butlin earned a trip to First Division Newcastle, and from the moment the draw was made the local and national press were in the grip of Malcolm Macdonald mania. Macdonald would be facing his old side for the first time since his transfer eighteen months previously.

Macdonald, already a hero of the Newcastle terraces, was never backward in coming forward, and turned the occasion into a personal crusade to put one over his old teammates. Despite the odds against Luton winning, several trainloads of supporters made the long trip north and were confronted by a partisan capacity crowd of 42,170 in a three-sided St James' Park. The Town, having failed to register their proposed new orange and black second strip with the Football League, had no such problem with the FA, and so turned out in their new shirts and shorts, purchased by director Eric Morecambe, for the first time.

New-look Luton had to endure an early onslaught, with Macdonald, made captain for the day, missing an early chance. Out of the blue, the Town scored when John Aston beat Magpies goalkeeper Iam McFaul when through on goal. Extraordinarily, Luton then scored again. Alan Slough cut the ball back to Aston, who banged it into the top corner for a picture goal. Not surprisingly, it was 'backs to the wall' stuff in the second half. John Moore, imperious throughout, was called upon to defend with unorthodox parts of his anatomy! The only disappointment for travelling fans was that the trains arrived back too late for them to relive the highlights on *Match of the Day* in those pre-video days.

The fifth round saw Luton travelling again. Bolton were chasing promotion from Division Three and were unbeaten at home for almost a year. Another partisan crowd greeted the trainloads of Luton supporters, who swelled the gate to 39,556. The Hatters took control from the start, and Alan Garner's second-half header earned a quarter-final place for only the fourth time in the club's history.

Although Luton were drawn away yet again – this time to Sunderland – that disappointment was tempered by the fact that, at the time, the Hatters' away record was better than their form at home. They had already won at Sunderland in the league, and the week before the cup-tie had won the return at Kenilworth Road 1-0.

Confidence was therefore high but, as in 1959 – when Nottingham Forest were thrashed 5-1 just prior to the Cup final – perhaps it was bordering on over-confidence. Sunderland rested several first-choice players for the league game, but they were back for the quarter-final. A colossal crowd of 53,151 packed the Roker Park terraces, a figure that was never subsequently exceeded. It was almost 40,000 higher than the number who turned out for the league meeting earlier in the season. Sadly, the red and white stripes tore into a surprisingly limp Luton, winning 2-0 and going on to lift the trophy after beating Leeds in the final.

With the Cup dream over, the Town could only muster two wins from the final ten league games as the season ended in another huge anticlimax.

During the 1973 close season the Luton directors formulated a five-year plan, at the end of which it was hoped that the club would be back in the top division. Had they known this objective would be achieved four years early, they might have come out in a cold sweat, because the club's finances were far from being on a firm footing following the V & G collapse.

It was decided to install 1,200 seats in the Bobbers Stand over the summer at a cost of £8,000. This was not the most popular initiative ever taken by the club, as it meant displacing many spectators who had stood in the same spot for decades. The work should have been completed by the start of the 1973-74 season, but delays meant that for some weeks that part of the ground resembled a builders yard. To add insult to injury, the take-up rate for the new section was slow and empty bright orange plastic seats are difficult to disguise on match-days.

On the playing side, Harry Haslam dispensed with the services of Alan Slough and Viv Busby, who both rejoined their former boss Alec Stock at Fulham. The only notable signing was the improbably named Tom Finney from Crusaders in Belfast.

New-season hopes drained away in ninety awful minutes at Nottingham Forest, when the Town went down 0-4. It was back to the drawing board for Haslam and his coaches. In effect, the pre-season work had to be re-started and crammed into the week before the visit of Carlisle.

Kenilworth Road Classics: **Luton v Carlisle** – 6-1

Football League Division Two, 1st September 1973

Due to the shocker at Nottingham, only 7,231 turned up for the first home game, the lowest for seven years. The game saw the baptism of the Town's new official first-team strip of orange and navy blue. The supporters had been promised a vote on the new strip, which did not happen, but it was unveiled anyway.

The stay-at-homes missed a treat, as the Town netted six times in 23 minutes midway through the first half. The hero was £13,000 signing Tom Finney, who had been combining pipe-fitting with part-time football in Belfast only a month before. Finney launched himself at a John Aston cross to head the first goal. Peter Anderson then dummied the Carlisle defence and drove the ball past ex-Hatters keeper Alan Ross. Finney hit the third from a Don Shanks pass, and Aston added number four with one of those shots that only arrow into the top corner when everything is going right for you. Striker Barry Butlin dropped deep to provide the through ball for Anderson to net the fifth, before belting in number six himself after Finney's shot had been blocked.

The scoring then stopped, although the Carlisle goal led a charmed life in the second half. The visitors even netted one themselves, though afterwards their disconsolate manager Alan Ashman said, 'I'm startled. I'm stunned. In all my career I have never before gone in six down at half-time. It's not nice. I don't want it to happen again.'

Haslam refused to let the players have their traditional Monday off, saying there was still much to do. As for Carlisle, they recovered to the extent that they would be promoted along with the Hatters.

LUTON: *Horn, Shanks, Thomson, Anderson, Faulkner, Garner, Jim Ryan, John Ryan, Butlin, Finney, Aston.*

CARLISLE: *Ross, Carr, Gorman, Ternent, Green, Winstanley, Train (Delgado), Owen, Clarke, Laidlaw, Martin.*

~~~~~~~~~~

Finney trumped his two goals against Carlisle with another one in the 3-1 win at Bristol City the following week and the equaliser in a midweek 1-1 draw at Notts County. Although his sensational start was not maintained, the Town's early season form was, and a 1-0 win at FA Cup-holders Sunderland was followed by a devastating 3-0 home win over Blackpool which pushed the Hatters up into a promotion spot.

Match sponsorship came to Kenilworth Road for the first time when Vauxhall Motors plus Shaw & Kilburn sponsored the league game with Swindon on 13th October. Free match programmes were given to all spectators by the sponsors.

Haslam, mindful of the fact that the Town had flattered to deceive in previous seasons, paid £100,000 to Burnley for Alan West, whose debut at Orient coincided with the end of the winning run, 0-2. The Town endured a wobbly spell but, riding their luck, picked up valuable points courtesy of last-minute own-goals – Don McAllister of Bolton in a 2-1 home win –

and goals by on-loan players – John Sims in the 2-1 home victory over Sheffield Wednesday.

Haslam bought Jimmy Husband from Everton for £70,000, but his debut too ended in defeat – at home to West Brom, who better mastered an icy pitch. Perhaps Haslam took the hint. Either way, he did not buy any more players that season.

An objective view, rather than a rose-tinted one, was that Luton were just an average side competing in a poor division. This was evidenced by Jack Charlton's Middlesbrough, who were steaming away at the top and who were clearly too good for the opposition.

Barry Butlin's return, following a broken jaw, signalled better fortunes, as three 1-0 wins in a row testified. But a sign of how poor the general standard was can be seen from Luton's next six games. They only won one, and could have expected to be pushed down the table. That they were not suggests everyone was fighting to avoid promotion.

After a 0-4 home thrashing by Division One Leicester in the FA Cup – which gave a stark example of what to expect should Luton get promoted – they beat Crystal Palace the following week and went back to second. They stayed there for the rest of the season, no matter how well or badly they played.

Easter, so often disastrous, earned only two points from three games, but a 3-0 home win over Millwall and further slip-ups by fellow challengers meant Luton needed only one point from the final two games to clinch the runners-up spot. Butlin headed an early goal at West Brom, but Albion levelled from a controversial penalty towards the end. Concussed Luton centre-half John Faulkner held the defence firm in those last nail-biting minutes before the referee's whistle signalled promotion. The final game, at home to Sunderland, was played in a carnival atmosphere. Goals flew in from all angles, though Luton ended up losing 3-4. The supporters who engulfed the pitch at the end did not give a jot that their team would never have gone up in any normal season.

The Town were back in the top division for the first time since 1960. They became the first Football League team to have fallen from Division One to Division Four and then bounce all the way back again. Although the directors were delighted with the progress made on the pitch, they were secretly scouring the balance sheet. Money was still tight, yet fans would clamour for top-class signings and to hell with the consequences.

Funds were somehow made available for Haslam to buy both teenaged Futcher twins from Chester for £125,000. The manager predicted that one of them, Paul, was destined to be a future England international, but the transaction would probably not have gone ahead but for chairman Robert Keens being hospitalised with double pneumonia. The rest of the Board were perhaps not so prudent, but it was evident to everyone that at least £50,000 had to be spent on the ground. The main outlay was on digging up the pitch to lay new drainage, but money was also needed for new crush barriers on the Kenilworth Road terrace, the replacing of the wooden terracing at the Kenilworth/Bobbers Stand corner, new police boxes at either end of the stadium, and fences in the enclosure to enable season tickets to be sold in that section.

Realising that the club needed to re-kindle its youth policy in order to survive in the longer term, the most significant arrivals in the summer of 1974 were of ex-player David Pleat and Uruguayan Danny Bergara on the coaching staff. Both were instructed to nurture, and add to, the crop of promising youngsters coming up through the ranks.

These worries behind the scenes were of little consequence to the average supporter, who merely wanted to be entertained. The visit of Liverpool – in Bob Paisley's first game in charge – on the opening day, together with the media scrum, brought home the fact that Luton Town were back in the big time.

Although the Town lost bravely, 1-2, it soon became apparent that the team was out of its depth. It took ten games to record a first victory. That was against fellow new-boys Carlisle, who were also struggling, on the day top scorer Barry Butlin was sold to Allan Brown's Nottingham Forest for £120,000. Money talked.

The loss of Butlin was keenly felt and the team went into free-fall. By mid-December the Town had only picked up nine points and looked likely to break the record for the lowest points total recorded in the top flight.

KENILWORTH ROAD CLASSICS: **Luton v Wolverhampton** – 3-2

Football League Division One, 28th December 1974

On 7th December 1974 at Chelsea, Harry Haslam sent on the youngsters. As well as re-introducing Steve Buckley in place of Bobby Thomson, he blooded eighteen-year-old Paul Futcher. Although Luton lost 0-2, travelling fans saw a star in the making. The following week's game at Liverpool was lost by the same score but on 21st December the first win for three months was recorded when Derby, the eventual champions, were seen off 1-0 at Kenilworth Road.

In a desperate bid to increase the strike tally, Haslam introduced Paul's twin brother Ron into the fray at leaders Ipswich on Boxing Day. Ron, signed as a makeweight to keep his brother from feeling homesick, was drafted in to replace Adrian Alston after surprising the manager by scoring 22 reserve goals. The top versus bottom clash was, frankly, grim viewing as the Town put up the shutters. Fortunately, Ipswich had an off day and spectators were streaming out long before the end, fed up with the endless succession of Luton back-passes. With thirty seconds left, Hatters winger John Aston, in a rare foray over the halfway line, crossed the ball with his left foot from the right wing, and Ron Futcher glanced in a header for an undeserved win. Hundreds of cushions rained on the field at the end.

For the visit of Wolves two days later, the twins kept their places and a holiday crowd of 19,642 rolled up to see them. Wolves were in mid-table, but had not lost for six weeks and were confident after beating high-flying Everton at Molineux on Boxing Day.

Wolves scored first in the 23rd minute, when Francis Munro headed home a John Farley corner, but then the Futcher twins took over. Paul found his brother with a long ball out of defence. Ron side-stepped Munro to equalise. In the 44th minute Ron headed in John Aston's centre for the second. With Aston beating Wolves' right-back Nigel Williams with ease, the Town took charge in the second half, only for Barry Powell to equalise in the 68th minute.

That might have been the signal for heads to drop, but attacks rained down on the Wolves defence, while at the other end Paul – with a mixture of skill and heart-stopping cheek – kept Wolves dangermen John Richards and Steve Kindon at bay.

Five minutes from the end Alan West centred for Ron Futcher to head the winner. The scenes at the finish were reminiscent of a cup final win.

LUTON: *Horn, John Ryan, Buckley, Anderson, Faulkner, Paul Futcher, Jim Ryan, Husband, Ron Futcher, West, Aston.*

WOLVES: *Parkes, Williams, Parkin, Bailey, Munro, McAlle, Hibbitt (Daley), Powell, Richards, Kindon, Farley.*

~~~~~~~~~~~

The Hatters still had a lot of catching up to do. By March they had forced themselves off the bottom and were attempting to claw their way out of the bottom three. Three straight wins helped the cause and provided supporters with some of the most exciting games at Kenilworth Road for years. After Carlisle were beaten 2-1 at Brunton Park, home games against champions Leeds and Arsenal provided marvellous entertainment. In front of capacity crowds the Hatters were roared to victory as they attacked in droves to claim maximum points.

The Easter games pitched Luton at Derby and Wolves, but the Hatters were thrashed on both occasions. Champions-in-waiting Derby won 5-0, with Roger Davies scoring all five, while at Molineux the Town lost 2-5 after being 2-1 up. Worse was to come when Luton lost at fellow strugglers Tottenham. Alfie Conn's winner was blatantly offside and Paul Futcher was sent off for arguing the matter a little too volubly.

The Town were now back to square one, but three more wins from three games set up a grandstand finish. Everton, Leicester and Birmingham were swept aside on waves of all-out attack. Following a home draw with Manchester City on the final day, the Town were where they wanted to be, out of the bottom three, at the expense of Tottenham.

The problem was, Tottenham had one game left – at home to Leeds, the deposed League Champions and European Cup finalists. Tottenham, needed only a draw to climb back above the Hatters and send them down. Many Luton fans trekked to White Hart Lane, and were shocked to see Spurs play like world beaters to win 4-2. Conspiracy theories abound to this day.

The Town were therefore relegated but gained many friends along the way. Had their performances in the first half of the campaign matched those in the second, they would have qualified for Europe. It would be unfair to say that the Luton directors 'had chased a dream' but the money spent in the vain attempt to keep Division One football in Luton was sure to cause problems that would reverberate around the club in ways not dissimilar to those of the Vehicle & General crisis of five years before. Players were still on Division One contracts, but attendances would plummet, no matter how well the Town did on the field.

The manager, players and supporters were upbeat about the prospects, in the light of recent form and the youngsters in the team, supplemented by local lads Lil Fuccillo and Andy King.

The 1975-76 season started well enough, with three wins from the first four games, but one win from the next fourteen drove the team towards the foot of the table. Injuries to Alan West and John Aston had not helped but that, one suspects, was only part of the problem. Rumours of major riffs at board level over the worsening money situation could hardly be kept secret.

Unrest was first sensed when Eric Morecambe resigned from the board citing 'pressure of work'. His departure came when Haslam was refused permission to sign ex-Scotland and Celtic winger Jimmy Johnstone on a free transfer because the club could not afford him. This was quickly followed by the resignation of three more directors, leaving chief executive Denis Mortimer to finally air the financial problems in public.

The situation was worse than anyone dreamt. The club had trade debts of £340,000, an overdraft of £383,000, and the bank had failed to cash the club's latest weekly wages cheque. This meant the remaining directors had to put their hands in their pockets to keep the club afloat. Rumours of the electricity being cut off turned out to be true.

A meeting of creditors gave the club 28 days to come up with some money. That meant a player being sold quickly. The Town had pre-empted this and were hoping to sell Peter Anderson to Antwerp. Unfortunately, news of Luton's plight leaked out just as Haslam was hoping to extract the biggest possible fee from the Belgian club. Instead he had to go cap in hand to get the best price possible. He had asked for £105,000. After all, Aston Villa had bid £150,000 for the player a year before, but in the end Haslam had to settle for £55,000, which was just about enough to solve the immediate cash crisis.

Supporters rallied round and pledged to buy up the 100,000 £1 shares (in the event less than 10 per cent were sold) that were put up for offer. The groundswell of support meant fans turned up in great numbers for the next home game. Unfortunately (or fortunately if you were Alan Slough), that game was a testimonial for the ex-Town player and, quite rightly, all the money paid at the gate that evening went to him.

The whole affair had clearly got to the players, because once the axe was lifted, performances improved to the extent that the team embarked on a seven-game winning run over Christmas and into the New Year. That run included a 5-1 victory at Charlton, where Peter Anderson made his last performance for the Hatters and scored twice. One wonders what would have happened if Anderson had played a stinker and, in turn, watching Antwerp officials had called off the deal. It does not bear thinking about.

The winning run lifted the Town into the top eight. Although they never dropped any lower, many observers felt they could have made a more determined push for one of the top three slots. It was most frustrating when good home performances were followed by 0-3 away defeats – that score was repeated no fewer that five times.

As the season drew to a close, the vultures started circling, casting envious eyes over the Luton youngsters. Knowing that the club was still in dire straights Everton put in a joke bid of £35,000 for Andy King which the Luton board reluctantly had to accept.

KENILWORTH ROAD CLASSICS: **Luton v Bristol Rovers** – 3-1

Football League Division Two, 19th April 1976

The Town's penultimate game was a meaningless Easter Monday clash with Bristol Rovers, who were safe from relegation and arrived fresh from beating Southampton at Eastville two days before.

Let Ricky Hill now take up the story. 'Over Easter 1976, David Pleat kept on asking me if my boots were clean, which puzzled me, but the reason for him asking soon became clear when, on the day of the Bristol Rovers home game, assistant manager Roy McCrohan called me in from playing pool with the other junior pros to tell me I was in the first team squad and would be substitute that afternoon. This came after only thirteen reserve team appearances.

'I took my place on the bench and as a dull game entered its final quarter, with the score deadlocked at 1-1, our centre-half John Faulkner, who had just returned to the side after a long lay-off with a bad knee injury, went down hurt. Without getting off his seat physio Reg Game knew that "Maxie's" knee had gone again and immediately ordered him off. I could sense the anticipation in the crowd as I came on as the majority of supporters had not seen me before.'

None of this seemed to affect seventeen-year-old Hill as, with almost his first touch, he played a marvellous through ball to Brian Chambers to put the Town into the lead. Moments later the ball was played into Hill's path by Jimmy Husband (a rare event for him to pass to anyone in the box, according to Ricky). A crisp low shot into the net later, and the crowd went mad acclaiming a new hero. Ricky turned nonchalantly to walk back to the middle, but after a couple of steps he was submerged by his teammates. A star was born.

LUTON: *Barber, Price, Buckley, Chambers, Faulkner (Hill), Paul Futcher, Husband, Fuccillo, Ron Futcher, West, John Ryan.*

BRISTOL ROVERS: *Eadie, Parsons, Day, Taylor, Pulis, Williams, Britten, Smith (Stephens), Evans, Staniforth, Fearnley.*

~~~~~~~~~~

With the directors desperately trying to reduce the club's overdraft, Harry Haslam did his bit over the summer of 1976 by getting rid of some of the older and more highly paid players. With all the promising home-grown youngsters pushing through, he knew the future was bright. The only new signing was ex-Scotland and Celtic striker Dixie Deans, who cost £20,000. Deans did not look like a footballer, let alone an international striker, but he became an instant hit when scoring both Luton goals in the opening-day 2-0 home win over relegated Sheffield United.

The Town were exasperatingly inconsistent, typified by a fine win at promotion favourites Wolves and a dire 1-4 home defeat by Southampton. Fans did not have a clue as to which Luton side was going to turn up.

Dixie Dean's light shone brightly for a while as he scored a few important goals, especially with his head, which was all the more remarkable as he was only 5ft 5in tall. He also took over in goal from the injured Keith Barber at Notts County, and his unconventional display inspired the Hatters to a 4-0 win. Unfortunately, Deans' haphazard time-keeping was aggravating his manager, and when he knocked a man off his bicycle with an apple thrown from the team coach after training, Haslam had to intervene to keep the story from the local press, who would have loved a 'Man knocked off bike by apple' headline.

The final straw came at Bolton in December when Deans got himself involved in petty arguments on the pitch which led to his dismissal. The ten men could not hold onto their one-goal lead and eventually lost 1-2, much to Haslam's ire. Deans never played for the Town again.

Following defeat at Orient on Boxing Day 1976, the Town dropped to fourteenth. It is difficult to put a finger on how and why the team suddenly transformed itself, but the next three months became one of the golden periods in the club's history. Chelsea were walloped 4-0 at a snow-covered Kenilworth Road on 29th December, and although Luton then lost 0-1 at Bristol Rovers, they notched a 3-0 win at Sheffield United in front of the *Match of the Day* cameras. Win piled upon win. The seventh straight victory was at Fulham, who were relishing their George Best and Rodney Marsh days. Unfortunately, Best missed this game, while Marsh turned out for the last time in Fulham colours. The Luton juggernaut won yet again through goals from Aston and Husband.

KENILWORTH ROAD CLASSICS: **Luton v Wolverhampton** – 2-0

Football League Division Two, 5th March 1977

Seven straight wins, fourteen points, and it was now getting serious. A crowd of 19,200 gathered to see Wolves, who had themselves gone twelve games undefeated and who lay third. Relegated the previous season, Wolves were anxious for a quick return and carved out five good openings almost before the crowd had settled into position.

Gradually, the Luton defence took control. Paul Futcher and John Faulkner snuffed out the Wolves strikeforce of John Richards and Alan Sunderland, while Brian Chambers and Lil Fuccillo nullified the threat posed by Willie Carr and Kenny Hibbitt. This left Alan West free, behind Husband, Aston and Ron Futcher, who constantly interchanged positions to confuse the Wolves rearguard.

The breakthrough came after 35 minutes when Ron Futcher headed on a free-kick from full-back Steve Buckley. Husband was the first to react with a crisp half-volley. The Town went 2-0 up ninety seconds later when Fuccillo drifted inside and casually floated the ball over the head of goalkeeper Pierce from a tight angle.

Although Wolves stepped up the pressure, Luton came nearest to scoring, when Geoff Palmer threw himself to fist a shot from Ron Futcher round the post, which went unnoticed by the referee.

The win lifted Luton to fourth. Haslam, who had received the 'Manager of the Month' award beforehand, attributed the Town's rise to 'Our team work and our attitude to the game, as well as our front line looking a lot better than our opponents'.

LUTON: Aleksic, Price, Buckley, Faulkner, Paul Futcher, Chambers, West, Fuccillo, Husband, Ron Futcher (Geddis), Aston.

WOLVES: Pierce, Palmer, Parkin, Munro, McAlle, Daley, Hibbitt, Patching (Gould), Carr, Richards, Sunderland.

~~~~~~~~~~

The winning run stretched to nine when substitute David Geddis, on loan from Ipswich, scored the only goal four minutes from time in the next game, at home to Oldham.

The Town could not make it ten. Plymouth – who would be relegated – fought a 1-1 draw at Kenilworth Road, but that proved to be blip. Ron Futcher scored another late goal, this time breaking the hearts of Hereford at Edgar Street, a result which took Luton into the top three. Carlisle were then thrashed 5-0 at Kenilworth Road. Where would it all end? With a 0-1 defeat at Southampton! Saints' Alan Ball netted in the second minute and that was that. A dismal Easter followed, with only one point earned from three games. The Hatters had shot their bolt and drifted down to sixth, albeit only four points off a promotion place.

The late 1970s was a time when football was gaining in popularity in the USA. Many English players were tempted to move there, if only for the money on offer. The Town would not normally have been happy at play-ers migrating for the summer months, fearing injury and the players return-ing stale after twelve months continuous football. In the 1977 close season, though, they positively encouraged Ron and Paul Futcher, and Alan West to join Minnesota Kicks in a complicated lease-purchase which earned the Hatters a profit of £118,000. As luck would have it, a car accident pre-vented Paul Futcher from taking part, but his place was snapped up by Paul Price.

The club could hardly blame their American loanees if they returned stale, because the rest of the squad embarked on a 33,000-mile round trip of the USA, New Caledonia, New Zealand and Fiji. The party flew from Heathrow to Los Angeles and then to St Louis, where the local NASL side were beaten 3-2. From the sunny States it was on to New Zealand, where it was mid-winter, and three wins were recorded out of four games. Next it was humid New Caledonia and Fiji, where three further games were played and won.

The exhausted party eventually arrived home after one of the longest tours in football history. After very little respite it was back to pre-season training, ready for another determined tilt at the Second Division title.

Pre-season training was hindered by the absence of the three loan play-ers who, under the terms of the agreement with Minnesota Kicks, were not due back until after the English season had started. It was therefore a makeshift side that took on Orient on the opening day of 1977-78. A crowd of 8,061 were greeted by an unfamiliar line-up, although the Town won 1-0 with a second-half goal from full-back Steve Buckley.

With West and Price back in the squad for the trip to Oldham, the team had a more familiar look. Luton lost unluckily 0-1, and to add insult to injury, Paul Futcher was ordered off for a foul. Ron Futcher was next to return, so it was a full-strength side that won 3-1 at First Division Wolves in a League Cup-tie. The goals came from Jim Husband, £35,000 summer signing Phil Boersma, and substitute David Carr.

KENILWORTH ROAD CLASSICS: **Luton v Charlton** – 7-1

Football League Division Two, 3rd September 1977

Fresh from that cup win at Wolves, Luton welcomed Charlton to Kenilworth Road. Gary Heale made his debut in place of the injured Phil Boersma. A 9,061 crowd saw the Town take the lead after twenty minutes when Husband finished off a well-worked free-kick routine. Ten minutes later, Buckley – who was fast earning a goalscoring reputation – fired home a rocket shot to put the Town two goals up.

The second period saw Luton in unstoppable form, leaving Charlton goalkeeper Jeff Wood shell-shocked. For the record, Ricky Hill put the Town three-up with a long-range dipper. Husband netted a fourth after weaving his way through the Charlton defence. Heale confirmed a memorable debut by heading in, and Husband took his personal tally to four – his penalty-kick trickled over the line before he headed in a John Faulkner cross. Charlton netted in the final minute when Mike Flanagan beat Luton goalkeeper Milija Aleksic from the spot.

Harry Haslam was obviously happy with the biggest win for twenty years, less for the goals than for the manner in which they were created. Husband was given the match ball as, in the words of Haslam, 'He has had it all afternoon so he might as well keep it.' Charlton coach Harry Cripps vowed 'It will never happen again'.

LUTON: *Aleksic, Price, Buckley, Fuccillo, Faulkner, Paul Futcher, Husband, Hill, Ron Futcher, West, Heale.*

CHARLTON: *Wood, Curtis, (Gritt), Warman, Campbell, Berry, Tydeman, Powell, Burman, Flanagan, Peacock, McAuley.*

~~~~~~~~~~

The good form continued through the autumn. Following a 1-0 home win over Fulham in mid-October the Town were up to second. To increase the feel-good factor, the club's finances were stated as 'much improved'. The overdraft had been slashed and the Town were almost living within their means.

From this feeling of relative strength, everything started to unravel. There were back to back defeats at Blackpool and Bolton, and long-term injuries to Phil Boersma and Paul Futcher. Futcher had been involved in his second car crash in a matter of months, but this time the immediate prognosis was that he would be lucky ever to play again. That he was back in ten weeks astonished everyone, considering his injuries, although in the eyes of many he never quite regained his former dominance.

Before long it was rumoured that Harry Haslam and new board member David Evans were at crossed swords. Evans, the wealthy boss of the Brengreen Group which employed 10,000 people was – by his own admission – blunt. When he came up against the similarly straight-talking Haslam sparks were always likely to fly.

Haslam maintained that Evans had told him to 'Change your coaches, or your players or I'll be after your blood each week'. Following a slanging match after an awful 1-3 defeat at Mansfield, the manager got the Board to ban Evans from the dressing rooms before and after games.

As rumours of these spats started to spread throughout the footballing world, Haslam found himself offered the vacant manager's position at Millwall, not to mention the chief scout's role at Manchester United. Although he turned both down, the first step had been taken on the slippery slope.

Out of the blue, chief coach Roy McCrohan announced that he was to join the exodus to the USA and become assistant manager of Detroit Express. It was not long before the Town reluctantly accepted an offer they could not refuse from Derby for popular full-back Steve Buckley. County manager Tommy Docherty said he now had the best full-back pairing in the country in David Langan and Buckley, which in the minds of Luton supporters only plunged the knife deeper.

The third rapid departure came in late-January 1978, when Haslam confirmed he was off to manage Sheffield United. Only days earlier he had confirmed in the club's match programme that the rumours of his departure were untrue and that he was set to sign a new contact. When Haslam read the small print of that contract he realised that he would be worse off than before. On learning of this, Sheffield United stepped in and offered a contract reputed to be worth £100,000 over five years.

The Town made little effort to make Haslam change his mind. Instead they offered the job to David Pleat, who had jumped from being reserve-team coach to chief coach – following the departure of McCrohan – and was now in line for the top job. To complicate matters, Pleat was invited by Haslam to join him at Bramall Lane, but after a couple of days' deliberation he decided to stay at Kenilworth Road.

Pleat soon discovered the pitfalls that lay in wait. Although he had the ears of the younger players, the older professionals were a bit sniffy about saying 'boss' to someone barely older than themselves. The new man stood his ground, and was soon orchestrating the departure of certain senior players to the States. Pleat was determined to be his own man and to create his own team.

The season was already dead from the players' point of view. Though the Town finished thirteenth, that was an illusion. In this freakish season

Luton were one of seven teams on 38 points. Blackpool, who had been in the top half just two weeks earlier, went down with 37.

Pleat set about ringing the changes, overseeing one of the biggest culls of players ever seen at the club. To fund his purchases, Pleat needed to sell. He persuaded Manchester City to part with £350,000 for Paul Futcher and a further £80,000 for Ron.

Awash with money – in Luton terms – Pleat recruited virtually a new team. Winger David Moss came from Swindon, Mark Aizlewood from Newport, Bob Hatton from Blackpool, Kirk Stephens from Nuneaton, Steve Sherlock from Manchester City, and the awkward – in more ways than one – Chris Turner from Peterborough via New England Tea Men. Luton supporters were disappointed if a day went by without news of yet another arrival.

Probably the steal of the summer proved to be defender Mal Donaghy from Larne. Bigger clubs than the Town, notably Celtic, expressed interest, but Pleat, showing admirable foresight, waited for the Larne manager to go on holiday before putting in a bid of £15,000. The Larne directors thought (wrongly) that Donaghy was out of contract and reluctantly agreed. When the manager returned he was said to be spitting feathers!

When all was done, Pleat and his coaching staff – Ken Gutteridge and ex-Hatters favourite John Moore – could reflect that the club was well rid of its potentially troublesome old heads. His own buys, and up and coming stars, would now be put to the test. He hoped that much-travelled striker Bob Hatton would help to groom Brian Stein, one of the few successes of the previous season, following his arrival from Edgware Town. Pleat did, however, warn that it might take time for the changes to pay off and pleaded for patience from the fans.

KENILWORTH ROAD CLASSICS: **Luton v Oldham** – 6-1

Football League Division Two, 19th August 1978

In view of the comings and goings over the summer, it was a bemused 8,043 customers who filed in to Kenilworth Road to see David Pleat's new-look side. As the players waved to the crowd before kick-off, most spectators were trying to work out who was who. No fewer than seven players were making their debuts, a figure only exceeded in the opening game of the 1946-47 season.

At half-time those same fans must have been scratching their heads. The Latics had taken the lead through Ian Wood early on and looked to be in control.

Whatever Pleat said in the dressing room, it worked. Fifteen seconds after the re-start Bob Hatton took a long ball from Chris Turner to level. Seconds later David Moss put the Town in front, and that was followed by a three-goal salvo midway through the half. Brian Stein netted from close in after a shot came back off the post, Lil Fuccillo banged in a penalty, and Moss hammered in a long cross from Mal Donaghy. Bob Hatton headed his second and Luton's sixth in the final minute.

LUTON: *Aleksic, Stephens, Sherlock, Donaghy, Turner, Aizlewood, Hill, Fuccillo, Stein, Hatton, Moss.*

OLDHAM: *McDonnell, Wood, Edwards, Blair, Holt, Hurst, Gardner, Taylor, Young, Halom, Chapman.*

~~~~~~~~~~~

The bubble quickly burst. The next games, at Crystal Palace and Newcastle, were both lost. At Kenilworth Road, though, the Hatters were a different side, as proved when Charlton visited and returned to London following a 3-0 defeat, with Hatton, Stein and Hill on the scoresheet.

With the team boosted by the return of Paul Price and Alan West from a summer playing in the USA, a 0-2 defeat at Bristol Rovers was seen as a massive disappointment. This was reflected when the crowd dropped to 7,752 for the visit of Cardiff the following week. The Bluebirds included ex-Luton goalkeeper Keith Barber – on loan from Swansea – but there was no happy homecoming as Luton went one better than the 6-1 misery inflicted on Oldham. Beaten seven times, the disgusted Barber decided to call it a day. He did not play league football again. For the Hatters, scores of 6-1 and 7-1 surely marked the limit for routs in one season!

KENILWORTH ROAD CLASSICS: **Luton v Notts County** – 6-0

Football League Division Two, 21st October 1978

On 21st October Notts County were one place above the Hatters in seventh spot. The crowd, after the early season excitement, had dropped, and only 8,651 were present to see the deadlock broken after 22 minutes when Hatton rounded off a four-man move. The Town went further ahead just before the interval when Stein headed home a cross from the dangerous David Moss. The second period turned into yet another rout with another four goals coming in a twenty-minute spell. Alan West, Moss, Stein and Lil Fuccillo were the players whose efforts counted, but it could have been more had County goalkeeper McManus not performed heroics.

'A majestic performance,' said David Pleat afterwards. 'We always looked as though we were going to score goals.' The supporters could reflect on 25 goals scored in just six home games. Luton stood fourth.

LUTON: *Aleksic, Price, Aizlewood, Hill, Turner, Donaghy, West, Fuccillo, Stein, Hatton (Jones), Moss.*

NOTTS CO: *McManus, Richards, O'Brien, Benjamin, Stubbs, Mann, McCulloch, Masson, Hooks, Hunt (McVay), Vinter.*

~~~~~~~~~~~

The problems were away from home, where Luton never got the knack of winning. And once they surrendered their dominance at home, they began to fall down the table. Following a 1-3 loss at Brighton just before Christmas, only three teams separated the Hatters from the relegation places. Pleat's pre-season warning was coming home to roost.

That game against Brighton marked another turning point, for the player of the season at that stage, Lil Fuccillo, had his leg broken by Albion's Paul Clark, who was not even booked. The Town contemplated legal action against the Brighton player, but that would not have helped Fuccillo who now faced a long lay-off.

Despite their league problems, the Town enjoyed their longest run in the League Cup during 1978-79. Wigan arrived in August without a league win to their name, following their election from the Northern Premier League that summer. They had, however, beaten Tranmere in the first round, after a replay, and were looking forward to a crack at the 'big boys' who entered the competition at the second-round stage. The corner count was 11-0 in the Town's favour, which gives an indication of the balance of play, but they only had two goals by Brian Stein to show.

Another Division Four side, Crewe, were the next visitors, and they also opted for defence in depth. The Town were regularly thwarted by Crewe goalkeeper Peter Caswell until early in the second half when the Town scored twice in three minutes. Mal Donaghy up-ended Steven Wilshaw in the box to let Crewe back into contention but Luton held out.

Their reward was a trip to Aston Villa, which brought on a mild dose of cup fever in Luton. Villa were mid-table in Division One and were building a side that would win the championship a couple of years later. A crowd of 32,727, including a fair few from Luton, saw Villa dangerman Andy Gray fire a shot which was well saved by Milija Aleksic before he was carried from the field with a knee injury following a clash with Mal Donaghy.

Minus their talisman, Villa were, quite honestly, a shambles. Luton fans could smell an upset, especially as the home crowd started to get on the backs of their team. Hatton had a goal disallowed for offside, while Moss was denied a penalty by a lenient referee who awarded an indirect free-kick in the area for obstruction. The goal the Town deserved finally came in the 66th minute. Fuccillo slid a perfect pass to Hatton which bisected Villa's twin centre-halves, leaving Hatton to drill the ball first time into the corner of the net. Villa began pumping balls forward, where the tall Chris Turner – enjoying his best game for the club – won everything. In the dying moments West embarked on a fifty-yard run down the left before crossing to Moss, who laid the ball back for Stein to score. Ironically, this was the Town's first away win since David Pleat took charge ten months earlier.

The Hatters were now through to the quarter-finals for the first time. They faced another difficult tie, this one at Leeds, who sat ninth in Division One. Leeds were not the power of old, but they still boasted a team crammed full of internationals and household names. The Hatters supporters swelled the Elland Road attendance to 28,177. Just as the Town players thought they had reached half-time with the game goalless, a long hopeful cross from Leeds defender Paul Hart eluded everyone, allowing Trevor Cherry to steal in at the far post. Leeds stepped up a gear after the turnaround and immediately scored again when Currie curled a brilliant shot round Jake Findlay in the Luton goal. Eddie Gray extended the lead on the hour, and when Paul Price was penalised for allegedly holding back Ray Hankin, Frank Gray stroked the ball home from the spot. Trailing by four goals, the Town's only consolation was when Stein netted in the 88th minute. At the end, the Luton supporters waited for two hours to get out of the car park, allowing them plenty of time to mull over the end of their Wembley dreams.

Goalkeeper Milija Aleksic was transferred to Tottenham after falling out with Pleat. Aston Villa's Jake Findlay eventually replaced him. The unpredictable but potent match-winner David Moss suffered from a groin strain which reduced his effectiveness as the season wore on, and Brian Stein went four months without scoring a goal. If that was not bad enough, Pleat was having problems with Chris Turner, who made it clear that he wanted to go back to the States. Rather than keep an unhappy player, Pleat allowed Turner to join New England Tea Men.

The Town's luck on the field could be summed up by the performances against West Ham. At Kenilworth Road three late breakaway goals gave the Hammers a flattering 4-1 win, whilst at Upton Park an own-goal by David Carr secured a rather fortuitous victory, with the Hatters complaining about three genuine penalty appeals that were waved aside.

David Pleat was desperate to limp through to the end of the campaign while staying out of the bottom three. Mercifully, Luton benefited from four own-goals in successive games which earned enough points to stay up. After safety was assured in the penultimate match, Pleat spoke of his 'many sleepless nights'. Luton finished eighteenth, just two points above the drop zone. Incredibly, no team in the division exceeded the Town's 46 home goals. Thank goodness for that Indian Summer.

David Pleat had anticipated that it would take three years to stabilise the club and looked forward to entering his second season free from the injury worries that had dogged him in 1978-79. It was the start of a new era for the Town, with new managing director John Smith ringing the changes. Smith, a career football administrator poached from Leicester, was determined to exploit the new marketing age and scrutinised the club from top to bottom in an attempt to maximise profits. Out went the orange strip, which met with the approval of David Pleat who had never been enthusiastic, and in its place came a white shirt with blue and orange stripes.

On the field, Pleat spent £200,000 on giant Mansfield centre-half Mike Saxby, to replace Turner, and at the conclusion of one of the first transfer tribunals was instructed to pay Orient £150,000 for Republic of Ireland midfielder Tony Grealish. Orient had originally wanted £350,000, but Pleat quickly learned how to play the tribunal system, as he would time and time again in the future.

With the squad suitably strengthened, it was a disappointment that the opening day of 1979-80 saw a dull 1-1 home draw with Cambridge. But by the fifth game, a 5-0 thumping of Swansea at Kenilworth Road, the Town had moved up to top spot for the first time since 1970-71.

Hooliganism was rearing it head, and the club announced it was considering installing seats in the enclosure to combat it. Chairman Denis Mortimer said, 'We realise that some people want to stand on terraces to watch games and there are still some supporters that no longer go to matches because they can't stand in the Bobbers any more. It has been discovered, though, that trouble rarely breaks out among supporters who are sitting down and I can see the day, perhaps in ten years or so, when clubs will decide that it is in their best interests to make everyone sit down.'

A 3-1 win at Fulham bore all the hallmarks of the cavalier approach that would become such a feature of David Pleat's teams at Luton. Typical of this approach were back to back home wins over Bristol Rovers and Sunderland. The Town were 3-0 up at the interval against Rovers, and beat the Wearsiders 2-0 in a televised game in which David Moss could do no wrong.

Having sampled wrestling and baseball on the Kenilworth Road pitch over the years, the supporters were now treated to six-a-side cricket as pre-match entertainment in the autumn of 1979. It made a change from police dog handlers or silver bands, but you could not let your attention slip for one moment, otherwise a cricket ball was likely to pole-axe you.

Luton went top again after winning 2-1 at West Ham. Pole position was maintained for a month, despite a spate of home draws. These included a 1-1 result against QPR which produced the highest crowd of the season at that stage – 19,619.

As Christmas approached, the Town went off the boil a little and the unbeaten home record fell to Birmingham City. But they bounced back and, with only a few seconds remaining in the Boxing Day derby at Vicarage Road, full-back Kirk Stephens stole in on the far post to convert Bob Hatton's long cross. It was probably the sweetest victory of Luton's season: it was also Basher's first goal for the club.

KENILWORTH ROAD CLASSICS: **Luton v Chelsea** – 3-3

Football League Division Two, 1st January 1980

This game produced a performance by the Hatters which was typical of the cavalier style of play encouraged by David Pleat, although the bone-hard pitch was only passed fit by the referee after much deliberation.

The attendance was 19,717 and they enjoyed a goal-feast between two committed sides. Chelsea scored first through Mick Fillery's twenty-yard drive, but Mal Donaghy – playing in midfield in place of the injured Tony Grealish – smacked in an equaliser off the underside of the bar. It was his first league goal for the Hatters.

Mike Saxby headed the Town ahead a minute from the interval. Ian Britton equalised soon after the restart, and then Chelsea were awarded a penalty for handball. Furious protests pressurised the referee to consult his linesman, who had signalled for a throw-in before the handling took place. The spot-kick was then overturned.

A rare header from Moss, from a long throw from Paul Price, put the Town in the driving seat once more, only for Clive Walker to run through the Luton defence to make it 3-3. The breathless game ended with Donaghy heading against the bar in the final minute.

LUTON: *Findlay, Stephens, Donaghy, Aizlewood, Saxby, Price, Hill, West, Stein, Hatton, Moss.*

CHELSEA: *Borota, Locke, Sparrow, Pates, Chivers, Bumstead, Britton, Fillery, Harris, Langley, Walker.*

~~~~~~~~~~

Home draws were too frequent to keep Luton at the top, and through February and March the away wins dried up. This left the Town in a supporting role amongst the promotion contenders. If one particular game pinpointed the failure to win promotion, it was the home defeat by Cardiff on 14th March 1980. A miserable evening, poor refereeing, clogging opposition – which produced the only major injury crisis of the season – plus missed chances made it a game to forget.

Easter brought a 4-1 win at doomed Charlton, followed by what was becoming a ritual 1-0 win over Watford. With the last seconds ticking away at Stamford Bridge, Chelsea equalised after a scramble which saw the ball hit just about every player on the pitch and the woodwork before bobbling into the net.

With the relaxation of Football League rules banning shirt advertising, Luton became the first southern club to enter into sponsorship of this kind. The £50,000 deal with Tricentrol, which would include the sponsors' name on the club's shirts, was announced in February 1980.

The sponsors, never mind the club, were therefore desperate for promotion, but in a four-pointer at Birmingham, the Blues stole the points with a 1-0 win in a game of missed penalties and missed chances. That result meant eventual promotion for Birmingham and a sixth position for the Hatters.

In view of the injury problems confronted during David Pleat's first season in charge, it is remarkable that no fewer than eleven players made 39 or more league appearances in 1979-80. Injuries may not have been a problem, but Pleat's next task was to turn some of the ten home draws into wins. Four more points would have clinched promotion.

The Oak Road end becomes all-seater in 1986

Aerial view in 1985, following the laying of the artificial surface

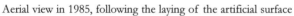

The new executive boxes in use during their first season

Mike Newell takes on the Manchester United defence on the artificial surface

Ashley Grimes curls in a free-kick in the 1988 Littlewoods Cup semi-final with Oxford

Lars Elstrup scores the vital second goal against Derby to secure safety from relegation
on the final day of the 1990-91 season

Scott Oakes is chaired off after netting a hat-trick against West Ham in
the FA Cup quarter-final replay in 1994

The Kohlerdome. The dream of chairman David Kohler

Carl Griffiths and Steve Howard celebrate a goal against Torquay
during the 2001-02 promotion season

A modern aerial view of the ground

The author, in this view from the 'New Stand' 2005

The 'New Stand' in 2005

The Oak Road end, and boxes, 2005

The 'Holy Grail'. The land adjacent to Junction 10 of the M1.
The new home of Luton Town?

Chapter 4

The Fourth Quarter-Century

1980-2005

The talk at Kenilworth Road over the summer of 1980 was the Safety of Sports Grounds Act. This would apply to all Division Two clubs in the coming season and all would require a safety certificate before staging football matches. The 'stadium', as it was now called, had received scant attention, so the list of improvements, and the subsequent cost, was large.

Chief executive John Smith confirmed that the Kenilworth Road terraces would be split into three sections. That nearest the railway line, and holding 3,500 spectators, would now be for away fans only. The other two sections would be for home or casual supporters. Significantly, there would be no inter-change permitted between the various sections.

The Oak Road end was also to be split into three sections, both ends of the ground were to have new non-scaleable fences installed, and improvements were to be carried out in the Main Stand. These included new exits to ensure that the whole ground could be evacuated within two and a half minutes. The total cost was put at £380,000, of which £185,000 would be paid by the Football Grounds Improvement Trust.

In normal circumstances this would have imposed a serious financial burden, albeit just about manageable, but news had also been received that the long-rumoured A505 Luton to Dunstable relief road was to become reality. If so, it could cut short the Town's stay at Kenilworth Road, making any ground improvements short-lived but just as expensive. The works were due to start in 1985. The plan was for the railway track to be moved closer to the rear of the Main Stand (on club-owned land) in order to accommodate the new road. This, in turn, would rob the club of its main entrance, various hospitality suites and car parking, and create intolerable financial problems.

The club asked why the railway track had to be moved. It was rarely used, and then only for freight (passenger trains ceased running in 1965 following the 'Beeching axe'). Moreover, it was in any case likely to be closed when the new road was built. Not so, said British Rail, it was still highly profitable! When the Luton Board submitted a £6 million compensation claim for the compulsory purchase of its land, it was deemed 'unrealistic' by Bedfordshire County Council. This war of words was likely to go on and on.

Manager David Pleat, however, had a quiet summer compared to the two previous ones. Only one player came in and one went out. Bob Hatton had stated on his arrival that he only intended staying for two years, otherwise he would become 'part of the furniture'. He kept his word and moved to Sheffield United for the £50,000 which the Town paid for him in the first place. That money went on well-travelled Yugoslav international Radomir 'Raddy' Antic, and marked the first of Pleat's many forays into the foreign transfer market. Antic's best position was sweeper but as Pleat did not normally play a sweeper system, perhaps he had other plans.

The opening fixture of 1980-81 was at FA Cup holders West Ham. The euphoria generated by parading the trophy got to the home players, and despite being in front, two late penalties, expertly slotted in by David Moss, sent the 28,033 Upton Park crowd home deflated.

Three days later Steve White – signed in December from Bristol Rovers before becoming the forgotten man – scored his first goal in an iffy 1-0 home victory over Watford. 'Barbarous Seville' was the headline in the *Watford Observer*. The barb was aimed at referee Alan Seville, who had refused to play the advantage rule in one particular Watford attack, when Mike Saxby had tried to pull back Hornets' Luther Blissett.

Derby then broke away twice to steal a 2-1 win at Kenilworth Road. The defeat sparked a run of just one point from three games, and but for Frank Bunn's last-minute equaliser against Wrexham, it would have been no points at all.

The season took off in the fourteenth game at the most unlikely place – Cambridge. David Moss's penalty had been cancelled out before half-time. Clive Goodyear headed his first goal for the club early in the second period before Moss limped off injured to be replaced by Antic. With the Town's goal under siege Jake Findlay was injured in making a brave save. With the one substitute permitted in those days already on, Luton were down to ten men and so put Mal Donaghy in goal. But the team shielded Donaghy and even scored a third goal through Brian Stein just before the final whistle.

KENILWORTH ROAD CLASSICS: **Luton v West Ham** – 3-2

Football League Division Two, 15th November 1980

The Hatters never looked back after that win at Cambridge. Sheffield Wednesday were trounced 3-0 in a televised game at Kenilworth Road before Watford were beaten 1-0 for the fourth time in a row, this time at Vicarage Road. Pleat attributed the previous patchy form to a reaction following the failure to win promotion in May.

West Ham were sprinting away with the division and had lost only once – to the Town on the opening day. They therefore had a score to settle and several thousand London fans swelled the attendance to a best of the season 17,031. Before kick-off, the Town's new scoreboard – reputed to be the most advanced in Europe – was officially switched on. The £100,000 out-lay had been met by Wallspan Bedrooms, who were owned by future Town director Terry Bailey.

Luton attacked from the start and were rewarded when a through ball from Ricky Hill was touched off by Steve White to the onrushing Brian Stein, who hit a scorcher from twenty yards. Five minutes later White again fed Stein, who this time took the ball around Phil Parkes in the West Ham goal. In difficult wet conditions West Ham reduced the arrears with a close-range header from Trevor Brooking.

In the second half West Ham messily equalised from the boot of Brooking. His first shot had hit Findlay, his second hit a post, and the third crept over the line. But with five minutes left, Kirk Stephens centred, Hill met the ball with a flying header, and Moss thumped home the winner.

So ended a memorable game, full of everything good in football and without a hint of malice. West Ham would only lose two more games as they raced to the title.

LUTON: *Findlay, Stephens, Aizlewood (West), Saxby, Price, Grealish, Donaghy, Hill, Stein, White, Moss.*

WEST HAM: *Parkes, Stewart, Lampard, Martin, Bonds, Holland, Devonshire, Brooking, Pike, Goddard, Cross.*

~~~~~~~~~

Victory over West Ham lifted the Town to tenth. A run of draws (two) and wins (four) up to New Year shot the team up another four places. Lil Fuccillo, out for two years following his two leg breaks, scored on his comeback in the 4-2 walloping of Preston. Christmas belonged to Brian Stein, who scored both Luton goals in the win over Chelsea, and three in the 4-2 victory at Bristol Rovers.

Luton failed to win in January, but supporters got their first sight of Mick Harford. He was wearing the colours of Newcastle and scored the only goal of a game in which Moss squandered another penalty. When Grimsby left with both points in another 'four pointer', Luton slipped to tenth.

After experimenting with a Sunday morning kick-off for the first time, which produced a sleepy 0-0 draw at Orient, David Pleat had to re-jig his system. He introduced a sweeper, with Raddy Antic the ideal man for the job. The tactics worked to perfection as the Town won 1-0 at Notts County.

A three-game winning run before and over Easter sent confidence soaring. QPR were thrashed 3-0 at Kenilworth Road in probably the best display of the season, Bristol Rovers were beaten 1-0, and a 2-0 win at Chelsea – Luton's first at Stamford Bridge since 1957 – lifted the Town to third with just three games to go.

It seemed that Luton had come good at just the right time, but they blew it when losing 1-2 at home to lowly Oldham. It was an eventful game, remembered for Latics forward Rodger Wylde, who should have been dismissed for elbowing and play-acting. His antics helped spark a pitch invasion towards the end.

A draw at Swansea – who would be promoted – and a 3-0 win at Bolton concluded the season. Luton were left to rue the dropping of so many home points to inferior opposition. Having said that, the Town were only two points off a promotion place and getting closer. Third time lucky?

Perhaps other-worldly spooks were responsible, for – as one might expect with an old football ground – Kenilworth Road can lay claim to its own ghost. It was reported that maintenance engineer Fred Bunyan, in the early morning when he was the only one in the ground, often saw wispy smoke wafting into the air near the corner of the players' tunnel and the dressing rooms, as if someone had a cigarette alight. So that's what happened to the old Main Stand!

The 1981 close season merry-go-round left many supporters scratching their heads. Popular local lad (and Wales international) Paul Price was sold to Tottenham for £250,000, while former skipper Alan West, certainly not over the hill, went to Millwall for £45,000. To top it all, the swap arrangement with Brighton, involving Republic of Ireland international Tony Grealish and veteran Brian Horton looked ill-conceived. Pleat, however, was proved right. Horton turned out to be the final piece in the jigsaw.

KENILWORTH ROAD HEROES: **Alan West**

Alan West enjoyed more than 300 first-team appearances for the Town. Yet if he had heeded medical advice, his playing career would have been cut short in 1973.

Born in Hyde, West was playing for his local school team when he was spotted by a Burnley scout and invited along for trials at the age of fourteen. He signed apprentice professional forms, joining one of the best youth set-ups in the country, and starred alongside Dave Thomas, Steve Kindon and Mick Docherty in a team that won the FA Youth Cup in 1968.

'I made my first team debut in the 1969-70 season at home to Stoke City in the same side as Ralph Coates and Willie Morgan,' he said. 'And in all I appeared in over fifty games for Burnley, mostly in Division One, as well as winning Under-23 international caps whilst I was there.'

Burnley suffered relegation in 1971 after selling one player too many. It was Alan's turn to move on in 1973, when Sunderland bid £100,000. But after three days of medical checks at Roker Park he heard devastating news. 'I was told by the Sunderland medical people that I had a vertebra in my back out of place and that if I continued playing I would be in a wheelchair within two years. I was sure that there was nothing wrong and when Luton manager Harry Haslam came in for me soon after I jumped at the chance as I was anxious to prove my fitness.'

West joined Luton for £100,000, and made his debut in October 1973 in a 0-2 defeat at Orient. But promotion to Division One was secured that season, leaving Sunderland behind on the way.

'The enduring quality of the Luton side at that time was the team spirit. We had no big stars in the side but played for each other with a good blend of defence, midfield and attack bringing out the best in each other. I still feel a bit aggrieved that we were relegated from Division One in 1975 as in the second half of that season, especially at home, we steamrollered sides and I have not experienced an atmosphere like it before or since. Although I played in three really good sides at Kenilworth Road, finishing up in the David Moss, Brian Stein era, it was a shame that I did not play longer in Division One.'

For four consecutive summers West played in the USA for Minnesota Kicks, pitting his wits against the likes of Eusebio, Pele, Beckenbauer, Cruyff, George Best and Gerd Muller, which must go some way in compensation for not turning out regularly in the top division.

'After we failed to get promotion after two near misses, I though that at thirty I was past my best and felt that the youngsters coming through meant that perhaps a move was in my best interests. I was under no pressure to leave the club and David Pleat was very good about it, but I decided to join Millwall where my old teammate Peter Anderson was manager. As it turned out, Peter was sacked and when George Graham came into the club, I didn't fit into his plans and joined Hitchin Town where I had four happy years as player-manager. I obviously had some regrets at leaving Luton when I did, just as the club was about to win promotion to Division One!'

West now looks on Luton as his home. He is happily settled in the town and is minister at the Luton Christian Fellowship.

~~~~~~~~~~~

In goal, Jake Findlay was taking the eye of Scotland manager Jock Stein with his shot-stopping abilities, while both full-backs, Kirk 'Basher' Stephens and Mark Aizlewood, had become crowd favourites on account of of their cavalier forays upfield and their biting tackles. Mike Saxby had developed into an excellent 'stopper', ably assisted by Mal Donaghy, who effectively swept along the back line.

Horton slotted into the holding midfield role, where his abilities as skipper, forceful tackler and clever passer allowed Ricky Hill to push forward, where he formed an almost telepathic relationship with ace scorer Brian Stein. Alongside Stein, Steve White – after a fairly slow start following his big-money signing from Bristol Rovers – had at last found his feet. Making up the regular eleven were winger David Moss and play-anywhere Yugoslav, Raddy Antic.

Moss was absent from the opening game of 1981-82 through injury. His place was taken by Godfrey Ingram. Dunstable-boy Ingram had been predicted to go far after catching the eye with England Schoolboys, but he had somehow lost his way and was destined to become only a bit-part player at Kenilworth Road.

The Town's first opponents were promoted Charlton, who had six players making their debuts. Luton romped to a 3-0 win, which from this season onwards earned three points instead of two.

The next game saw the Town make football history. Their match at QPR was the first league game to be played on an artificial surface. With the Town 0-1 down at half-time, few Luton followers approved Rangers' Omniturf, but 45 minutes later it was suddenly a superb idea as Mark Aizlewood and Ricky Hill scored the goals to secure the points.

Although the away form stood up, the next two home games were surprisingly lost. But before the supporters could get too despondent Watford were seen off 4-1 at Kenilworth Road in a game that saw David Moss net the first two of his eventual eleven penalties that season.

Kenilworth Road Classics: **Luton v Grimsby** – 6-0
Football League Division Two, 17th October 1981
By the time of Grimsby's visit, the Town led the table on goal-difference, but were mindful of how the Mariners had beaten them the previous season. It was quickly apparent that Grimsby had arrived bent on a point, but Lil Fuccillo's rocket shot opened the game up. When Brian Stein was tripped by Dean Crombie, David Moss's penalty atoned for his miss at Blundell Park the previous year. Trevor Whymark hit the crossbar for Grimsby, which proved expensive, as Steve White gave Luton an unassailable 3-0 interval lead.

The chatter at half-time was the form of White, so often the butt of the crowd since his arrival from Bristol Rovers, which got so bad that at one stage he had put in a transfer request. White ensured he would never again be abused from the terraces, scoring three further goals to bring his match tally to four, and nine for the season so far.

Grimsby were not as bad as the score. They won the corner count!

Luton: Findlay, Stephens, Aizlewood (Bunn), Horton, Saxby, Donaghy, Hill, Fuccillo, White, Stein, Moss.

Grimsby: Batch, David Moore, Czuczman, Kevin Moore, Crombie, Waters, Brolly, Mitchell, Ford (Kilmore), Whymark, Drinkell.

~~~~~~~~~~~

Disaster struck in the next home game, in which Crystal Palace were beaten 1-0. Mike Saxby turned in the penalty area and went down in a heap. The knee injury he sustained effectively ended his Town career.

One man's tragedy is another's opportunity, as young Clive Goodyear stepped into the breach. After being groomed by Mal Donaghy in his early games, Goodyear played so well that he saved David Pleat the necessity of buying an expensive replacement.

When the Hatters won 3-1 at Norwich over Christmas, they were so far ahead of the rest at the top it was difficult to see how they could be caught. It took a succession of blank Saturdays because of the weather, coupled with a glut of away draws, to allow main challengers Watford to close the gap. In late March the Hornets even overtook the Town for a few days, but as they had played several games more the correct pecking order was soon restored.

Easter brought a 1-1 draw at Cambridge – where 5,000 Luton supporters transformed the Abbey into a home game – and a 2-0 home win over Norwich. Goals from Brian Stein and short-term signing Billy Jennings sealed a victory which, in retrospect, clinched promotion.

The Hatters, however, lived dangerously in the next games. Newcastle were 2-0 up at Kenilworth Road before a hat-trick from Stein, including two terrible but effective penalties, stole the points. Chelsea drew at Kenilworth Road in a game that could have gone either way, and a last-minute penalty save by reserve keeper Alan Judge earned the Town a point at Rotherham.

KENILWORTH ROAD CLASSICS: **Luton v Shrewsbury** – 4-1

Football League Division Two, 30th April 1982

A home win over struggling Shrewsbury would clinch promotion back to Division One. A tense crowd of 14,563 gathered on a balmy Friday evening and transmitted their anxiety onto the pitch, where it became obvious that the Shrews would be playing for a point. Nerves were settled when Brian Stein latched onto a belted clearance from Jake Findlay to lob the Town into the lead.

Hearts sank when Ian Atkins, with just about the Shrews' only real attack, equalised on the hour with a neat volley, but when Raddy Antic was brought on a few minutes later the Town started to look a team again. It is now written into Kenilworth Road folklore how Ricky Hill volleyed a beauty after a corner had been headed on to him by Mal Donaghy. Further goals from Steve White and David Moss secured a flattering victory. The supporters did not care. The Hatters were up.

LUTON: *Findlay, Stephens, Goodyear, Donaghy, Money, Hill, Horton, Fuccillo (Antic), Stein, White, Moss.*

SHREWSBURY: Wardle, MacLaren, Griffin, Keay, Johnson (Petts), Turner, McNally, Tong, Bates, Atkins, Cross.

~~~~~~~~~~~~

The championship was sealed when Luton beat FA Cup finalists QPR in the next home game. An award ceremony preceded the penultimate match, against Barnsley at Kenilworth Road. The curtain came down with a 3-2 win at Cardiff which sealed a record breaking year with 88 points won and only four defeats recorded along the way.

Unopposed in the championship race, after two years of near misses, the Hatters felt that they had a side more than capable of holding its own at the top level. Even so, David Pleat spent hours trying to entice young Paul Walsh from Charlton. Walsh was coveted by most of the top clubs in the country, but the persuasive tongue of Pleat finally won the day. There was a heavy price to pay: Steve White, the previous season's second leading scorer, was off-loaded to the Valley as part of the deal. Pleat felt he now had the best attacking pair in the country, in Walsh and Brian Stein, especially with winger David Moss providing the ammunition.

Luton's opening fixture in 1982-83 was at FA Cup-holders Tottenham, where after twenty minutes all Pleat's bold promises seemed to be in tatters. Spurs had shot into a two-goal lead, to the delight of the packed White Hart Lane crowd of 39,180. Making his Spurs debut that day was one-time Pleat target Gary Mabbutt, who took only three minutes to open his account for his new club, heading in a Glenn Hoddle free-kick. Hoddle set up the second as well, threading a pass through for Mick Hazard to make simple work of beating Jake Findlay.

The Town players had to learn fast, and gradually started to make an impact on the game, with Stein, in particular, causing problems to the Tottenham defence. It was Stein's direct run and shot that panicked John Lacy into knocking the ball into his own net for the first Hatters goal, and then piercing Spurs' square home defence to tap in the second.

Afterwards Pleat warned that better teams than Tottenham would not fritter away a two-goal lead, and he was right. Three days later West Ham were the first visitors to Kenilworth Road. It was men against boys. An uncharacteristic Hammers side, using physical power, soaked up Luton's attacks and scored two second-half goals. This time there was no fightback and no happy ending.

KENILWORTH ROAD CLASSICS: **Luton v Notts County** – 5-3
Football League Division One, 4th September 1982
In those days Luton supporters fretted if the team went two games without a win, and a nervous crowd of 9,071 – the smallest of the season – turned up to see if the Town could break their duck and overcome Notts

County, who had drawn their opening two matches. The Magpies, managed by the wily Jimmy Sirrell, had played together for a while and had caused a few upsets the previous season, their first back in Division One. They also possessed the quickest player of his day in John Chiedozie who, according to Pleat, 'could catch pigeons'. One drawback was that Chiedozie often reached the by-line before his strikers had time to lumber up to the penalty box.

Walsh, only nineteen, headed in a Ricky Hill cross before County's giant centre-half Brian Kilcline put away a corner. Worse was to follow when Chiedozie scampered past the stretched Luton defence and hammered County in front. Hatters defender Richard Money had to leave the field after breaking his nose in a clash with Trevor Christie, but before substitute Mike Small could take his place Hill had slammed in from a corner to level the scores.

In the second half David Moss shot the Hatters ahead from a free-kick routine, paving the way for Walsh's bit of magic. He set off for goal, avoiding two foul tackles from Pedro Richards, before skipping past Kilcline and goalkeeper Raddy Avramovic to bring the house down. Walsh's hat-trick was completed soon after, when he reacted quickly to a low Moss cross and edged in front of the Notts defenders to steer the ball in. County pulled one back through Mark Goodwin's header, but that did not stop the crowd rising to give the players a standing ovation at the end.

LUTON: *Findlay, Stephens, Money (Small), Horton, Goodyear, Donaghy, Hill, Stein, Walsh, Antic, Moss.*

NOTTS CO: *Avramovic, Benjamin, Kilcline, Richards, Worthington, Hunt, Goodwin (McParland), Mair, Chiedozie, Harkouk, Christie.*

~~~~~~~~~~

The good work was undone with a 1-4 setback at Aston Villa. But when the Town's forward line was on song, then the crowd was in for a goal feast. This was demonstrated when the Hatters played a pulsating 3-3 draw at champions Liverpool. Among the talking points were tremendous goals, three different players keeping goal for Luton, and a fortunate late leveller from the Reds. Yet the hard facts were that after five games the Hatters were down in eighteenth position.

Another day, another game, and this time Brighton were spanked 5-0 at Kenilworth Road, with Stein netting a hat-trick and Wayne Turner scoring with an overhead kick to lift the Hatters into the top half. With so many goals flying in at both ends, it was no surprise that the TV companies wanted a slice of the action, and the cameras were again in evidence when Luton visited Stoke. Once again the nets bulged, the Stoke goalkeeper was sent off, and with the score at 4-4 the Hatters were awarded a last-minute penalty – but Moss wasted it.

Following a 1-1 home draw with Manchester United, a 3-2 win at Birmingham pushed Luton up to eighth. All seemed well, but that was to be as good as it got. The top sides slowly got to grips with the team's style of play. Pretty 'wall passes' broke down when defences made sure – by fair means or foul – that the player of the first pass did not receive the return. Professionalism versus innocence had only one outcome: the Town were increasingly muscled out of games. They went eight long games without another win, before Manchester City were beaten 3-1 at Kenilworth Road. The three points were costly, as Brian Stein broke a bone in his foot which effectively kept him out of regular contention until the season's end.

Pleat tried several alternatives to the badly missed Stein, including loanees David Geddis and Steve White. But not until the signing of the well-travelled Trevor Aylott in March did the forward line rediscover its threat. By then it seemed too late. Even with the signing of young centre-half Paul Elliott from Charlton, relegation looked inevitable by Easter. Four straight defeats, culminating with a 2-5 mauling at Watford on Easter Monday, probably sealed the Town's fate to most football-watchers.

On the following Saturday a last-gasp Moss goal saw Luton beat Aston Villa to spark a six-game unbeaten run which enabled the team to claw its way out of the relegation positions. With three games to go, a home victory over mid-table Everton would just about ensure survival, and hopes soared when Ricky Hill headed an early goal. Inexplicably, as half-time approached Luton collapsed. The final score, 1-5, was bad enough, but to make matters worse all the other strugglers won, turning a drama into a crisis! From a position of relative safety, the Town suddenly found themselves back in the relegation mire.

Luton's last two games were in Manchester. After losing 0-3 at Old Trafford, they then had to return to take on City, who were themselves embroiled in the dog fight at the bottom. The mathematics were simple. Only a Luton win would condemn City to the drop. Anything less and City would survive at the Hatters' expense.

A crowd of 42,843 – bettered only by the Manchester derby – packed Maine Road to see a sterile affair with the home side content to guard the point they started with. In the second half the Hatters had to push up, but with the minutes ticking away they had not created any chances. Pleat sent on substitute Raddy Antic for Wayne Turner, and five minutes from time the Yugoslav scored one of the most important goals in the club's history. Brian Stein, playing his first game for three months, saw his cross pushed out by City goalkeeper Alex Williams to the edge of the box. Antic fired it back, with Williams deflecting the ball past defenders who might otherwise have cleared it. The delirium at the end was captured by the TV cameras, and included Pleat's ecstatic jig across the pitch for posterity.

Nor was that the Town's only achievement in this momentous season. Coach John Moore guided the Town's youth squad to the FA Youth Cup semi-final, where they lost to Norwich. This was the furthest the Hatters had gone in the competition, which had started in 1952.

No sooner had the euphoria of staying up faded, than something more catastrophic than mere relegation shook the supporters rigid. It was leaked by the Football League that the club had made preliminary enquiries to move to Milton Keynes. Frantic fans mobilised to form 'Supporters of Luton Town FC (1983), and within a short time over 18,000 signatures were collected in a bid to kill the proposed move.

From their point of view, the Town's directors did not know which way to turn. Mindful of the loss of amenity which would result from the A505 relief road, they had investigated fifteen sites in the Luton area in order to relocate. The question of land at Lewsey Farm had again reared its head, but even though the necessary infrastructure was in place – by way of wide access roads – residents' opposition to a planned football stadium was implacable. Ironically, the council had privately given approval, but with an election in the offing, they threw their hands in the air. A possible site was identified at the Brache estate off Park Street, owned by Vauxhall Motors, but again the Luton Borough Council said no.

The club ran up large expenses surveying sites at Skimpot, Chaul End, Houghton Hall at Houghton Regis, Wardown Park(!), Wigmore Valley, Dallow Road Hills, Laportes, Sundon, Stockwood Park, Leagrave Park, Luton Hoo, Stopsley Common and Vauxhall Motors' land at Toddington. The sites were either too small, not economically viable, or were liable to be turned down by one or other of the local authorities.

It was at this stage that Milton Keynes Development Corporation proposed building a multi-purpose sports stadium. The land itself would be free, so all the club had to do was finance the stadium. This clearly had its appeal, as there would presumably be no planning problems or residents' protests to worry about.

On the other hand, if the club were to build a new stadium in Luton, they would need 'enabling development' alongside it – in the form of shops, flats, hotel etc – to fully fund the project. This would have posed problems at, say, the Brache, so the directors were possibly pleased when that site was turned down.

Out of the blue the council reversed its decision and asked the club to submit plans for the Brache. Whether this was bowing to political pressure from voters who happened to be Hatters supporters, or was intended to flush out the plans for Milton Keynes – by calling the directors' bluff – is open to surmise. But a letter from the club published in the *Luton News* left the fans in no doubt. It claimed that the eleventh-hour change of heart by the Luton Borough Council was 'too little, too late', and stated categorically that a move to Milton Keynes was now the only option.

The same letter was reprinted in the match programme for the visit of Birmingham on 12th November 1983, but by this time a supporters' rally had been organised at Pope's Meadow. It was attended by 2,000 who, after listening to various speeches, walked at funereal pace to the ground. Chief Executive John Smith was quoted as asking where the 18,000 who signed the petition had disappeared to!

Perhaps a buy-out was the solution. A consortium of local businessmen formed a takeover group 'HALT', aimed at keeping the club in Luton at all costs. They approached the directors, only to be informed that the price required for them to walk away from the club was £5 million. And so the saga rumbled on.

Against this unwelcome background, David Pleat was battling to strengthen his side to avoid another stomach-churning climax, and he made a good job of it. His only summer signing of note was the experienced goalkeeper Les Sealey from Coventry, Jake Findlay having fallen out of favour. The early season form in 1983-84 was so good that after beating Southampton in late October the Town were in the dizzyingly high position of fourth.

Although they were sunk 0-6 at Liverpool the following week, Luton bounced back and by Boxing Day – following a 3-0 win at Notts County – they actually hit third spot and sights were increasingly set on a European place.

Sadly, the Hatters had flattered to deceive. Over the next 23 games the players picked up a win bonus just three times. That was relegation form in anyone's language and, but for the points already in the bag, the trap door could easily have awaited.

The off-field saga of Milton Keynes obviously did not help. Many staunch supporters opted to boycott Kenilworth Road until the Board publicly disavowed its intention to relocate to Buckinghamshire. Among society at large, football was increasingly regarded as a second-class pastime. Hooliganism was rife, and when you add the poor crowds attracted to Kenilworth Road, with its backdrop of high fences and cattle pens on the terraces, and games contested in a morgue-like atmosphere, we can hardly be surprised that the players felt less than inspired.

Long-term injuries to Ricky Hill and David Moss forced Pleat to blood several youngsters before they were really ready, and well though the newcomers played, they obviously lacked the experience and savvy of the men they replaced.

In 1982 Ricky Hill had become the first Luton player selected to play for England since the 1950s, while a year later Brian Stein and Paul Walsh created another Luton 'first' when they both won caps for England against France in Paris. Unfortunately, neither player was on top form domestically, and both had stinkers in the Parc des Princes. The experience shattered Stein's confidence and it was quite some time before he was back to his best. That in turn made matters worse for Pleat as he attempted to arrest the Town' slide down the table.

Pleat was no doubt pleased to see the end of the campaign, which left Luton just three points above the drop zone. Considering all that was going on around him, it is to his credit that he rejected approaches from Aston Villa and QPR over the summer, when it would have been easier to walk away from the Town's multitude of problems.

Financial problems had reared their head again in the course of the season, and the club's bankers needed assurance that a 'star name' would be sold. Pleat was obviously key to all this and he drove a hard bargain with Liverpool for Paul Walsh. Had the Reds been privy to the Town's parlous state, they would surely not have paid anywhere near the £763,000 that eventually changed hands. The fee was a Luton record at that time, but every penny had to satisfy the club's bankers. Even when Pleat agreed with Coventry to swap Kirk Stephens for Ashley Grimes, the directors were rebuked as the bank were expecting Stephens to be sold, not Grimes to be bought.

The purse strings were loosened slightly though, with the decision to install 1,500 seats in the enclosure during the close season, although it reduced the Kenilworth Road capacity to 20,100.

Kenilworth Road was not a nice place to be in the summer of 1984. The team was in free-fall and results were likely to get even worse with the loss of Walsh, plus the departure of veterans Raddy Antic and Brian Horton as they embarked on the first steps of football management. The Milton Keynes saga dragged on, with supporters still boycotting the club in numbers, and there was bickering behind the scenes at board level as to the future direction of the club.

The 1984-85 season opened with a 2-0 home victory over Stoke, but Pleat knew the Potters were weak – so weak they would be relegated with the fewest points in memory. The Town won only two more games over the next three months, leaving them stranded in the relegation zone. When centre-half Paul Elliott broke his leg in a Milk Cup home tie against Leicester, the Town were down to the bare bones and in need of help from somewhere.

Tired of the personal abuse heaped upon him, plus the pressure to lead from the top with a cash injection, Chairman Denis Mortimer resigned both from the chair and from the Board. Director David Evans took his place as chairman and, along with a newly co-opted director Terry Bailey, loaned enough money to provide Pleat with a substantial transfer pot. The new regime also successfully renegotiated the club's overdraft.

Temporarily freed from his shackles, Pleat brought in Steve Foster from Aston Villa, David Preece from Walsall, Mick Harford from Birmingham for an eye-watering £250,000, and finally Peter Nicholas from Crystal Palace – all in the space of six weeks. The Town now had a fighting chance.

It was now that the Milton Keynes debacle took a surprising turn. It transpired that two rival schemes were competing against the Town's bid for a sports and leisure complex. One of these was not dependent on a football club being in situ. Milton Keynes Borough Council had reassessed its options and decided it no longer wanted a football club, the Hatters or anyone else, on its doorstep. Local residents had been up in arms in protest, fearing mass hooliganism. How times change, as twenty years on they were saddled with Wimbledon!

The complicating factor was that the decision to import a football club was not for the Borough Council to make. That belonged to Milton Keynes Development Corporation, who had encouraged the Town to submit plans in the first place.

All this came to light when Bedfordshire County Council – under whose jurisdiction the A505 relief road was being built – proposed plans for the road to be laid, the railway line re-aligned, and the club to retain its amenities. It would cost around £1.3 million for the works to be carried out at Kenilworth Road, but the County Council would pay.

Matters came to a head in late January 1985 when the Milton Keynes Development Corporation rejected the Hatters' proposal as too grandiose and plumped for the scheme that did not involve a football club. It is note-worthy that the alternative stadium was never built. Instead, the National Hockey Stadium was eventually erected on the site allocated.

A shocked David Evans, in typically bullish fashion, demanded £2.3 million compensation from Bedfordshire County Council, which was £1 million more than the cost of the council's plans. The club's situation would be unchanged and it would be left once more seeking alternative sites within a 25-mile radius of Luton.

The supporters knew the battle had been won and champagne corks popped all over the town. The 'stay aways' now clamoured for season tick-ets in the days leading up to the visit of Tottenham to Kenilworth Road. With all the pent up fears and anger released, the crowd of 17,511 – the biggest of the season – created a marvellous atmosphere The four new signings played together for the first time and the team would have won but for a late equaliser from Spurs' Graham Roberts.

Although results started to improve, the rise up the table was hindered by a long run in the FA Cup. Stoke, after a replay, and Huddersfield were despatched before an energy sapping three-game thriller finally put paid to Watford. This produced a quarter-final clash with Millwall from Division Three.

The clash with the Lions saw one of the worst, if not *the* worst night of football violence ever seen in this country. With the game being televised, a much wider audience than would normally have been the case watched appalled by the destruction and violence on show. Whether or not the game should have been all-ticket is immaterial, as eye-witness reports say Millwall 'supporters' left London from the morning onwards drunk and hell-bent on trouble. A ticket-only entry would have made little difference as the hooligans broke into the ground long before the start.

This writer sat in the Bobbers Stand at the time, and I can confirm that the individuals who invaded the pitch and started ripping up seats all around me before kick-off were not Millwall supporters. When Lions manager George Graham came over to appeal to them, they did not have a clue who he was. It was a night out for every yob in London!

The game was almost incidental, and was played out in an unreal atmosphere with crowd invasions and fighting punctuating what little action there was on the pitch. The sour mood seemed to affect the Millwall players more than Luton's, and they were never really in the game, which was settled by a Brian Stein strike after 31 minutes.

The repercussions were felt for weeks afterwards. Prime Minister Margaret Thatcher demanded answers and action. There was a real danger that an example would be made of the Hatters to pacify Thatcher, who could never understand the passion for football in this country. At the FA hearing the Town were ordered to erect fences all around the ground. These would have severely restricted the view of seated spectators in the Bobbers Stand and enclosure. On appeal, the Town successfully argued against the fences, and in the end were completely exonerated from complicity in the riot.

Riot or not, Luton were in the last four of the FA Cup. The Town's first FA Cup semi-final since 1959 would be against league leaders Everton at Villa Park. Pleat, understandably, viewed the Cup run as a diversion from the infinitely more important task of guaranteeing First Division survival. He was heartened when the Town won three vital games before the semi-final, which lifted them out of the bottom three.

More than 18,000 Luton supporters trekked up the M1 to Birmingham hoping for an FA Cup and Division One survival double. The Town were without the cup-tied Preece and Nicholas, but they were not outplayed, and only glaring misses from Emeka Nwajiobi prevented the underdogs from taking a substantial first-half lead. As it was, they were only one goal to the good – a rocket from Ricky Hill which flew in via a post.

With five minutes left, a rainbow suddenly appeared, which the Luton supporters looked on as a good omen. Unfortunately, the omen was aimed at Everton. Within a minute, Harford was penalised for pushing, and from the free-kick Kevin Sheedy drove in the equaliser. Television replays showed that no foul had been committed, but the goal knocked the stuffing out of the Luton players who were now faced with extra-time. There was now only one team in it. Everton powered forward and Derek Mountfield nodded in the winner after 114 minutes. Afterwards, the media covering the game awarded the game to Luton on moral grounds.

The Cup dream over, it was back to more pressing matters. Would the dashing of the Wembley dream help or hinder the players?

The answer was soon clear. In a titanic struggle, goals from Nwajiobi (two) and David Moss earned a 3-1 home victory over fellow strugglers Norwich. The previous season had seen Manchester United win 5-0 at Kenilworth Road in front of the live television cameras. Naturally the cameras were back, but this time the Hatters won the game in the last minute when Harford threw himself at the ball in a crowded penalty area. It was the first victory over United since 1937.

Two quick home games, six points better off, and at last Luton supporters believed relegation could be averted. The players blotted their copybook when Nottingham Forest won at Kenilworth Road in the next game, but a draw at West Ham and a home win over Arsenal left Luton on the brink of safety. Three more points at Aston Villa should banish the nightmare completely.

So, less than a month after heartbreak in the FA Cup, it was back to Villa Park. Villa has scored nine goals in their previous two games, but their forwards hardly made a dent in the new Luton back four of Tim Breacker, Steve Foster, Mal Donaghy and Mitchell Thomas.

It must be said that the Town did not play as well against Villa as they had against Everton, but there again Villa were not in the Toffees' class, as proved by the fact that the Merseysiders had already clinched the league title. The only goal came after 21 minutes, when Brian Stein smacked the ball home after it had been miscontrolled by Villa's Gordon Cowans. Fifteen points from the eighteen at stake since the semi-final defeat put paid to relegation fears with four games left to play. The supporters could not make up their minds whether the Cup disappointment was a blessing in disguise.

KENILWORTH ROAD HEROES: **David Moss**

Aged sixteen, David Moss had the choice of joining either Swindon or Oxford, but despite being Oxfordshire born and playing for Oxfordshire Youth, he decided to 'go over the border' and sign for his childhood favourites Swindon Town. Working his way through the ranks, he made his league debut at home to Hull in January 1972. He became a regular in 1973-74, just in time to see Swindon relegated to Division Three.

During the next four seasons he regularly finished as top scorer, despite playing wide, and with several clubs taking notice David Pleat nipped ahead of Stoke to bring Moss to Kenilworth Road during the summer of 1978.

'I well remember making my Luton debut at home to Oldham in August 1978 as I was one of seven players making their first appearance that day. I also recall scoring twice in the 6-1 win. That first season was a bit of a struggle for Luton and after the turn of the year I was never fully fit due to a pelvic problem. As I was regarded as having the ability to turn games, I played on when I probably should not have done but I do remember coming on as substitute in a crucial game at Preston towards the end of the season with Luton being 0-2 down, laying on the Town's first goal and then scoring probably my best ever goal for the equaliser.'

After the traumas of Moss's first season, David Pleat's team started to take shape and, after two narrow failures, promotion to Division One was achieved in 1982.

'We had a great squad around that time. I fondly remember such players as Ricky Hill, who was a joy to watch and work with, Bob Hatton who helped turn Brian Stein into the player he became, Brian Horton for his leadership qualities, and Kirk Stephens who made the transition from non-league football to Division One look easy. The promotion season and the one that followed were definitely highlights of my career, with the game at Liverpool early in 1982-83 probably the best I appeared in, as we played them off the park and were unlucky to come away with only one point in a 3-3 draw.'

After seven seasons with the Town, during which he had become a true crowd favourite with his mesmerising wing-play and the many memorable goals scored, he rejoined Swindon, where he made a further four League appearances before retiring.

~~~~~~~~~~~~

1985 marked a low ebb in English football. Luton's problems with Millwall paled into insignificance in the light of the Bradford City fire and the Heysel tragedy, both within weeks of each other. The Government was probably correct in its anti-football stance, with hooliganism rife and outdated stadiums proving to be death-traps. The whole football world needed to wake up before the game as we knew it disappeared into oblivion.

The complexion was a little more rosy at Luton, however, with the outlook buoyant and the atmosphere unrecognisable from that of only a few short months before. Pleat, elevated to the Board in March 1985, had spent wisely, strengthening the spine of the team and adding older home-grown talent such as Brian Stein and Ricky Hill, who had both – after much spec-ulation – signed new contracts. There was also the cream of coach John Moore's 1983 FA Youth Cup squad to call upon.

The summer of 1985 saw feverish activity at Kenilworth Road. For once it had nothing to do with the transfer market, which was relatively quiet. The activity was caused by the Town's decision to install an artificial surface. Laid over ten weeks at a cost of £335,000, it was manufactured by En-Tout-Cas and was said – thanks to advances in technology – to be far superior to the surface laid at QPR by Omniturf in 1981.

David Pleat and the players put on a united front, professing to enjoy playing on an artificial surface. They trotted out the approved words, that the pitch improved their skills and how it was consistent in all weathers. Privately they were not so keen.

The club were pleased with their investment, as the cost had been effec-tively met by a new sponsorship agreement with Bedford Trucks. Within a short time they were enjoying extra income of £3,000 per week, as they hired out the pitch for American football, hockey, bowls, lacrosse, concerts, boxing matches and even police dog training. The pitch could be used '24/7': the only threats to its use were fog and occasional snow lying so thick outside the ground that people could not get to it. The number of local firms and Sunday football teams shortly claiming to have played on a First Division football ground became incalculable and provided lasting good public relations.

The Hatters baptised the new surface on the opening day of 1985-86 against Nottingham Forest. It had not properly bedded down and every kick sent a small spiral of sand into the air, but onlookers seemed impressed. Brian Stein became the first goalscorer on the Town's artificial turf in what ended as a 1-1 draw.

The Town were entering their centenary season in good shape, both on and off the field. Crowds were slightly up, which bucked the national trend, as the players tried to put on a show for the supporters. The first ten games brought three wins and three losses, but the campaign was transformed with, of all things, a home draw. Manchester United arrived in early October having won ten out of ten, and were set on overtaking the best ever winning start, established by Spurs in 1960. In a frantic game, watched by an audience of 17,454, the Town more than held their own, and but for a glaring miss by central defender Paul Elliott, 1-1 might have become 2-1.

KENILWORTH ROAD CLASSICS: **Luton v Southampton** – 7-0

Canon League Division One, 19th October 1985

David Pleat was still on a search for more firepower. In the summer he had lost out on Frank McAvennie, who preferred West Ham. In the days before the visit of Southampton, Pleat was quoted as saying that he was frustrated by the lack of goals which the general build-up play deserved. Equally frustrated were the Luton fans, half of whom – having watched Manchester United – now stayed away. They missed a treat, as the Hatters went goal crazy, making a mockery of Pleat's misgivings.

Seven goals were slammed past England goalkeeper Peter Shilton without reply, making it the most miserable day of his career. He was offered no protection by his defenders from the moment Mick Harford and Brian Stein exchanged passes to set up Emeka Nwajiobi after five minutes. Ricky Hill and Harford combined to put in Stein to double the score, and when Hill sidefooted home the third the contest was as good as over.

Harford dragged another England international, Mark Wright, in circles as the Town stepped up a gear in the second half. When Steve Foster's shot was blocked, Stein followed up to make it 4-0. David Preece touched in at the far post, with substitute Ray Daniel knocking in a sixth. Stein's hat-trick was completed in the final minute when he converted a penalty after Harford had been shoved by Wright.

At the post-match press conference Pleat was dumbstruck: 'Just write about the football; it spoke for itself.' Saints manager and former Hatters centre-half, Chris Nicholl, refused to hide: 'It was just rank bad defending. My defenders badly let me down. I was always an honest player but there are a few in the dressing room who can't look me in the face right now.'

Exonerated from blame was Glenn Cockerill. He was making his debut for the Saints after turning down Luton and probably regretting the decision. Also blameless was Shilton, who had not conceded seven since he was a nineteen-year-old at Leicester. He had kept the score down with a string of fine saves: 'No one likes letting in seven but I don't think I made a bad mistake for any of them. There is no self pity. I don't want to talk about how I felt after the match, but I can tell you the dog was in its basket when I got home!'

LUTON: *Sealey, Breacker, Thomas, Nicholas, Foster, Donaghy, Hill, Stein, Harford, Nwajiobi, Preece (Daniel).*

SOUTHAMPTON: *Shilton, Baker, Wright, Bond, Dennis, Case, Lawrence, Armstrong, Townsend, Cockerill, Moran.*

~~~~~~~~~~

The Town never looked back after this, and although never threatening to catch the top three – Liverpool, Everton and West Ham – they seemed firmly established as a top-ten side, which seemed barely credible after all that had gone on a year before.

An abundance of riches in central defence meant that the fit again Paul Elliott could not regain his place. Steve Foster was showing the form that had won him England caps. When Aston Villa offered £400,000 for Elliott, it was too good to turn down, and some of the proceeds went on buying striker Mike Newell from Wigan for £85,000.

Safe in the league, this was exactly the kind of season in which Luton could make a determined chase for the FA Cup. The road to Wembley started in January with a trip to Second Division Crystal Palace. The original match was postponed because of frost, but went ahead two days later on a bog. In between, Selhurst Park's tenants, Charlton, also played a Cup-tie on the pitch.

The game was won on the wings, with Ricky Hill and Brian Stein marauding down the right with Mitchell Thomas and David Preece inter-changing down the left. The Town's opening goal was scored by Stein, who headed in a Thomas cross, but it was not until just before the end that the tie was made safe when Preece fired home.

The reward was a visit from Third Division Bristol Rovers. The Pirates arrived without three first-choice defenders, all injured. To take on a First Division side on top form, on an artificial surface where ball control and playing to feet were paramount, meant that Rovers did not stand a chance. This was one game where the Cup was not going to be a great leveller. Two goals in each half left Rovers' manager Bobby Gould warning that the Town were well equipped to go all the way to Wembley.

Next up were Arsenal at Kenilworth Road. This tie certainly caught the imagination, judging by the long queues snaking round the ground after tickets went on sale. Bad blood during the recent league encounter at Highbury (won by Arsenal 2-1) was bound to add spice to the occasion. Record receipts of almost £60,000 and a press box full of Fleet Street's finest certainly made this the game of the season.

The teams shared four goals in an ill-tempered first half. A bad injury to Brian Stein would keep him out until April. Accusations by Arsenal manager Don Howe that Luton players – and in particular Mick Harford – employed 'bludgeoning' tactics hardly reduced the temperature. That said, the Hatters carved enough chances in the second half to have won. The normally blinkered London press corps agreed, but that verdict was hidden amongst many column inches of quotes from Arsenal players and man-agement regarding the Town's supposed rough play!

The much-hyped replay was postponed when Highbury's under-soil heating failed, and when at last it received the go-ahead the quarter-finals were just four days away. Highbury was a farce, and presented a priceless advert for an artificial pitch. The players slithered around on a surface that would never be deemed playable today. No goals were scored, although the Gunners had the best of the chances, especially in extra-time.

There were no golden goals, penalty shoot-outs, or restrictions on the number of replays in those days. The tie had to be fought to a finish. The toss of a coin brought the second replay back to Kenilworth Road just 48 hours later, again a situation that would not be tolerated today. This time the Hatters steamrollered their opponents, winning 3-0, and Mark Stein – playing his first game of the season, deputising for the injured Marc North – scored once and forced Arsenal centre-half David O'Leary to put through his own goal. Don Howe, shortly to lose his job, agreed that the Town were worthy winners.

Before Luton could draw breath they had to face Everton at Kenilworth Road. Everton, the defending champions, were neck and neck with Liverpool at the top of the table, but most importantly they would be fresh while the Hatters would be playing their fourth game in seven days.

The Town obviously had a score to settle – following the previous season's semi-final defeat – and 15,529 gathered to see Mick Harford pounce when Ricky Hill's shot was parried by Neville Southall in the Everton goal. When Mark Stein skipped through on the hour to double the lead, Luton fans truly felt that Wembley was their destiny. Unfortunately, Everton were not considered the best team in the country for nothing and, following a clever substitution, they replied almost instantly through Graeme Sharp. It was backs to the wall for the Luton defenders, and the inevitable equaliser fell to Adrian Heath after Gary Lineker's overhead kick could have gone anywhere. It might have been even worse, as Lineker wasted two simple opportunities in the final minutes.

The replay, just four days later, saw Lineker make amends in front of a crowd of 44,264, skinning Foster and Donaghy before scoring an early goal. Lineker was then brought down by Sealey, seemingly outside the area, but when the keeper saved the spot-kick it seemed to light a fire in Luton's bellies. Luton substitute Ray Daniel shook the woodwork and, with Foster joining the attack, the Everton supporters were howling for the final whistle long before the end.

Everton had dashed Luton's Cup hopes two seasons running, but the Town exacted revenge ten days later, beating the Toffees 2-1 to effectively deny them the title. Luton eventually finished ninth, the best since 1958.

If everyone thought that the summer of 1985 was eventful, then that was almost calm compared to the events of twelve months later. Work at the ground included the roofing of the Kenilworth Road end, the installation of seating in the Oak Road end and – most controversially – altering the Bobbers Stand to install executive boxes. These changes, which represented the biggest upheaval to the structure of Kenilworth Road since 1937, were not without their problems.

Roofing the Kenilworth Road terrace was initially frowned upon by the local authority, as it was 50ft high, but as there were no complaints from residents, the building works were, reluctantly, allowed to proceed. But these works necessitated the demolition of those houses backing onto the terrace, some of which housed the club's offices.

Rebuilding the Maple Road entrance and the offices to the rear of the Main Stand – to be carried out as part of the A505 relief road compensation – were still ongoing. This meant the club had to hire premises in Dunstable Road on a two-year lease to serve as administrative offices in the interim. As can be imagined, this was a logistical nightmare.

Although supporters could understand the monetary incentive behind converting the Bobbers Stand, it did not please the displaced season-ticket holders, who were to be shunted behind the Oak Road goal. They preferred their existing view from the side, and with the best seats in the Main Stand and enclosure already taken, they were the principal losers.

While all this was going on, the club lost its manager. David Pleat decided to throw in his lot with Tottenham. Chairman David Evans tried his hardest to keep Pleat, and gentle persuasion turned to outright acrimony for a time, but Spurs were determined to get their man and their man was determined to go. The wound was then re-opened when Pleat enticed full-back Mitchell Thomas to White Hart Lane. Although the sale was eventually settled by tribunal, Luton supporters could not help but think that the club had lost out. They knew from experience that Pleat was the master tribunal operator, the Town having benefited from his astute dealings many times in the past.

As if losing the manager and rebuilding the ground was not enough, the club now decided to implement a card-carrying 'members-only' policy. In essence, this meant keeping out away supporters, all of them, whether skinheads or nuns.

A nationwide membership scheme had been aired by the Conservative Government as a hooligan deterrent for some months, and who better to test the water than a prospective Conservative MP in the shape of Luton Town Chairman David Evans. The Hatters supremo was naturally accused of trying to feather his own political nest, but he retorted that local shopkeepers would be able to go about their business without fear of hooliganism and that families could return to Kenilworth Road to watch the Hatters in peace and comfort.

The Millwall riot was still fresh in the mind and Fleet Street was initially sympathetic, as it had been over the artificial pitch. Attitudes could quickly change though.

This was the situation confronting new manager John Moore, who had been promoted internally from his position of coach. Moore, who had originally joined the Town as a player in 1965, turned down the chance to join Pleat at White Hart Lane and was rewarded for his loyalty with the top job at Kenilworth Road.

Moore recruited former Fulham manager Ray Harford (no relation to Mick) as his assistant, and ex-playing colleague Jim Ryan as coach. The new regime presided over a Town side that would prove difficult to beat, even though – with long-term injuries to Mick Harford and David Preece – it was not likely to score too many goals.

The ban on away fans was strictly enforced at the start of 1986-87, but its first real test came when Luton were paired at home with Fourth Division Cardiff City in the Littlewoods (League) Cup. The Football League had sanctioned the Town's experiment for league games, but for cup-ties they invoked the rule that 25 per cent of tickets should be available to the away side. Cardiff had maintained that 5,000 supporters were prepared to travelled to this, a second round midweek tie, and were about to be deprived. Luton refused to budge and were thrown out of the competition.

That decision provoked more column inches in the national press than anything else in the club's history. The consensus was still generally sympathetic, especially in view of a major disturbance at Bradford City's temporary home at the Odsal Stadium, where Leeds were the visitors. Cardiff were also cheekily demanding £25,000 from the Football League as compensation for their 'lost' game.

A meeting of Football League clubs agreed to enforce the rules regarding cup-ties, but allow Luton the opportunity to play the tie at Ninian Park or at a neutral venue. When the Town refused either option, the sympathy started to wane a little. It waned faster when Margaret Thatcher threw in her oar and made it clear that David Evans had her complete support. The press was coming to the view that Evans was out to score political points by being stubborn and awkward.

The tide turned completely when Liverpool and Everton, the big two, started moaning about the artificial pitch. It gave the Hatters too much of an advantage, they claimed. Coupled with the ban on away supporters, Luton were starting to feel like pariahs.

KENILWORTH ROAD CLASSICS: **Luton v Liverpool** – 4-1
Today League Division One, 25th October 1986
In the absence of the injured Mick Harford, the goalscoring mantle had fallen on ex-Wigan forward Mike Newell, signed the previous season. He was, unfairly in the view of many, compared unfavourably with Harford and the restlessness of the crowd was beginning to affect him. The visit of League champions and FA Cup holders Liverpool was not expected to end a famine that had seen only one goal scored in six hours play. The Hatters had failed to beat Liverpool since 1962 and a full house of 13,140 turned up fearing the worst but hoping for the best.

Liverpool started by employing an offside trap, using giant Dane Jan Molby as sweeper, and hoping to catch the Hatters on the break. When Newell beat the offside trap and the lumbering Molby to plant the ball past Bruce Grobbelaar in goal, the Luton supporters sat back expecting a backlash. It did not come. Instead Newell doubled the lead, hammering in a low cross from Mal Donaghy.

By now the ground was rocking, and just before the interval Grobbelaar hit a weak clearance to David Preece, who switched the ball to Ricky Hill, who made no mistake from close in. Luton's first victory over Liverpool for 24 years was clinched early in the second half when Hill's header hit the bar and Newell dived to head the ball over the line for his hat-trick.

The Reds pulled one back when Molby, pushed into midfield to prevent further personal embarrassment, was upended in the box by Steve Foster. Molby netted from the spot. At the final whistle the teams trooped off, while Liverpool manager Kenny Dalglish went away to prepare for his future attacks on the Kenilworth Road artificial surface.

Newell, now a Luton hero, went home clutching the match ball after letting slip that as a boy in Liverpool he was an avid supporter of the Reds. He had even been on their books for a time. Skipper Foster revealed that the Town had anticipated that Liverpool would use a sweeper, and had arranged a full-scale rehearsal against the youth team who were instructed to use the same system. 'And we only beat them 3-1!'

LUTON: *Sealey, Johnson, Grimes (Wilson), Nicholas, Foster, Donaghy, Hill, Brian Stein, Newell, Mark Stein, Preece.*

LIVERPOOL: *Grobbelaar, Venison (Johnston), Lawrenson, Hansen, Molby, Beglin, Nicol, Whelan, McMahon, Walsh, Rush.*

~~~~~~~~~~

Beating Liverpool made headlines for all the right reasons – the quality of the Town's football. It was the first of four straight wins that pushed Luton up to fourth, and though they eventually slipped back to seventh, that was still the highest in the club's history.

The club had worried that the FA, in the event of a home tie, would follow the Football League in insisting a quarter of the available tickets be allocated to away supporters. The FA proved to be more flexible, however, and when the Town were paired with Liverpool they allowed a couple of hundred visiting supporters into the Main Stand. It also helped from a crowd-problem point of view that the game was televised live.

Liverpool, thrashed 1-4 three months earlier, thought they had seen the last of Luton's plastic pitch for one season. As before, they played it tight and, unlike before, got the draw they wanted.

On the day of the Anfield replay, severe weather threatened the north of England. Fearing that the players' coach might encounter impassable roads, the club decided to fly to Liverpool, only to discover on arrival at Heathrow that there were no flights out. Luton's players found themselves stranded, unable to get to Anfield on time. The game therefore had to be called off, despite Anfield's pitch being perfectly playable.

Liverpool, and in particular manager Kenny Dalglish, were scathing in their criticism of the unprofessional Town who, of course, should have made arrangements to travel up the day before. From a Luton point of view, the moaning went over the top – to the extent of counting the number of pies that had to be disposed of – before the press got bored.

When the game eventually went ahead, the Hatters were even more disadvantaged than usual. They had to contend with a contemptuous, vociferous home support, in addition to the might of the best team in the land. That Luton's defence held firm for 120 minutes to force a second replay speaks volumes for the resolve of the players, and made John Moore – who had contemplated resigning after the postponement debacle – a very proud man.

The Town won the toss of the coin to stage the second replay two nights later, and this time Luton hammered Liverpool, with Brian Stein proving that you could bend free-kicks on an artificial surface. Mick Harford netted the second from the spot after Stein had been tripped, and Newell added a pile-driver. Boy, did Dalglish moan after this one!

Luton had just three days in which to gloat before hosting QPR in the next round, and four days after that they lost at Loftus Road 1-2 in a replay.

This string of exhausting cup-ties had little or no effect on league form. Coming seventh was some achievement, and but for surprisingly losing at home to Oxford in their penultimate game, they would have finished fifth.

As for the controversial membership scheme, it had not generated the extra customers that David Evans and his co-directors anticipated. On the contrary, crowds were slightly down. That, plus the cost of implementing the scheme and the ground improvements, meant that the club was drifting back into the red. Nipping the problem in the bud, Luton appointed two new directors, Brian Cole and Mike Watson-Challis, who each made funds available.

The resignation of manager John Moore was a bolt from the blue. He professed to not liking the high-profile nature of the job, but privately he was annoyed at the constant sniping about his style of play, not to mention the artificial surface and the away supporters ban, which were out of his control.

The Town again appointed from within, inviting Ray Harford to take over. He lured Brighton's Danny Wilson to strengthen the midfield, but having done so learned that Aberdeen had offered £350,000 for Peter Nicholas. Although Alex Ferguson had just left Pittodrie for Manchester

United, European competition for the Dons was more or less guaranteed, so the deal suited everyone, apart from a new manager who now needed a another new midfielder.

Little did anyone sense that this would be the most momentous season in Luton's history, especially when the team picked up only two points from the first five games. Player-power perhaps exerted itself, because Harford then reverted from his preferred 4-4-2 system to the tried and trusted attacking formula that the players had been used to.

The sixth game was at Oxford. Brian Stein headed the Town in front, and although Neil Slatter equalised, full-back Tim Breacker slammed in a low drive before the interval. Emeka Nwajiobi scored with a diving header seconds after half-time, and Ricky Hill netted a fourth before Mick Harford lobbed a fifth from 25 yards. Oxford's late consolation was not enough to satisfy manager Maurice Evans who called it 'The worst performance since I have been here. Some of our players looked as though they were ready to walk off after Luton went 3-1 up. Luton won because they were better than us in every department.'

Oxford and Luton then went their separate ways. By the time of the return, in February, Luton were eighth and Oxford were falling through the trap door.

KENILWORTH ROAD CLASSICS: **Luton v Oxford** – 7-4

Barclays League Division One, 6th February 1988

As had happened at the Manor, Luton set off at a dash. This time Mick Harford hammered them into an early lead. The goals then followed thick and fast, hardly giving the crowd of 8,063 time to breathe. Breacker set up Brian Stein before Dean Saunders pulled one back for Oxford from the spot after a handball. Darron McDonough volleyed in the Town's third before Foyle reduced the deficit once more. If anything, the second half was even more breathless. Mark Stein netted an eleven-minute hat-trick, Richard Hill and Les Phillips replied for Oxford, and Mick Harford completed the scoring to make the final tally 7-4. In addition to the eleven goals, the woodwork was hit three times, several efforts were cleared off the line, and both goalkeepers played blinders. Ray Harford called it 'A freak result which was probably great for the fans but I would sooner win 3-0 than 7-4'. Maurice Evans was simply shell-shocked.

The aggregate eleven goals was Luton's highest in the top division, and had only been exceeded three times in the club's long history. With both games against Oxford being broadcast to a worldwide TV audience of 200 million, the television companies were rubbing their hands. Eighteen goals had hit the net in three hours. Certainly no time for the armchair supporter to get bored.

Nor were Luton and Oxford done for the season. They were due to meet in the Littlewoods Cup, and this will be recalled in due course. All that need be said now is that the Town finished the league in ninth position, which meant a top-ten place for three seasons in a row.

LUTON: Sealey, Breacker, Johnson (Grimes), McDonough, Foster, Donaghy, Wilson, Brian Stein, Harford, Mark Stein, Allinson.

OXFORD: Hardwick, Hebberd, Bardsley, Briggs, Caton (Whitehurst), Rhoades-Brown, Shelton (Mustoe), Hill, Phillips, Saunders, Foyle.

~~~~~~~~~~~~

1987-88 also saw Luton enjoy an extended run in the FA Cup for the fourth year running. The road to the Twin Towers started at Fourth Division Hartlepool. Goals from Micky Weir and Darron McDonough earned a 2-1 win. Southampton seemed to be cruising to victory in the next round, when Colin Clarke's long cross deceived Les Sealey in the Luton goal. Fortunately, late goals from Darron McDonough and Brian Stein tuned the tie. QPR were then knocked out after a replay, with Warren Neill putting the ball into his own net at Kenilworth Road for the second season running.

KENILWORTH ROAD CLASSICS: **Luton v Portsmouth** – 3-1

FA Cup, Quarter-final, 12th March 1988

Division One strugglers Portsmouth were the quarter-final visitors. With cup games coming thick and fast, the Town had relented and segregated a section of the Kenilworth Road terrace for 2,000 opposition supporters. Pompey took their full allocation, swelling the crowd to 12,857.

The game got off to an explosive start. A 'route one' kick from Les Sealey saw the ball headed on by Harford to Danny Wilson. The Pompey defenders backed off, leaving Wilson to cut inside and let fly with his left foot. The second goal was similar. Again Harford was instrumental. Mark Stein nipped in, drifted away from two defenders, and buried his shot. Pompey pulled a goal back before the break when a seemingly offside Terry Connor crossed for Mick Quinn to turn the ball in.

With the game finely poised, Quinn was sent off for elbowing Luton skipper Steve Foster. The game was effectively over, but to make sure, two minutes from time Harford headed in a pin-point Tim Breacker cross.

LUTON: Sealey, Breacker, Foster, Donaghy, Grimes, Rob Johnson, McDonough, Allinson, Wilson, Mark Stein, Harford.

PORTSMOUTH: Knight, Gilbert, Blake, Ball, Hardyman (Mariner), Horne, Dillon, Fillery, Hilaire, Quinn, Connor.

~~~~~~~~~~~~

Sadly, the Hatters fell at the semi-finals once more, going down 1-2 to Wimbledon at White Hart Lane, despite Mick Harford scoring first. The

Town were wobbling at that time, also losing 1-4 to Reading at Wembley in the final of the Simod Cup. All supporters were hoping that the Town would make it third time lucky in the Littlewoods Cup final.

Having been excluded from the 1986-87 Littlewoods Cup for refusing to admit away fans, the trip to Wigan in September 1987 represented Luton's first game in the competition under its new guise. A goal from Micky Weir, signed from Hibs, on his full debut earned the Hatters a first-leg win, and a second-leg hat-trick from Mick Harford removed all doubts.

Unlike Wigan, the next opponents – Coventry – demanded their full allocation of tickets at Kenilworth Road. The police nervously advised the Town to play elsewhere. Fulham's Craven Cottage was mooted, but the Metropolitan Police wanted £20,000 to police it, so the tie was eventually switched to Filbert Street, Leicester, which made it almost a home game for Coventry and their fans. That could not prevent the Hatters winning 3-1 on a quagmire of a pitch to set up at tie at Second Division Ipswich. Luton were without six injured regulars for the trip, but a sweetly executed goal from Brian Stein in the fourth minute confirmed a place in the quarter-finals.

The segregation row had been settled by the time of the visit of Bradford City two months later, the turning point of which came when Bantams goalkeeper Paul Tomlinson handled the ball, dribbled it out of the area, and then dribbled it back again before picking it up. An indirect free-kick was awarded by the eagle-eyed referee. It was touched to Steve Foster, who fired in. Mick Harford doubled the score later.

The Town were through to the semi-finals for the first time. Their opponents were Oxford, winners of the competition two years earlier, but battered and bruised from 2-5 and 4-7 thrashings in the league already this season. For the first leg, the Manor pitch was covered in thawing snow. This seemed to suit Luton, who scored first when Brian Stein exchanged passes with Harford and fired in from twenty yards. Just 33 seconds after the break, Oxford keeper Alan Judge's long clearance saw Dean Saunders outpace Mal Donaghy and tumble to the ground. The referee, forty yards behind play, pointed to the spot. Saunders sent Sealey the wrong way to maintain his record of scoring in every round.

When Saunders and Donaghy tussled again, a second penalty was awarded, to the disgust of the Luton players. This time Sealey heeded the advice of Danny Wilson – who had played with Saunders at Brighton – and dived the right way to save. The drama was not yet over. Saunders went down a third time, which looked the most blatant foul of the lot, but the referee waved play on. Afterwards, Saunders expressed surprise that the referee had given the first penalty from so far away, and admitted that the second was no more than a little bump!

KENILWORTH ROAD CLASSICS: **Luton v Oxford** – 2-0

Littlewoods Cup, Semi-final second leg, 28th February 1988

It was just three weeks since the Town had beaten Oxford 7-4 in the league, but this second leg was not a foregone conclusion. Oxford quite liked Luton's artificial surface and had won on it twice previously, so this would be no pushover.

The game was switched to Sunday afternoon to accommodate a live TV audience. Even seasoned pros like skipper Steve Foster felt tense, trotting out the old cliché about it being only half-time. When the teams lined up, Luton were heartened to see Oxford's creative midfielder Trevor Hebberd back as a sweeper. The Hatters stuck to their own game plan, attacked from the start, and by the interval were two goals up. Brian Stein headed into the top corner, and Ashley Grimes curled a left-foot free-kick over the wall for the second. There was no way back for Oxford.

LUTON: Sealey, Breacker, Grimes, McDonough, Foster, Donaghy, Wilson, Brian Stein, Harford, Mark Stein, Rob Johnson.

OXFORD: Judge, Bardsley, Briggs, Caton, Dreyer, Hebberd, Hill (Shelton), Phillips, Rhoades-Brown (Leworthy), Foyle, Saunders.

~~~~~~~~~~

Luton had to prepare for the Littlewoods Cup final with a mini-injury crisis. Les Sealey had injured a shoulder against Sheffield Wednesday, Mal Donaghy had torn ankle ligaments during the Mercantile Credit Centenary celebration game at Wembley, and Darron McDonough had hurt himself in training two days before the big clash against Arsenal. Manager Ray Harford agonised over the fitness of Ricky Hill, out with a broken leg since Christmas, and David Preece, who had just one game under his belt since injuring his ankle seven months previously. In the event, Donaghy was declared fit, Hill and Preece were included, and nineteen-year-old local lad Kingsley Black was preferred to Mark Stein up front.

On hearing he was to be on the substitutes' bench, Mark Stein stormed out of the team's hotel, and but for the calming influence of older brother Brian, he might never have returned to the fold. Arsenal's future Hatter Steve Williams was also inconsolable on hearing that he would not be playing. To the disgust of manager George Graham, he stormed off never to return.

Over 35,000 Luton supporters raised the Wembley crowd to a virtual capacity 95,732, in what was the last season of all-standing behind both goals. The stadium was decrepit, but still magical.

Luton took an interval lead through Brian Stein's cool shot from Steve Foster's clever pass. Shortly after the break Stein was thwarted by a flying save from Arsenal goalkeeper John Lukic, whereupon the Gunners netted twice in three minutes through Martin Hayes and Alan Smith.

When Arsenal's dominance was rewarded by a soft penalty, the Luton supporters feared the worst, but Andy Dibble pushed Nigel Winterburn's spot-kick round a post.

It was now the Town who gained a second wind, and an error by Arsenal's Gus Caesar led to Danny Wilson stooping to head the equaliser. In true *Roy of the Rovers* style, Brian Stein crashed home the winner in the final seconds. The Town had won a cup after 103 years of trying. It was an overdue reward for the 1960s' crash down the divisions, virtual bankruptcy in the 1970s, and the guts needed to admit to being a Luton fan during the pariah years in the 1980s.

As Wembley was virtually a home ground for Luton during 1987-88, the Littlewoods Cup final line-ups deserve a mention.

LUTON: Dibble, Breacker, Rob Johnson, Hill, Foster, Donaghy, Wilson, Brian Stein, Harford (Mark Stein), Preece (Grimes), Black.

ARSENAL: Lukic, Winterburn, Caesar, Adams, Sansom, Rocastle, Thomas, Davis, Richardson, Groves (Hayes), Smith.

~~~~~~~~~~~

The Town played 58 competitive matches during that unprecedented 1987-88 season. It was a frantic and expensive time for Luton supporters, who were punch-drunk with the sheer number of games and the intense media hype attending everything the club did or said. Following the celebration dinner at the London Savoy, an open-top bus carried the joyous players through the streets of Luton. The league season was not yet over, and a lap of honour preceded the next home league game, against relegated Watford.

That summer it was back to the stark realities of life at Kenilworth Road. The Town staged their biggest and most spectacular event on the artificial surface when hosting a boxing match between Barry McGuigan and Tomas Da Cruz. On the same bill was the new sensation Nigel Benn, but he cried off, leaving the Town to bemoan the consequent fall in attendance from 15,000 to 8,500. The Luton Board withheld £70,000 as compensation for the lower attendance, which provoked a war of words between boxing promoter Frank Warren and the Town's David Evans, with High Court writs flying around. The dispute took a year to settle, with the only winners being – as to be expected – the lawyers.

On the playing side, Ray Harford realised his team was ageing. Brian Stein, who had not kicked a ball since firing the winner against Arsenal, was the first of the 'old school' to depart, signing for French club Caen over the summer. Chelsea's Roy Wegerle, John Dreyer from Oxford, Alec Chamberlain from Everton, and Arsenal misfit Steve Williams were signed, with Williams commanding a Luton record outgoing fee of £300,000. To balance the books, Mark Stein went to QPR for £300,000, and Andy

Dibble – understandably – was not prepared to go back to the reserves. He dropped a division and signed for Manchester City for £240,000. Also off was Mal Donaghy – reluctantly as far as Luton were concerned. He had been enticed by a move to childhood favourites Manchester United. The Hatters were well compensated, to the tune of £650,000, but were sad to lose the quiet Northern Irishman, who had won 58 caps for his country whilst at Luton.

Once again, the Town were slow out of the blocks in 1988-89, and it was only when Ray Harford ditched his 4-4-2 system yet again that the Town gained enough points to prevent them being dragged into the relegation dogfight.

The change of formation brought out the best in Roy Wegerle. For a time the South African was almost unplayable, especially on the artificial surface. Alas, his light did not burn brightly for too long.

West Ham were beaten 4-1 and Southampton received their ritual thrashing, 6-1, both at Kenilworth Road, but these wins were rarities, and they dried up completely from February, when the Town went ten games without a victory, dropping from a comfortable thirteenth to a worrying eighteenth in the process.

Luton found the Littlewoods Cup more to their liking. Fourth Division Burnley sensed a giant-killing after a 1-1 draw at Kenilworth Road in the Town's first defence of the trophy, but inspired by skipper Steve Foster – who had seventeen stitches inserted in head and thigh wounds over the two games – Luton triumphed with a scruffy goal from Ricky Hill.

The Hatters faced another partisan crowd in the next round at Leeds, unbeaten under new manager Howard Wilkinson. Goals from Danny Wilson and David Oldfield made the game safe long before the dismissals of teenager Julian James and manager Ray Harford.

Another Division Two side, Manchester City, with Andy Dibble in goal, were the visitors in the next round. Roy Wegerle played a blinder, and the score, 3-1 to the Town, was met by a volley of moans from City manager Mel Machin, leading to the *Luton News* running the headline: 'Pitch scores three goals.'

In the quarter-finals the Hatters hosted a Southampton side that had crashed 6-1 in the league only two weeks before. The Saints were determined to avoid a repetition, and fought back to equalise after Ricky Hill had headed in a David Preece free-kick on seventy minutes. Apparently, the noisy celebrations coming from the Southampton changing room at the end spoke volumes, ensuring that the Town players needed little motivation for the replay.

Luton had the better of the first half, the Saints the second, but no goals. In extra-time, Mick Harford – back after suspension – headed home and Ricky Hill thundered in a 25-yard effort eight minutes later. Rod Williams then set up a grandstand finish with a goal two minutes from time. In a frantic finale, brother Ray Wallace was dismissed for a second bookable offence.

In the semi-finals, West Ham were – like the Hatters – a side showing poor form in the league but who could do no wrong in the cups. In the televised first leg at Upton Park, Mick Harford headed the Town into the lead just before the interval and Roy Wegerle scored at the near post just afterwards. Both goals were blamed on the Hammers' keeper, Allen McKnight. When Julian Dicks hauled back Wegerle, Danny Wilson fired a third from the spot.

Trying to retrieve a three-goal deficit in the away leg is next to hopeless, and when the Hammers' early burst fizzled out, Harford and Wegerle extended the winning margin to five.

Nottingham Forest were the opponents at Wembley, and all older supporters looked forward to avenging the 1959 FA Cup final defeat. This would not be easy, bearing in mind the current form of the two sides. The Town had earned only one point from eight games since the semi-final and were nudging the relegation places, while Brian Clough's Forest were up to fourth and chasing the leaders.

On the day, however, form seemed to count for little. Luton took an interval lead through Mick Harford's strong header and it took an error by goalkeeper Les Sealey to allow Forest back into the game. Charging out of his goal, when he should have stayed put, Sealey brought down Steve Hodge for a penalty which was converted by Brian Clough's son Nigel. Forest smelled blood and it came as no surprise when further goals – from Neil Webb and Clough – made the final score 1-3. It was the Hatters' first defeat in the competition since 1985.

There were still six league games to play and only a complete reversal of form would enable the Town to escape the drop. Just 8,610 turned out for the visit of Coventry, who twice pegged back Hatters goals to leave them with just one point when they hoped for three.

As for the trip to lowly Newcastle, Luton had only one league win at St James' Park to their name, back in 1937-38. The game was dire, no goals, no nothing, but the Hatters were delighted to come away with another point.

Two home games in three days were just the tonic, for they could make or break the season. But Derby had lost only four times on their travels, while Charlton had just beaten Manchester United in their bid to avoid the drop. Considering the Town had scored only six goals in ten games, it was a welcome shock when Derby were beaten 3-0. Now all Luton had to do was beat the Addicks.

KENILWORTH ROAD CLASSICS: **Luton v Charlton** – 5-2

Barclays League Division One, 2nd May 1989

Much of the credit for the Town's new-found confidence was down to Terry Mancini, hired by manager Ray Harford on a short-term contract to liven up the dressing room and inject a few fresh ideas. His motivational abilities were certainly going to be needed for the relegation dogfight against Charlton.

The attendance of 10,024 was rewarded when Danny Wilson headed in following an interchange between Kingsley Black and Mick Harford. The lead was increased when Harford's cross was headed into his own goal by Colin Walsh. The goal was later credited to Kingsley Black, but this writer was sitting behind the Oak Road goal and was as near to putting the ball in the net as Black was!

Just before half-time, two more goals in three minutes sealed the outcome. Wilson grabbed his second, stabbing home a David Preece centre, and Harford got the goal he deserved from Wegerle's cross. Charlton scored two of the three second-half goals, to make it 5-2, but that did little to ease manager Lennie Lawrence's dismay.

LUTON: *Chamberlain, Breacker, Foster, Beaumont, Dreyer, Wilson, Hill, Preece, Black (Cooke), Wegerle, Harford.*

CHARLTON: *Bolder, Humphrey, Caton (Williams), Shirtliff, Pates, Reid, Walsh, McKenzie, Mortimer, Lee, Crooks (Jones).*

~~~~~~~~~~~

Luton were almost safe, but there were some heart-stopping moments to come. After losing 0-1 at West Ham in the penultimate game, Luton entertained high-flying Norwich still needing a win to be certain of staying up. Danny Wilson, who had never missed a spot-kick for the Town, did just that after ten minutes, and with the nerves jangling Mick Harford headed against a post. Fortunately, the referee awarded another penalty for a push seen by no one else, and this time Wilson buried the ball.

Norwich pressed late on, but even if they had equalised Luton would have been safe. Defeat for Luton – when other results came in – would have sent them down. It was that close.

At the end of the season the Town bade farewell to Ricky Hill, who signed for Le Havre to sample Continental football as his career drew to a close, but that was overshadowed by the revelation that the Town's directors were considering a 'sale and leaseback' of Kenilworth Road to the local council.

The sale price was £3.25 million, with a leaseback for seven years at a peppercorn rent. It was seen by supporters as akin to selling the family jewels. The Board insisted the transaction was good business for the club, as it involved paying back all director and bank loans which were imposing high commercial rates of interest. With the small crowds the Town were attracting, that interest was not being covered, let alone the capital being repaid. As things stood, the club was sinking deeper and deeper into debt with no hope of reversing the situation.

The trouble with this sort of transaction is that you can only do it once. You can't sell something twice. Unless care is taken, it would not be long before the spiral of debt starts to rise again, this time with no security to fall back upon – apart from directors' guarantees. For their part, the Luton Town directors agreed that future loans to cover transfer fees would not attract interest, as transfers would be regarded as speculative transactions and that all board members should underwrite the risk. Some supporters argued that all loans by directors should be interest free, irrespective of their purpose.

KENILWORTH ROAD HEROES: **Ricky Hill**

Born in London in March 1959, Ricky Hill wanted to be a footballer as soon as he could kick. At Anson Road Primary School in Cricklewood and Sir John Kelly Boys School in Neasden football became an overriding passion, but it was brother Ian who encouraged him him to turn out in Sunday games, albeit against much older boys.

'I apparently dropped a slab of concrete on my left foot when I was young and broke a toe nail which meant I could not kick with that foot. So I learnt to kick with my right to become two-footed and dreamed of being the one player in a hundred who would make it as a professional,' explained Hill.

Luton's reserve-team coach David Pleat received a routine call from a sports master at Hitchin School, to remind him of a match against the Sir John Kelly School in the National Pepsi-Cola Schools Under-16 Trophy. The Hitchin team included a few possibles, and after watching the game Pleat invited three players back for trials, including an 'overweight boy with a clever football brain and fine control' – Ricky Hill.

'After trials I was asked to sign forms for Luton, which I was happy to do, in November 1975. As Luton had such a big squad at the time I was not always guaranteed a reserve team place but I was prepared to bide my time. Over Easter 1976 David Pleat kept on asking me if my boots were clean which puzzled me, but the reason for asking soon became clear when on the day of the Bristol Rovers home game, assistant manager Roy McCrohan called me in from playing pool with the other junior pros to tell me I was in the first team squad and would be substitute that afternoon. This came after only thirteen reserve team appearances.

'I took my place on the bench and as a dull game entered its final quarter, with the score deadlocked at 1-1, our centre-half John Faulkner – who had just returned to the side after a long lay off with a bad knee injury – went down injured. Without getting off his seat, physio Reg Game knew that "Maxie's" knee had gone again and immediately ordered him off. I could sense the anticipation in the crowd as I came on as the majority of the supporters had not seen me before.'

None of this seemed to affect Ricky. Almost his first touch was a marvellous through ball to Brian Chambers to put the Town into the lead. Moments later the ball was laid into Hill's path by Jimmy Husband. Hill fired low into the net, and a new hero was born.

Hill retained his place for the final game of that season, and also for the first five games of 1976-77, scoring two goals, before he received the first major setback of his career:

'We were down to play Fulham on the following Saturday, which I was really looking forward to, as a full house was expected due to George Best and Rodney Marsh being in the Cottagers side. On the day before the game Roy McCrohan had told me that manager Harry Haslam wanted a word and I was then given the news that as Jim Ryan had now returned to Kenilworth Road after a summer playing in the USA, his experience was going to be needed against Fulham and I was to be relegated to the bench. By way of consolation, Harry did say that next time I was in the first team I would be in to stay.'

Apart from a couple of substitute appearances that season, it was back to the reserves to continue to learn his trade, but Haslam was right in his prediction that once back in the side he would never again be dropped. Hill returned against Notts County at the end of April 1977, scoring twice in a 4-2 win, and was then – apart from injury – a permanent fixture in the side for the next twelve years.

'During my first few seasons at Kenilworth Road we started to build up a formidable squad of players, and with David Pleat replacing Harry Haslam in the manager's chair, the style of play changed a bit and we were really unlucky to miss out on promotion from the old Division Two in 1980 and 1981. With no disrespect to the players who had been in the side before, the signing of Brian Horton in the summer of 1981 was the final missing ingredient that enabled us to walk away with the championship the following season with an exceptional team. Brian was good for me as he enabled me to go up and support the attack more, safe in the knowledge that he was my back-up and was always in the right place at the right time. He knew the game, had the ability to influence others and was the manager's eyes and ears on the pitch. We had a brilliant team spirit and utter belief in ourselves and my link up with Brian Stein that season, where we had an almost telepathic understanding of where each other was on the pitch, was instrumental in our success. Great days.'

The Hatters took the First Division by storm the following season, and were the darlings of the television companies due to the cavalier style of play. Nonetheless, the Town were faced with a last-day showdown at Manchester City with the loser to suffer relegation.

Says Hill: 'None of the players doubted our ability to play in the top flight and relegation was not on our minds. We had a low-key trip to Henlow Grange before the game and we were so confident of the result that we pooled some money together to get a bet on, but no one would accept it. We treated it as just another game. On the day, our team work was solid with no outstanding individuals but as the game wore on we badly needed a goal as City were looking less and less likely to hurt us. Then the ball fell at the feet of substitute Raddy Antic in a packed penalty area. Raddy was the one player you would hope the ball would fall to as he had the technical ability to strike it low with either foot. City's goalkeeper, Alex Williams, got his hand to the ball but only succeeded in deflecting it past two defenders on the line. We hung on for the final five minutes and at the final whistle angry City supporters stormed on the pitch and I received a thump around the ear for my troubles, and then in the tunnel the City players were saying things they probably regretted the day after.'

So ended a memorable season for Hill, who had made his England debut as substitute for Tony Morley in a European Championship qualifier in Denmark, and then started against West Germany in a friendly at Wembley: 'To be quite honest I found the pace of international football comfortable and it was great to be on the same pitch as players such as Karl-Heinz Rummenigge and Peter Briegel who I was up against.'

Luton slowly consolidated in Division One after that, with Hill instrumental, but then came a couple of setbacks in his career: 'I had suffered hamstring problems before, but after a Cup game against Watford in January 1984 I was training ready for the replay when my leg seized up. It took ages before someone diagnosed a calcified hamstring which eventually involved an operation to cut away the extra bone growth. This meant that I missed the remainder of the season.'

During the Hatters' most successful spell, finishing in the top ten three years running, Hill suffered a recurrence of his hamstring problem in 1986. He was not out for long, but then broke an ankle and suffered ligament damage at Everton on Boxing Day 1987 which kept him out as the team marched to Wembley in the Littlewoods Cup.

'Although I was not fully match fit I was lucky enough to make it back just in time for the final which was obviously the crowning point of my career at Luton. The penalty save by Andy Dibble was the turning point as to go 3-1 down would have killed us. Instead we were lifted and went on to win the game with the clincher coming in the final minute. The only sad point was that we were not allowed to show our skills in Europe due to the ban on English clubs taking part.'

Approaching thirty, Hill fancied playing on the Continent and was given a verbal assurance that he could leave at the end of the 1988-89 season. He could go on a free transfer, to reward his long service and loyalty. In fact, a fee was demanded from Le Havre, which left a sour taste at the time but was soon forgotten.

It was only the wretched state of the club's finances that prevented Hill returning to Kenilworth Road under Jim Ryan a couple of years later: 'I had a brilliant time in France and earned more money than I had ever earned before. During my time at Luton I was aware that I was a bit of a pauper when listening to some of the other players in the England dressing room, but I did not want to leave the family atmosphere and job satisfaction at Luton. I certainly had opportunities to leave, both legal and illegal, but remained loyal which I never regretted, and went through the whole of my career without an agent.

'I learnt a lot in France about coaching and fitness training which I use today but after my English playing colleague, John Byrne, decided to leave because of personal problems I took the opportunity to return to England and join up with David Pleat who was then at Leicester. I was warned not to go, as the place was in turmoil and in retrospect it was not a good career move.'

Pleat did not last long at Leicester. When Brian Little took over, Hill was given a free transfer, and soon received an invitation from Rodney Marsh do some coaching in the USA for Tampa Bay Rowdies: 'Shortly after my arrival the other coaches were sacked and I was put in charge. We reached two National Championship finals and I was voted "Coach of the Year", but then I fell out with Marsh and returned to England and played for Chertsey while setting up a Soccer School in Harlesden.'

Hill flitted between coaching jobs on both sides of the Atlantic before the call came in 2000 to take charge at Kenilworth Road, a job he had craved for years. Unfortunately, that dream job turned sour, which was just as sad for his legions of supporters who genuinely wanted him to succeed.

~~~~~~~~~~

The dismantling of the 1988 Littlewoods Cup-winning side continued. Steve Foster joined his old Brighton teammate Brian Horton at Oxford, who he was now managing, and Rob Johnson signed for Leicester in part-exchange for tough midfielder Mick Kennedy.

Ricky Hill's move to France hit the buffers when Chairman David Evans – just before handing over the chair to long-time Hatters fan Brian Cole – demanded a fee of £50,000, even though Hill claimed he had been told by the manager he could leave on a free transfer. As Hill still had a year left on his Luton contract, there was not much he could do. As Le Havre would not pay, he allegedly settled the account out of his signing on fee.

Considering the financial restructuring that had taken place in the summer of 1989, it seems odd that a record outgoing fee of £600,000 was then paid out to Odense for Lars Elstrup, a Danish international forward. It was queried even more when – no sooner had the money been paid – the Hatters were reported as in dire straits again. The club's bankers refused any more directors' 'guarantees'. Cash injections from player sales or director involvement would from now on be the only acceptable currency.

Talismanic striker Mick Harford was on the long-term injured list, hence the reason for boosting the strike force. But when another forward was sold to balance the books – Roy Wegerle moving to QPR for £1 million – then you were back to square one.

No sooner was Harford restored than Elstrup needed cartilage surgery, keeping him out until the last few games of the season. Moreover, three central defenders all succumbed to injury within weeks of each other, leading to frantic requests to Manchester United to borrow former favourite Mal Donaghy. Danny Wilson and David Preece were just about holding the midfield together, but two men on their own could not stem the tide and it was not long before the team was staring relegation in the face.

With problems on the field, the Town did not want their dirty linen aired in public. After supporters started getting on the manager's back, a national tabloid quoted Chairman Brian Cole as saying that Ray Harford 'Lacked the charisma or the ability to relate to the fans in the right way'.

The upshot was Harford leaving 'by mutual consent', quickly followed by the chairman stepping down – none of which enhanced the image of the club with the footballing public at large.

Caretaker boss Terry Mancini oversaw a 1-4 capitulation at Brighton in the FA Cup, whereupon applications for the hot seat were considered. On the recommendation of director David Evans, the Town once again promoted from within, and appointed Jim Ryan.

Ryan's first game saw lowly Luton scrape a draw at table-topping Liverpool, with young Kurt Nogan scoring on his debut, and for a time the new manager conjured up enough points to lift the team out of the relegation spots. He had to do this, however, with no money to spend. When Mick Harford was sold to Derby for £480,000 – 'too good to turn down for a thirty-year-old with a history of injury' – the promised re-investment in the team did not materialise. The Board needed to spend the funds elsewhere.

The financial situation was now desperate, with the club losing money hand over fist on a weekly basis. A consortium consisting of director Ray Pinney and ex-chairman Denis Mortimer was all set to take over, but pulled out at the last minute. That scuppered Jim Ryan's hopes of securing Ronny Rosenthal, who promptly became a goalscoring sensation at Liverpool instead.

With the season drawing to a close, and Luton back in the bottom three, a three-page expose in the *Luton News* offered a frank and bleak assessment of the financial problems facing the club.

The Board was fighting a losing battle to keep the club in the top division. This was admitted by Chairman Roger Smith, who had taken over from Brian Cole. The cost of implementing the 'members-only' scheme had been considerable, and the envisaged increase in local support had not been forthcoming. Although some of this cost had been recouped by the continued commercial use of the artificial surface at Kenilworth Road, hidden costs, such as players' signing-on fees, meant that the club was still losing around £6,000 per week.

Smith admitted that the Board had backed a dream, effectively buying the Littlewoods Cup, back in 1988, and were paying for it now. Salaries for players and staff had escalated, necessary improvements to the inadequate Kenilworth Road ground had cost a small fortune, funds to fight the A505 relief road case had to be found, and ongoing investigative costs for possible relocation were still in progress.

Desperate times needed desperate measures, and unless a 'Mr Big' was prepared to inject funds, a cull of the playing and administrative staff could not be avoided over the summer.

All this was reported with the Hatters looking odds-on to lose the First Division place they had earned in 1982. There were only three games left to rescue the situation. That meant nine points to play for, but Luton were already six points adrift of safety. In other words, while the Town needed to start winning, those above them needed to lose.

The situation had been exacerbated by points tossed away over a disastrous Easter. Goals from ex-Hendon striker Iain Dowie put Luton 2-0 up against Everton, but no one was surprised when the Toffees levelled the scores. The Town then capitulated at Nottingham Forest, losing 0-3 to a team which had gone eight games without a victory.

Of the three remaining games, two were at home. First up were defending champions Arsenal. Jim Ryan had a simple message: win at all costs and hope that fourth-from-bottom Sheffield Wednesday would slip up. Dowie fired the Town into the lead after Arsenal full-back Nigel Winterburn failed to control the ball. Full-back Tim Breacker then surged down the wing, played a wall pass with Danny Wilson, and crossed low for Kingsley Black to convert – 2-0.

The players trooped off to learn that Sheffield Wednesday had lost 0-1 at QPR, narrowing the gap at the bottom to three points.

Wednesday were due to be play doomed Charlton at Selhurst Park, while the Town would host FA Cup finalists Crystal Palace. Charlton boss Lennie Lawrence threatened to field a team of kids, but following objections from the Town to the Football League he relented.

Palace had just confirmed their safety, and with one eye turned towards Wembley, decided to close the game down. It was tedious stuff, frustrating too, when Danny Wilson hit a post, and when Nigel Martin saved the follow-up from Welshman Jason Rees.

News filtered through that Wednesday were in front at Selhurst Park. Luton's breakthrough goal was timed at 89 minutes, six seconds, and went in off the shin of Iain Dowie.

The situation was now set for a last-day showdown. The Town were at Derby, while Sheffield Wednesday were at home to Nottingham Forest. The Hatters had to win and Wednesday had to lose, it was as simple as that.

Many thoughts crowded through the minds of Luton supporters. How could the Town win at Derby when they had won away only once all season? The Rams were safe from relegation and boasted Peter Shilton, Mark Wright, Dean Saunders and a certain Mick Harford in their side. Sheffield Wednesday had a fair home record, but would Forest manager Brian Clough allow any of his players to roll over?

Five thousand sleepless Luton supporters converged on the Baseball Ground on a gloriously sunny day to see the Town take the lead after only 66 seconds. Ignoring the set-piece routines drilled into him, Tim Breacker fired in a free-kick from thirty yards out. When Kingsley Black tucked away a Wilson cross after eighteen minutes – coupled with news that Forest were winning at Hillsborough – the impossible seemed possible.

But on this day of topsy-turvy emotions, Derby pulled back the two goals, through Wright and Paul Williams, and only brilliant goalkeeping from Alec Chamberlain prevented the Rams taking the lead by half-time.

Sixteen minutes from time, local boy Kingsley Black scored again, this time with his 'wrong' foot. The players then sensibly shut up shop. The abiding memory is of hard-man midfielder Mick Kennedy setting off on a jinking run to nowhere, ending up by the corner flag, where his bulk shielded the ball for a few more valuable seconds.

By the time the final whistle sounded, everyone knew that Wednesday had lost 0-3. Cue celebrations long into the night.

KENILWORTH ROAD HEROES: **Mal Donaghy**

Born in Belfast in September 1957, Malachy Donaghy made an early name for himself as a Gaelic footballer, and while at school represented County Antrim. After becoming a clerk with the Post Office, Association Football began to dominate his thoughts and it was not long before

Donaghy was playing for Larne in the Irish League. He quickly won three 'Player of the Month' awards in succession.

Honours came thick and fast. He was voted 'Newcomer of the Year' by the Northern Ireland Professional Footballers Association, and was outstanding in his first international at Under-21 level against the Irish Republic: 'I was picked to play for the Northern Ireland Under-21 team to play Eire in Dublin and was apparently watched by David Pleat,' recalled Mal. 'He was obviously impressed and put in a bid of around £20,000 for me, but the Larne manager Brian Halliday wanted considerably more.'

As mentioned earlier, Pleat waited for Halliday to go on holiday, then stepped in with a bid which was accepted by the Larne directors, who were under the impression that Donaghy had not re-signed for them and could have left for nothing. 'Halliday was not happy, to put it mildly,' said Mal. 'But I do see him now from time to time, and he does talk to me.'

Luton had snared 'one of the best players to leave Northern Ireland in years' for a song, and from under the noses of Celtic, who had previously invited him over for a week's trial, not to mention Wolves, Sheffield United and QPR. 'We think we have something special,' reported David Pleat at the time.

Donaghy was homesick at first, but lodged initially in Shaftesbury Road with landlady Mrs Haughney, who made him welcome. Making his debut at left-half in a friendly at Oxford, Donaghy scored what was to be a rare goal in a 2-2 draw.

Although the Town struggled after a bright start during that 1978-79 campaign, they went close to promotion in each of the next two seasons. It was therefore third time lucky when the championship was won in 1981-82. 'The team that won promotion,' says Donaghy, 'was a dream to play in and although we were always liable to let in goals, such was the cavalier nature of our play, we were always likely to score more. I must admit, as a defender, that a 1-0 win was always better than 5-4, but the crowd always seemed to prefer the latter.'

By this time, Donaghy was a regular in the Northern Ireland team, having made his debut against Scotland in May 1980. He went on to win 91 caps, with 58 of them earned during his time at Kenilworth Road. That constitutes a club record that will probably stand for all time. Many of his international appearances were made at left-back, a position he only played during his early days at Kenilworth Road. So which was his favourite position? 'I was always happy to play wherever I was picked, but if pushed I preferred to play in central defence, playing off the big, ugly centre-half. I also played in goal on several occasions during my time at Luton, moving back to replace Jake Findlay, which I didn't mind as my previous life as a Gaelic footballer taught me good hand and eye co-ordination.'

The games where Donaghy deputised as an emergency goalkeeper were at Cambridge (which the Town won), at Charlton (which was lost), at Liverpool (which was drawn), at Manchester United (lost), and at home to Bolton (won).

1982 was a good year for Mal Donaghy: his son, Ciaron, was born, the Hatters were promoted to the First Division and he appeared for Northern Ireland in the World Cup finals.

He went on to enjoy central defensive partnerships with Clive Goodyear, Paul Elliott, and an enduring one with Steve Foster which would see the Town to glory in the Littlewoods Cup final in 1988.

During his time at Kenilworth Road, Donaghy was largely injury free, no doubt down to playing alongside the big, ugly centre-half. In fact, in his first nine seasons he was ever-present in six, and missed only six games in total from the other three. It therefore came as a shock when he was stretchered off the week before the biggest game of all, against Arsenal:

'We were playing in the Mercantile Credit Centenary competition at Wembley against Manchester United and I went into an awkward tackle with Peter Davenport and badly injured an ankle amongst other things. I have nothing but praise for physiotherapist John Sheridan and club doctor Bill Berry who worked on me non-stop during the following week in order to try to get me fit for the big game. I did eventually make it although it was a close run thing as I was only passed fit on the day of the match.'

That win over Arsenal was undoubtedly the highlight of Donaghy's time at Kenilworth Road, and it seemed likely that the unflappable defender would spend the rest of his career with the club. It surprised many when, early in the following season, Alex Ferguson came in with a £650,000 bid to take the 31-year-old to Old Trafford:

'I agonised over the decision for two weeks, as I had enjoyed ten great years at Kenilworth Road and was happily settled in Luton. If it had been anyone else apart from Manchester United I would have said no, but I supported them as a kid and in fact my only visit to England before signing for Luton was a trip to Old Trafford. It was a great wrench but in the end I decided to go although I did not burn all my boats as I kept my house on in Luton.'

After 483 senior appearances for the Town, he then made 119 senior appearances over the next four seasons for Manchester United, including six in the European Cup-Winners' Cup, although he was a non-playing substitute when United beat Barcelona in the final.

In a twist to the tale, Donaghy returned to Luton in December 1989 – in the final days of Ray Harford's reign – as a loan player. He made five further appearances for the Town, up to the appointment of Jim Ryan to the hot seat. It was during this time that Donaghy was awarded a testimonial for his ten years' sterling service to the club. That was in January 1990, when the Town took on Ricky Hill's Le Havre at Kenilworth Road.

By the end of 1991-92 Donaghy's appearances at Old Trafford were becoming few and far between, as Gary Pallister established himself. A telephone call from Ian Porterfield gave him the opportunity to finish his career at Chelsea with a two-year contract with the Premiership club.

'It was an ideal move for me and I used to travel to training with Mick Harford who was also still living in the Luton area. In fact, the Luton connection went further than Mick and myself, as Paul Elliott, Mark Stein and Alec Chamberlain were also at Stamford Bridge at the time. I played in 78 first-team games for Chelsea over two seasons but could only make the bench for the FA Cup semi-final against Luton at Wembley in 1994. After retiring from the playing side in 1994, I had the opportunity to go to Southend, but did not really want to step down a level and I faded into the background a bit, waiting for the right opportunity to come up.'

When it came, it took Donaghy to a coaching position with the FA of Northern Ireland.

It is worth recalling that Donaghy's Luton career would have been over before it began if he had listened to the 'bloke behind me' in the Bobbers Stand. 'He will never make a footballer, he is too long striding' (whatever that meant) was the shout that went up every time Mal came out of defence with the ball.

Perhaps that is why some of us are born to play football and others are born to spectate!

~~~~~~~~~~~

No sooner was the 1989-90 season over than rumours spread again regarding a new purchaser for the club. This time they were true, and in May 1990 a London property developer, 43-year-old Peter Nelkin, and his 31-year-old business partner, David Kohler, bought 60 per cent of the club for a reported £1.8 million. Controversial ex-chairman David Evans resigned immediately, with three other directors leaving two months later. Nelkin admitted he was no 'Mr Big' but would apply good husbandry to all aspects of the club, which meant that manager Jim Ryan would still have little or nothing to spend.

Out went Danny Wilson to relegated Sheffield Wednesday for £200,000, with Mick Kennedy going to Stoke. Ex-manager John Moore returned to the coaching staff, and would keep an eye on the bright crop of youngsters on the Town's books. Jim Ryan had been taken on as a coach by Moore in 1986, and now the roles were reversed.

The 1990-91 season started well enough, considering the restraints Jim Ryan was under, and on 29th September a fully fit Lars Elstrup netted a hat-trick in a 3-1 win at Norwich which shot the Hatters up to sixth.

Then the rot set in. Tim Breacker – Supporters Club Player of the Year – was offloaded to West Ham for £600,000 to appease the bankers, who were not prepared to let the club exceed their £1 million overdraft facility.

KENILWORTH ROAD CLASSICS: **Luton v Derby** – 2-0
Barclays League Division One, 11th May 1991

On 9th March 1991 the Town won at Aston Villa to record their third win in four games. This constituted a dramatic upsurge in fortunes. With ten games to play they were in a comfortable thirteenth spot. Unfortunately, the remaining ten games turned into a nightmare. Two draws were all they got from the first seven of these. Record signing Lars Elstrup had gone off the boil, and Iain Dowie had been sold to West Ham for £480,000, the second reluctant player to become a Hammer in a matter of months. The Town were leading at Coventry and Sheffield United, but lost both games, went down at home to Norwich and Wimbledon after having much of the play, drew 0-0 at home to Tottenham with John Dreyer missing a penalty, and were three up at Chelsea, only for the Blues to pull level.

But someone was smiling on Luton. This season only two clubs, not the usual three, would be relegated, due to restructuring the size of the divisions. There were still two clubs below the Town – Sunderland and Derby – and both still had to come to Kenilworth Road. Sunderland arrived with only one previous away win, but they doubled that tally with a 2-1 victory. Manager Jim Ryan kept the players in the changing room for an hour after the game to vent his frustration.

The penultimate game was at Everton. The Town hid behind a defensive barricade, but still lost to a second-half strike from Tony Cottee.

Since winning at Kenilworth Road, Sunderland had drawn two home games and were level on points and goal-difference with Luton, who had the advantage of having scored more goals. The situation was now reasonably straightforward. The Town had to beat already doomed Derby, and hope that Sunderland did not run riot at Manchester City.

This was all very well, but the Hatters had lost the habit of winning. And although Derby were already down, they still had Peter Shilton, Mark Wright, Dean Saunders and Mick Harford to contend with. A season's best crowd of 12,889 turned up hoping for yet another great escape. They let out a collective roar when it was learned that Sunderland were a goal down, but the silence was deafening when that score was updated to show they had now gone 2-1 ahead. If the scores stayed as they were, Luton would be relegated.

The breakthrough came just before half-time when Jason Rees's free-kick skimmed off the top of Mick Harford's head straight into the net. Mick obviously had his heart, or rather his head, in the right place. Just after half-time a bout of head-tennis following David Preece's corner led to Lars Elstrup shooting past a wrong-footed Shilton. In the end the win was unnecessary, as Sunderland ended losing 2-3. Luton could have lost 0-1 and still stayed up.

LUTON: *Chamberlain, Beaumont, Dreyer, McDonough, Harvey, Rees (James), Pembridge, Preece, Black, Farrell (Nogan), Elstrup.*

DERBY: *Shilton, Sage, Wright, Patterson, Forsyth, Micklewhite, G Williams, P Williams (Hebberd), McMinn (Cross), Saunders, Harford.*

~~~~~~~~~~

Within minutes of Luton confirming their survival, rumours swept around the bars in the ground that Ryan was about to lose his job and be replaced by out-of-work ex-Town manager David Pleat. The gossip was confirmed in the next day's newspapers, and on Monday morning Ryan was dismissed. It appeared that Peter Nelkin did not approve of his style of management and David Kohler did not approve of his style of football. The decision to sack Ryan had been taken weeks earlier, but was not made public while the Town were still scrapping for their lives. The final straw, according to the gossip, was Ryan's refusal to allow Nelkin's wife and young daughter into the changing room prior to the Derby game.

So, David Pleat returned to the club he had left in 1986. He insisted on greater autonomy than his predecessor enjoyed, and also on bringing in his own assistant, Colin Murphy, which meant no place for coach John Faulkner.

Pleat hoped to persuade Lars Elstrup to sign a new contract, but the Danish international wanted to return to Odense, who were promptly told the fee would be around £500,000. Elstrup said he would work as a bank teller for six months, and then join his local club for nothing which, of course, mortified the Town. In the end a cut-price £250,000 secured his transfer, which did not particularly please anyone.

The fans' fury at the sacking of Ryan reverberated around Kenilworth Road throughout the summer. It prompted the resignation of Peter Nelkin after the threats got too personal for his liking. David Kohler, however, decided to ride out the storm.

KENILWORTH ROAD HEROES: **Brian Stein**

Born in South Africa in 1957, Brian Stein was brought to England aged seven as his family fled the apartheid regime. Although football was important to the young Stein it was only when his brother Edwin persuaded him to join his team, Sudbury Court, that he started to develop his skills:

'After playing for Sudbury Court, where I scored seventy goals in a season I was spotted by Edgware Town and combined turning out for them with a job as an Executive Officer for the local Health Board. We played against Dunstable and John Moore, who was with them at the time, rec-ommended me to Luton and it was only a short time later that Harry Haslam and David Pleat convinced me that my future lay at Kenilworth Road.'

Only weeks after joining the Town, Brian was thrown into the deep end when appearing at Old Trafford in a League Cup second replay against Manchester City. 'I always remember that on arrival at our hotel in the afternoon before the game we were told to get some sleep. I obviously could not because of the anticipation of my first big game but thought it strange that we should be expected to sleep when only weeks before my pre-match ritual was eating fish and chips.'

Brian made his league debut shortly afterwards, as substitute for Gary Heale in a 1-3 defeat at windswept Mansfield in November 1977: 'Skipper Alan West came in for some stick from Harry Haslam for playing into the wind in the first half and then seeing the wind change round at the inter-val,' he recalled.

Stein's first goals in a prolific Luton career were not long in coming, with two banged in during the 4-0 rout of Sheffield United over Christmas 1977. With Haslam replaced by David Pleat later that season, the team was gradually rebuilt and Brian Stein became a regular. Learning from that wily old pro, Bob Hatton, Brian hit ten goals in 1978-79 in a side that struggled to make an impact. The following season Stein was ever present but left the main goalscoring responsibilities to Hatton and winger David Moss, who was enjoying a purple patch at the time.

Bob Hatton left Kenilworth Road in 1980 and Stein top scored the fol-lowing season, which also saw his first hat-trick – in a 4-2 win at Bristol Rovers.

By now David Pleat's rebuilding was complete and Stein top scored again as the Town won the Division Two championship in 1982: 'The game that probably sticks out more than any other is the home win over Newcastle towards the end of the season. We were 0-2 down to a Magpies side that was making a late bid for promotion but we managed to fight back to win 3-2. I scored all three that day and, in the absence of regular penal-ty taker David Moss through injury, hit two of them from the spot.'

Unfortunately, after a tremendous start to the next season, when Brian scored thirteen goals in only eighteen appearances, he broke a bone in his foot at home to Manchester City and played only a bit part in the second half of the season: 'The games in the early part of 1982-83 were a joy to play in but after breaking my foot I attempted to come back too early and only played a few games in the second half of the season. I did, however, play in the final game at Manchester City, which we needed to win to stay up. We were all up for it and the sheer tension of the occasion meant that just about everyone was in tears in the changing room at the end of the game. An incredible experience.'

By 1985, with the acquisition of Steve Foster, Peter Nicholas, David Preece, and Mick Harford, the Town had a team to compare with the best in the country: 'With just a shade more luck I think we could have won the league around that period. Liverpool were not the team they were, the division was wide open and I certainly feel we had more ability than Everton. We all mixed socially and had a great team spirit.'

Possibly the best spearhead in the club's history was the pairing of Mick Harford and Brian Stein: 'Mick was great to play with and he has kindly said the same about me. We taught each other and had awareness of the other's abilities which meant that we were normally playing to our full potential.'

During the club's heyday – when the team finished in the top half for three seasons running – the goalscoring exploits of Brian Stein were crucial: Goals that stick in the mind include his hat-trick in the 7-0 demolition of Southampton, and the free-kick he scored against Liverpool in an FA Cup replay. That goal came when the anti-plastic lobby was generating a head of steam. Curling free-kicks were considered impossible to execute on that type of surface. This writer, who was sitting behind the Oak Road goal that evening, directly in line with the free-kick, can certainly confirm that it bent!

The Harford-Stein partnership had its greatest day on 24th April 1988 against Arsenal. The Hatters had already lost at Wembley that season, to Reading in the Simod Cup, and might have made three appearances at the Twin Towers in one season, but for losing an FA Cup semi-final to Wimbledon.

Brian had played a major part in getting the Town to Wembley, scoring the all-important goal at Ipswich in round four, and netting in both legs of the semi-final against Oxford: 'The day before the big game we lost Darron McDonough through injury, which meant that teenager Kingsley Black was included. Manager Ray Harford gambled on Ricky Hill and David Preece, who had both suffered from long-term injuries and were hardly match fit, and when you remember that I was just coming back from a broken arm we were hardly favourites.'

Delicate arm or not, Brian scored twice, with the Hatters' winner coming in the final minute: 'We hardly gave them a kick in the first half but in the second period they came on strongly as we began to tire. When Arsenal were awarded the penalty, which Rocky [Rocastle] later admitted he was embarrassed about, I thought we were in for another Reading-type result but we fought back after Andy Dibble's spot-kick save and went on to deservedly win the game.'

It was a surprise when Brian was allowed to leave at the end of that season, considering that manager Ray Harford called him 'The best finisher I have seen in all my time in football'. Although Brian enjoyed his time in France, his appearances were cut short by a knee injury.

With David Pleat re-installed, the call to return came in 1991, which Brian accepted: 'The 1991-92 season was a major disappointment for me with the club relegated from the top flight. I think there were about eight games where we dropped points by conceding a goal in the final minute and I still feel we were good enough to stay up.'

After a period in non-League football Brian returned to Kenilworth Road once more, and at the time of publication of this book he was manager Mike Newell's assistant. Brian had been encouraged by Bob Hatton to follow his example and move on every couple of years. Mercifully, he did not heed that advice. If he had, the Luton supporters would not have been privileged to witness the most clinical finisher the club had ever seen in almost 500 first-team appearances.

~~~~~~~~~~~

Kenilworth Road was also about to undergo radical changes in the summer of 1991, with the return of grass, away fans, the building of the New Stand and the installation of seats in the lower half of the Kenilworth Road end. The club had bowed to pressure from both the Football League and the Football Association to rip up the artificial surface, and although a compensation package was agreed, which virtually paid for the relaying of grass, it could not hope to compensate for the loss of a facility that could be used 365 days a year.

When first laid in 1985, the visiting London press could find no real fault with it. It was only when Messrs Dalglish and Kendall, the managers of Liverpool and Everton, started moaning, that a groundswell of ill-will started to build up. The Town's home record was no better on plastic than it had been before. Nor had any fixtures been postponed in its six-year existence.

The 'members only scheme', or 'away fans ban', depending on your view, was certainly more controversial, and when combined with the artificial surface, made Luton Town the most reviled club in the country. The Millwall riot confirmed the justification for banning away fans. Regrettably, the high-profile Luton chairman and future Tory MP David Evans had the backing of Prime Minister Margaret Thatcher at a time when football in general was at it lowest ebb. It would, rightly or wrongly, be easy to deduce – as many did – that the scheme had been politically motivated.

The main dissenters were not football supporters, otherwise they would have seen that, after the first three months of rigorous adherence to the ban, it was gradually relaxed by the club. By 1991 away fans were being admitted, albeit not in huge numbers. The main purpose of the original decision had been achieved, inasmuch as hordes of yobs following the big-city clubs were no longer able to take a day out in the country and plague Luton Town.

The Hillsborough disaster of 1989, and the subsequent Taylor Report proposing all-seater stadia, meant that football had to change its ways. In these new circumstances, the need for a 'Luton Town' model was no longer needed. It had been a brave experiment but it had had its day.

From 1991-92, away supporters would now be seated in the Oak Road end, which meant displacing the Luton supporters from that area a second time. They would have to choose between the 715-seat capacity New Stand, or the new seats at the Kenilworth Road End, but for some it was one move too many.

Pleat used the Elstrup money on buying Phil Gray from Tottenham, and welcomed back Brian Stein after his three years in France. Nevertheless, the new campaign started dreadfully. The team went over 400 minutes before scoring a goal and six games before recording a win. The Hatters bowed to the inevitable and sold Kingsley Black to Nottingham Forest for £1.5 million, which may have helped the bank balance but did little to appease the supporters who could foresee a relegation struggle even earlier than usual.

As part of the Black deal, Lee Glover came on loan from Forest, only to be injured on his debut. Steve Thompson then arrived from Bolton for £180,000, but left after five games, which was all it took to confirm he was not up to First Division football. Trevor Peake signed from Coventry for £100,000, having just starred in a 5-0 thrashing of Luton by the Sky Blues.

KENILWORTH ROAD CLASSICS: **Luton v Oldham** – 2-1

Barclays League Division One, 14th September 1991

Pleat had talked about the need for a 'Mick Harford' type of player to lead the attack, and it therefore came as no surprise when £325,000 was spent on the best Harford type in the business ... Mick himself. After leaving Luton for Derby he had suffered relegation and was keen for the chance to show his skills at the top once more.

Harford's second coming earned a rapturous reception by the crowd prior to kick-off against promoted Oldham. But one swallow does not make a summer, and one man – even Mick Harford – could not make a team. The Town were forced on the back foot to repel the Latics strike-force of Ian Marshall and Graeme Sharp, but on 52 minutes Oldham took the lead. Neither Harford or anyone else could make any headway until Pleat made a double substitution. Paul Telfer and Kurt Nogan came on for Brian Stein and Darron McDonough. The fresh youngsters helped turn the game towards the Oldham goal, but with five minutes left the visitors still seemed likely to earn their third win in a row.

Nogan then crossed low for Harford – who had got in front of his marker – to poke in. For his party-trick Harford then performed an over-head kick into the roof of the net in injury-time to secure an unlikely win.

Pleat said afterwards, 'I have to be mean with Luton's money and I think I paid about £75,000 over the odds for a man of 32, but I knew what Mick had to offer and what he was really worth to us.'

LUTON: Chamberlain, Jackson, Rodger, Peake, McDonough (Telfer), Dreyer, Pembridge, Thompson, Preece, Stein (Nogan), Harford.

OLDHAM: Hallworth, Fleming, Barrett, Kilcline, Halle, Adams, Milligan, Henry, Holden, Sharp, Marshall (Ritchie).

~~~~~~~~~~~

Clearly, a 32-year-old Harford could not carry the team on his own. Pleat's other signings were mainly of the bargain basement variety, and frankly not good enough.

The victory over Oldham proved to be a flash in the pan. The next eleven games brought just four more points, and not surprisingly Luton were stranded at the bottom of the table. The supporters obviously felt the team was beyond redemption, because the visit of Coventry on 20th December – the first of three home games in a row – saw only 7,533 both-er to turn up.

On a cold night, those present saw a Coventry team that were so awful that it was hard to imagine how they had thrashed Luton 5-0 earlier in the campaign. The score might easily have been reversed, yet all the Hatters had to show for their total dominance was Harford's 55th-minute goal. But at least it brought three points.

Next up were champions Arsenal on Boxing Day. The all-ticket crowd of 12,655 was the highest of the season so far. With the game entering its final quarter, Pleat gambled by sending on a young recruit from Leicester, Scott Oakes. Within minutes Oakes' long diagonal pass was met on the vol-ley by Harford, and the ball whistled past David Seaman. With Trevor Peake shackling new scoring sensation Ian Wright, Luton held out for another unexpected three points. 'We were rubbish,' said Arsenal manager George Graham. The Town had simply not allowed them to play the way they wanted.

Two days later the fans returned to Kenilworth Road with a spring in their step. Chelsea – together with their most famous supporter, Prime Minister John Major – were beaten by a free-kick routine involving David Preece, Paul Telfer and Mark Pembridge, which left full-back Richard Harvey with a clear sight of goal from 25 yards. Shortly afterwards Pembridge was pulled down by goalkeeper Dave Beasant, and after heated

Chelsea protests, John Dreyer – with his familiar heart-stopping two-step run-up – slotted the ball home.

Under newly announced rule changes, Beasant should have been sent off, but he escaped with a caution. His teammate Tommy Boyd, though, was not so lucky when, with fifteen minutes left, he chopped down Telfer in the area when he was clear on goal and was red-carded. Instead of Dreyer taking the kick, Harford stepped up instead. Apparently, during the interval, Pleat – never easy with Dreyer's style – had instructed Harford to take any more penalties. One wonders how Pleat felt when Harford blazed his kick against the bar. At least the miss was not expensive.

Nine points from nine, three clean sheets, and off the bottom of the table. Things were looking up, but Pleat sounded a note of caution, pointing out that some tough away games loomed on the horizon. With only two points picked up on Luton's travels he was right to be wary.

After a 1-1 draw at Nottingham Forest, a last-minute killer at Liverpool condemned the Town to a 1-2 defeat. Last-gasp goals on the road became the bane of Luton's life that season. They totted up to ten dropped points by the end of a campaign where no away victories were recorded.

Pleat raised £400,000 when selling four players – David Beaumont, Sean Farrell, Graham Rodger and Darron McDonough – but when he tried to buy on-loan goalkeeper Steve Sutton he was blocked by the Board. The supporters, who approved of Sutton, probably interpreted this as the white flag being raised by directors unable to contemplate yet another season of financial struggle in the top division.

The Town's home form kept the campaign alive, however, and the team travelled to relegated Notts County on the final day knowing that a win – coupled with a Coventry defeat at Aston Villa – would mean escape from the jaws of disaster for the fourth season in a row. Some 5,000 Luton supporters were at Meadow Lane to see Julian James give the Town a 1-0 interval lead. In the second half future Hatter Rob Matthews netted twice to send the Town down. It was doubly galling to hear that Coventry had lost 0-2 at Aston Villa.

The Town had enjoyed ten seasons among England's elite, yet all but three of those seasons had been a struggle to survive. Still, it was fun while it lasted. Ironically, the television riches of the Premier League were about to be unleashed in 1992-93 and – had they stayed up – Luton's portion might have staved off relegation for a little longer. The reality, though, was that the Hatters were back in Division Two, which had been their home for most of their Football League career. Perversely, Division Two was about to be renamed Division One. All very puzzling!

Facing up to the new reality, David Pleat sold Welsh midfielder Mark Pembridge to Derby for £1.25 million. It galled Pleat that the lad should be sold to a club in the same division, but the Rams had money while the Town needed some. Pleat spent £160,000 of the proceeds (the figure set by tribunal) on Steve Claridge from Cambridge.

Just as the 1992-93 season was about to start, Chelsea's £300,000 bid for 33-year-old Mick Harford was accepted. Pleat agreed that he could hardly block the player's right to return to the top level, but bemoaned the timing.

Losing had become a habit, whatever the division, and the Town went six games before picking up a win bonus. The 2-1 victory at Brentford was the first away win for eighteen months, but was scant consolation as the Town were playing second fiddle at home to visitors who worked out that playing deep and attacking on the break worked wonders. It was not until late November that a home win was recorded, by which time Claridge had been sold back to Cambridge. The Town had been confronted by a large VAT bill which needed paying. More bad news came in the shape of a fatal road accident involving youngsters Paul Telfer and Darren Salton, which left the latter's career in tatters. 'We did it for Darren,' said David Preece after the televised home win over Watford.

Club owner and Managing Director David Kohler courted unpopularity in the eyes of many Luton supporters, who blamed relegation on his tight control of the purse strings. Now, it looked possible that one relegation could be followed by another, as had happened in the 1960s.

Kohler professed to be willing to sell his shareholding, but whenever potential buyers came forward the deals always foundered. Either the purchasers lacked the requisite funds or too many strings were attached by the seller. It depended on whose perspective you took, but for the foreseeable future David Kohler remained in charge and the fans' protests got louder and stronger.

David Pleat maintained a dignified silence. After the Town hit rock bottom in late January, the team suddenly went seven games without conceding a goal to equal a record set in 1923. With goals hard to come by, Pleat brought in Luton-born Kerry Dixon on loan. Rejected by Pleat as a youngster, Dixon had made a name for himself with Chelsea, and won England caps to boot, but a recent big-money move to Southampton had turned sour and the Saints were happy to offload him. Phil Gray and Kerry Dixon formed a potent partnership, with Gray scoring in six consecutive games, the best since Joe Payne managed seven in 1936.

With the season drawing to a close, a vital home win over promotion chasing West Ham, plus draws at Sunderland and Derby, had probably done enough to keeper Luton up. Only defeat at Southend on the final day, plus a freak sequence of results elsewhere, could have sent them down. Over 2,000 nervous supporters converged on Roots Hall to see a display of pace and power from Stan Collymore seal the points for the home side, who needed the win more than Luton did. The freak sequence of results elsewhere did not materialise, leaving both sides safe and jubilant at the final whistle.

The summer of 1993 was subdued. The supporters were not surprised to see Phil Gray sold to Sunderland for £800,000, as the club desperately needed the money.

The 1993-94 season opened with a heartening home win over Watford, but then four straight defeats left the fans calling for the head of David Kohler once more. With the introduction of Paul Dickov and Alan Harper, on loan from Arsenal and Everton respectively, and the emergence of teenager John Hartson, the tide slowly turned.

Kerry Dixon, who had been 'borrowed' for eight months, was finally given a free transfer by Southampton, who wrote off the £575,000 they had paid Chelsea in 1992. Dixon celebrated his new contract with a hat-trick against Stoke in a 6-2 home win, after the Potters had been 2-0 up.

Another consortium offered to buy out David Kohler, but after eight weeks of accusation and counter accusation, the deal fell through. In the meantime, Luton supporters and local businessmen Chris Green and Cliff Bassett joined the Board and injected funds. They took their places in time to witness a goal that rivalled that scored by Graham French against Mansfield in 1968. Against Derby on 22nd January 1994, Scott Oakes took possession fifteen yards inside his own half, accelerated through the Rams defence, shrugging off tackles, before firing in a shot on the run. A special goal that earned the Town a priceless 2-1 win.

For the first time in six years the Town enjoyed an extended run in the FA Cup which took them through to the semi-final stage. The run was, however, almost over before it started. Southend missed several first-half chances at Kenilworth Road, and were punished by Paul Telfer's second-half strike, which set up a money-making tie at Premier League Newcastle. Tony Thorpe, on his full Hatters debut, fired a 25-yard shot into the top corner. Although the Magpies levelled through a Peter Beardsley penalty, they were destined for a replay. Kenilworth Road was rocking when young Hartson, deputising for the injured Dixon, coolly rounded Mike Hooper in the Newcastle goal. Scott Oakes fired a second near the end to seal a mem-orable evening.

Next up were Cardiff, where in a belligerent atmosphere goals from Oakes and David Preece secured a 2-1 win. The crowd scenes afterwards were the subject of much recrimination over the following weeks, but most Luton supporters were just grateful to leave Wales in one piece.

The Hatters' allocation of 4,000 tickets for the quarter-final at West Ham was quickly snapped up. Luton strung five players across the middle to keep the Hammers at bay for ninety minutes. A full-house of 13,166 gathered at Kenilworth Road for the replay, and were treated to a thriller that swung end to end from the first minute to the last. Hammers keeper Ludek Miklosko tipped a Kerry Dixon header onto the bar and dived bravely to foil Scott Oakes, only for the Hammers' Martin Allen to break away to score after half an hour. For the first time in the competition Luton were behind, but not for long, as Oakes hammered in a right-foot-er after being set up by Preece and Dixon. Just after the interval Oakes took advantage of a chest-down by Dixon to fire the Hatters ahead. West Ham levelled at 2-2 through Ian Bishop, but then Hammers captain Steve Potts lost control on the halfway line. Oakes scampered down the pitch, drew the goalkeeper, and fired home for his hat-trick. At the end Oakes was chaired off the pitch for his performance – indeed the game of his life.

The Football Association decreed that both semi-finals would be staged at Wembley, which gave Luton supporters an unexpected chance to re-visit the Twin Towers. Some 26,000 of them swelled the crowd to 59,989 to see if the Town could overcome Chelsea.

Despite Kerry Dixon trying to put one over his old side, the Town were unable to deal with Tony Cascarino in the air and eventually lost 0-2 in a performance that had few plusses.

On the previous Saturday, Luton had beaten Peterborough 2-0 at home, which was hoped to have put paid to relegation fears. Unfortunately, the semi-final defeat prefaced a run of five straight losses without a goal being scored and suddenly alarm bells were ringing. Home draws with Millwall and Southend arrested the slide, but a win over fellow strugglers West Brom was vital because the final two games were at Bolton and Stoke.

KENILWORTH ROAD CLASSICS: **Luton v West Brom** – 3-2

Endsleigh Division One, 3rd May 1994

The final home game of a long season was a genuine 'six-pointer' with both sides needing to win to avoid the drop to the third tier. The season's biggest league crowd of 10,053 were met by a heavily watered pitch, by order of David Pleat, which had standing puddles on it. The supporters behind the Kenilworth Road goal were in sombre mood, as the last remaining standing section was to be converted to seating over the summer at a cost of £211,000.

The Town had only one goal to show for their first-half dominance, a twenty-yard effort from David Preece. The corner count was 11-0 in the Town's favour at the interval, but as was feared, West Brom came out fired up and levelled through Bob Taylor, who surged past John Dreyer and Trevor Peake before firing home. On the hour, Baggies defender Daryl Burgess was stretchered off with concussion after colliding with Luton goalkeeper Juergen Sommer, who also had to depart soon after. Albion keeper Stuart Naylor then broke a cheekbone after a clash with John Hartson. Substitute keeper Tony Lange's first task was to pick the ball out of the net after Julian James headed in from a corner by Ceri Hughes. A sweet first-timer by Hartson made it 3-1, only for Kevin Donovan to drive a shot against the post and Lee Ashcroft to hammer in the rebound.

The game ignited in the sixth minute of injury-time when the Town's Mitchell Thomas and West Brom's Gary Strodder were dismissed for fighting. Seconds later David Pleat was beaming, while West Brom chairman Trevor Summers threatened to report the Town to the Football League for over-watering the pitch. It proved to be an empty threat as West Brom won at Portsmouth on the final day to save themselves from the drop.

LUTON: *Sommer (Petterson), James, Peake, Dreyer, Thomas, Telfer, Harper, Preece, Hughes, Oakes (Thorpe), Hartson.*

WEST BROM: *Naylor (Lange), Parsley, Strodder, Burgess (Mellon), Darton, McNally, Donovan, Hamilton, Smith, Ashcroft, Taylor.*

~~~~~~~~~~

A relieved Pleat knew his younger players would be stronger and wiser in the coming 1994-95 season, and genuinely felt that the Town might finish up among the promotion or play-off places. He tried to bring in Crewe's Tony Naylor to add fire-power up front, but the player preferred to sign for Port Vale. Pleat eventually settled for speedy Dwight Marshall from Plymouth, at a fee of £150,000.

John Dreyer, a regular in the side for six years, moved to Stoke on a technical free transfer. In those immediate pre-Bosman days, if a player was offered reduced terms on a new contract, he was entitled to seek employment elsewhere. Pleat was not prepared to renew Dreyer's contract on identical terms – which would have enabled the Town to retain his registration – and so the big defender affectionately known as 'Tumble' departed. He was the second player to leave Kenilworth Road under these circumstances, with goalkeeper Alec Chamberlain moving to Sunderland the year before.

For once the Town were never in fear of relegation, and until Christmas harboured thoughts of the play-offs. It was a frustrating period, because fast, clever forwards like Scott Oakes and Dwight Marshall could catch home teams on the break, whereas at Kenilworth Road they were shackled by massed defences. Wins at Port Vale, Watford, Stoke – where Dreyer had a stinker against his old mates – Sheffield United, Wolves and Swindon pushed the club up to fifth. That they were not higher was due to winning only twice at home in the same period.

Without warning, bids started to appear for nineteen-year-old John Hartson. When Southampton offered £1.1 million plus ex-Town favourite

Iain Dowie they sparked an unseemly scramble that left David Pleat and the Board uncertain what to do. The club did not need to sell Hartson, so put a massive £2.5 million price tag on his head in the hope of flushing out the serious bidders. It worked, with Arsenal swiftly agreeing the figure to create a record price for a teenager and, of course, a record incoming fee for the Hatters. Much of the credit went to the Town's scout in South Wales, Cyril Beech, who was worth his weight in gold, having unearthed Mark Pembridge, Jason Rees, Ceri Hughes and now Hartson.

Pleat was promised some of the Hartson money but had difficulty in spending it. As soon as other clubs sensed that Moneybags Luton were sniffing around, the price went up, and Pleat had never been in the habit of throwing money around. Eventually he spent modestly, bringing in Rob Matthews – whose goals for Notts County had relegated the Town in 1992 – and the much-travelled John Taylor.

Having now solved the problem of winning at home, but at a cost of losing away, the team settled for mid-table obscurity. It was the first time since 1988 that Luton were not fighting a relegation battle, but it was worrying that the Hatters did not win any of their last six games and lost the last four.

'If you will it, it is no dream' was a quote attributed to Theodore Herzl that appeared in the brochure announcing plans for the Kohlerdome. The Kohlerdome, self-evidently the brainchild of David Kohler, would be a 20,000 all-seater covered stadium built on land adjacent to Junction 10 of the M1 motorway. The stadium, which would utilise the best ideas behind the BC Place Stadium in Vancouver and the Pontiac Silverdome in Chicago, was to have a revolutionary moveable grass pitch whereby it could be 'hovered' out in strips in six hours. This would enable the grass to grow naturally outside and, more importantly, allow the stadium to be multi-functional throughout the year. Planning application for the £30 million scheme was lodged with Luton Borough Council, even though Kohler did not own the land. It was part of the Luton Hoo estate and had already been promised to a rival developer, Wyncote Developments.

Before Kohler had time to counter the inevitable objections to his plans, he needed to find a new manager. David Pleat had joined up with Premiership Sheffield Wednesday. Although Tottenham had approached Pleat the previous season for the post of 'general manager', he was not yet ready to quit the training pitch. The Sheffield Wednesday job enabled him to enjoy fuller control as well as the opportunity to manage at the top level once more. Kohler was not prepared to accept the compensation on offer from the Owls. Pleat was still under contract and Kohler threatened injunctions to block his departure. Kohler was, he said, standing up for small clubs, who were always being bullied by the big boys.

The matter eventually went to tribunal, where it was determined that the Town receive £150,000 plus costs. This was a far cry from the £1 million originally demanded by Kohler, but substantially more than the £50,000 offered by Wednesday.

Despite receiving over forty applications for the vacant manager's position, the Town decided to promote youth team coach Terry Westley, who in turn brought in Mick McGiven as his assistant.

It was to be a summer of tribunals. Coventry were made to pay £1.15 million for Paul Telfer, while the Town were forced to part with £750,000 for Burnley centre-half Steve Davis. A tribunal also decided that David Preece could join Derby after it was established that the new contract on offer was not as good as his old one. Once again, an aggrieved David Kohler threatened to take the matter to civil court, but whatever the rights and wrongs, the clever midfielder has never been adequately replaced. Luton did eventually extract £75,000 from the Rams.

With money from the sale of Hartson and Telfer, Terry Westley enjoyed something denied to most of his predecessors – the freedom to buy. In addition to Davis, Westley recruited Gavin Johnson, Graham Alexander, David Oldfield, Darren Patterson and Bulgarian international Bontcho Guentchev, but despite the outlay the team was slow out of the traps in 1995-96, with only one win from the first nine games.

Injuries to Scott Oakes, John Taylor and new signing Patterson did not help, but it was not long before the supporters started calling for Westley's head. The team was disjointed and tactically naïve, and the signing of giant American goalkeeper Ian Feuer, plus Danes Johnny Vilstrup and Vidar Riseth for a combined fee of £875,000, only muddied the waters as the Town stumbled from crisis to crisis.

David Kohler was frustrated to be informed that the Department of the Environment had ordered a planning enquiry for the Kohlerdome, which was not likely to be heard until the summer of 1996. Kohler responded by putting his club shareholding up for sale at £3 million, and entered into talks with Milton Keynes Borough Council to see if they would be interested in his Kohlerdome.

After a woeful 0-4 defeat at Portsmouth in mid-December, the Town made the predictable decision to dispense with Westley and McGiven 'by mutual consent' and quickly recruited the ex-Bradford City, Middlesbrough and Charlton boss Lennie Lawrence. A safe pair of hands was needed.

As often happens when a new man takes charge, the players are anxious to impress and start winning, which must always make the previous incumbent scratch his head. Discounting a 1-7 mauling at Grimsby in the FA Cup, the Town went unbeaten in eight league games, which pushed them up to nineteenth, clear of the bottom four. The spark was undoubtedly generated by the speedy Dwight Marshall, but when he broke his ankle at Sunderland in late February, the goals stopped and the defeats started.

Lawrence was desperate for another pacy forward, and after baulking at paying £100,000 on Stevenage forward Barry Hayles, paid out £250,000 to Charlton for Kim Grant. Also arriving on loan were Paul Wilkinson and Graeme Tomlinson. The former broke a toe in his third game, and the latter broke a leg on his full debut. Clearly, this was not destined to be the Hatters' year.

After a 1-2 home defeat to Stoke, with both Potters goals coming in the closing minutes, everyone seemed to accept the inevitable relegation to a division last seen in 1969-70. It had been an awful campaign and considering that £2.5 million had been spent on players, an expensive one. Although some players had contractual clauses reducing their wages in the event of relegation, a cull was still required. Expensive imports Vilstrup and Riseth were allowed to leave, while Scott Oakes rejoined David Pleat at Sheffield Wednesday in exchange for £700,000 in an attempt to kick-start his career.

With everyone at Kenilworth Road expecting immediate promotion, the 1996-97 season started with three defeats, the last of which – a 0-5 thumping at Bristol City – saw Lennie Lawrence make a public apology for the performance.

Once the Town had familiarised themselves with their new surroundings they slowly climbed the table. They scaled the summit after a 6-0 home thrashing of Crewe and a 1-0 win at Millwall just before Christmas. Tony Thorpe had netted fourteen goals at this, the halfway stage, revelling in his new favoured position.

A cold snap meant the Town went from Boxing Day until 18th January without a league game. When normal service was restored, the players seemed rusty. Injuries to key players also took their toll and it was not until late February, when Preston were seen off 5-1 at Kenilworth Road, that the fans could say that the Town were approaching their pre-Christmas best.

KENILWORTH ROAD CLASSICS: **Luton v Brentford** – 1-0

Nationwide Division Two, 21st March 1997

Despite only two wins from eleven games since the turn of the year, the Town still clung on to second place. Brentford had been consistent until late February, but had then wobbled, having gone four winless games prior to this one. But they were still top. A win for the Town would see the clubs change positions, and such was the interest that it was switched to a Friday night to accommodate live coverage by Sky TV.

The crowd numbered 8,680, and they quickly saw why Brentford boasted the best away record in the division – with nine wins to their credit.

Marcus Bent's shot rebounded off the bar as they took early control. With the game about to enter its final quarter, Tony Thorpe – with twenty league goals already – turned inside his marker, Jamie Bates, before firing in a shot past Luton-born Kevin Dearden in the Bees goal.

There was time for Brentford's Joe Omigie to add to his pair of glaring first-half misses, but the Town hung on to reclaim top spot. A relieved Lennie Lawrence said: 'We were under the cosh early on, but got to grips and pushed them back in the second half. Tony Thorpe got us a goal out of nothing and then we battled away to the end. Give credit to Brentford, because they showed why they had the best away record in the league.'

LUTON: *Feuer, James, Thomas, Waddock, Davis, Johnson, Hughes, Alexander, Oldfield, Thorpe (Grant), Showler (McLaren).*

BRENTFORD: *Dearden, Hutchings, Ashby, Bates, Anderson, Bent (Dennis), Smith, McGhee, Asaba, Taylor, Omigie.*

~~~~~~~~~~

Victory over Brentford turned out to be a high spot. A sequence of frustrating home draws, plus a 2-3 defeat at Walsall, saw Luton drop to third by the end of the campaign, behind Bury and Stockport. The Town (and Brentford) now had to face the lottery of the play-offs..

KENILWORTH ROAD CLASSICS: **Luton v Crewe** – 2-2

Nationwide Division Two, Play-Off semi-final second leg, 14th May 1997
The Hatters' semi-final opponents were Crewe, who had somehow squeezed into sixth spot despite losing seventeen games, one of them 0-6 at Kenilworth Road. The first leg was at Gresty Road on a Sunday afternoon. This marked Crewe's fifth appearance in the play-offs in six seasons, so they were presumably used to the pressures, but the Town got first blood when David Oldfield netted from close range after three minutes to silence the capacity crowd of 5,467.

Then things started to go wrong. Already without the injured Ceri Hughes and Marvin Johnson, the Town were further depleted when Gary Waddock had to limp off after eight minutes. Crewe levelled after 52 minutes, whereupon Julian James – who had lost possession for the goal – got sent off for a second bookable offence. A disjointed and depleted Town then conceded a second goal, to Colin Little. In truth, the Hatters were lucky to get away with only a 1-2 defeat, as Dele Adebola hit a post when it seemed easier to score.

Lennie Lawrence knew that his team had got out of jail and that they could not play any worse in the second leg three days later. When Oldfield put the Hatters two up inside half an hour, the damage appeared to have been rectified. Unfortunately, Crewe hit back at once and Little pounced after Ian Feuer could only parry Adebola's shot.

With the game poised at 3-3 on aggregate, it was Crewe who stepped up a gear, and few Luton supporters had any complaints when Alex levelled on the night through Shaun Smith. Crewe held on to their aggregate lead and Lawrence admitted afterwards that the Hatters had been beaten by the better side over two legs. Crewe beat Brentford in the final at Wembley to win promotion to Division One for the first time in their long history.

LUTON: Feuer, Patterson, Thomas, Waddock (Fotiadis), Davis, Marvin Johnson, McLaren, Alexander, Oldfield, Thorpe, Showler (Marshall).

CREWE: Kearton, Unsworth (Johnson), Smith, Westwood, Macauley, Charnock, Whalley, Little, Rivers (Garvey), Murphy (Lightfoot), Adebola.

~~~~~~~~~~~

The one redeeming feature of the season was John Moore's youth team, which reached the semi-finals of the FA Youth Cup before going out to a star-studded Leeds. This was the furthest the Town had gone in the competition since 1983, when Moore's side were beaten by Norwich.

In view of their narrow miss, one bookmaker made the Town 8-1 favourites to win the title in 1997-98, and it was reported that one fan had placed £6,000 at those odds, such was the optimism running through the streets of the town.

Lennie Lawrence, however, knew that he had a tough job to galvanise the players, especially as the previous season's reasonable luck on the injury front was unlikely to repeat itself. In which case, his small squad would be found wanting. The departure of teenager Matthew Upson to Arsenal for an initial £1 million was not such a blow, as the young defender had only made one appearance for the Hatters, and that as substitute. As Luton now had no financial need to sell anyone else, it was a disappointment when Welsh international Ceri Hughes departed to Wimbledon for £400,000, plus extra based on appearances.

No sooner had the season started than the feared injury crisis struck, the like of which had not been seen for many years, leaving the team weakened throughout most of the autumn. At Bristol City in late September 1997 matters were so bad that none of the three named substitutes had played a league game between them, and the subsequent 0-3 defeat was even interpreted as a moral victory.

The supporters were less forgiving the following week, though, as table-topping Watford strolled into a four-goal lead inside half an hour. Lennie Lawrence came in for fearful stick from the home crowd, and at one stage the match looked like it would boil over. It probably would have, had the Hornets decided to chase more goals.

When Trevor Peake came off the substitutes' bench during the visit of Wrexham in September, he became the oldest league player in the club's history, beating the previous record set by Dally Duncan in 1947. But he was needed. With Luton spending £400,000 on re-signing Phil Gray from Fortuna Sittard, then seeing him crocked after just a few games, everyone wondered how many mirrors had been broken. The crisis did, of course, in the end subside, but the poor early results left the team playing catch-up. Try as they might, they could not quite lift themselves clear of the relegation positions.

Four consecutive home defeats in November – among them Luton's first FA Cup first-round exit since 1929 – saw terrace disquiet threaten to explode at the prospect of sinking back to the football basement. Three straight wins over Christmas offered some comfort, but not for long, as they ushered in four more rapid defeats. Lennie Lawrence was at his wits end, as he could not put his finger on the team's failings. The defence was all at sea one week, and the forwards firing blanks the next. He later admitted that this was the most stressful time in the whole of his long managerial career.

The turning point can be traced to the visit to Watford in mid-February. Watford were streaking away with the division and were seeking a rare double over the Town. After taking the lead just after the interval, they felt that the Hatters would self-destruct, but instead Luton bagged an equaliser just in time from an unlikely saviour – Marvin Johnson.

That point against the leaders was followed by another, this time at home to second-placed Bristol City. Results and performances were now pointing in the right direction, but just as light appeared at the end of the tunnel it was extinguished when top scorer Tony Thorpe was sold to Fulham for £800,000. Chairman Kohler cited continuing financial problems with the Town still losing £40,000 a week.

Despite this, goals in the last ten minutes from Andrew Fotiadis and Sean Evers earned a valuable victory at fellow strugglers Plymouth in the next game and pushed the Town up to nineteenth.

The need for an accomplished striker soon became acutely apparent, with a 0-1 defeat at Preston, followed by draws at home to Wycombe and at Burnley. In all three games the Hatters dominated possession, but the outcome was to drop into the bottom four yet again. Desperate for a loan signing, as transfer deadline-day approached, Lawrence tried to get Bradley Allen of Charlton and Gerry Creaney, who was out of favour at Manchester City, but neither could be enticed from their respective clubs. With the Town dropping to 23rd, following a 2-2 home draw against Grimsby, ex-Town boss David Pleat, now Director of Football at Tottenham, came up with a solution.

Pleat suggested that Spurs' twenty-year-old striker Rory Allen was exactly what Luton needed. The downside was that Allen had managed barely two reserve games since ankle surgery the previous summer, and his general fitness was therefore of some concern. In normal circumstances Lawrence would have said no, as he had enough walking wounded to worry about, but he was not about to look a gift horse in the mouth. Allen, for whom a great future had been predicted, was anxious to prove himself and was confident of scoring goals at Division Two level, starting in the next game against Walsall at the Bescot Stadium.

The Saddlers were not safe themselves, although they had games in hand on all the other strugglers. They had inflicted a 3-2 defeat on the Town a year before which virtually ended hopes of automatic promotion, and had won 1-0 at Kenilworth Road earlier in this campaign.

At the time Walsall included four Frenchmen – Roger Boli, Jeff Peron, Didier Tholet and Jean-Jacques Eydelie – and their play-acting and theatricals, especially in the first half, left the Town players irate. Fortunately, referee Bill Burns was not taken in by the antics.

Luton had somehow managed to sneak into the lead when Allen chased a lost cause and floated the ball to David Oldfield, who mis-hit a looping shot over James Walker in the Walsall goal. In the second half Walsall defender Adrian Viveash powered in a header from a corner, but just as Luton seemed about to capsize they scored two goals on the break. Oldfield ran through the Walsall defence before smacking a shot against an upright. Allen followed up to score. Then Dwight Marshall played a wall pass with Oldfield before netting from an acute angle. Although Walsall pulled a goal back, Luton battened down the hatches.

All the talk was of the contribution from Rory Allen and although he did not score in the 3-0 home win over York the following week, he did net the only goal in an unlikely win at high-flying Grimsby.

Having helped his new teammates to four wins from six games, Allen knew that – with two games to go – a draw at fellow strugglers Brentford would ensure Luton's survival and Brentford's relegation. In a highly charged game, 6,598 turned out to see the physical Bees attempt to intimidate the Hatters, but Dwight Marshall fired the Town ahead following a goalmouth melee. Brentford levelled when Andy Scott headed in at the near post. On the hour Allen took a long punt from goalkeeper Kelvin Davis in his stride, held off defender Jamie Bates, and drove in low to restore Luton's advantage. Although Carl Hutchings scored Brentford's second equaliser with ten minutes to go, the Hatters just about managed to hang on for their life-saving draw.

Rory Allen netted his sixth goal in eight starts when bagging the last-minute winner at home to relegated Carlisle on the final day, leaving Luton fans shuddering at the thought of what might have happened had the 'best loan signing in the club's history' not been lured to Kenilworth Road.

KENILWORTH ROAD HEROES: **Julian James**

Luton coach John Moore first spotted Tring-born Julian James playing in a county schools match at Hemel Hempstead, but thought he was already on Watford's books. Gratified to learn otherwise, he invited James to Kenilworth Road, and he eventually signed professional forms in June 1988.

James did not have long to wait for his full debut, which came as the Town were defending the Littlewoods Cup the following season at Leeds, where a hostile crowd awaited the eighteen-year-old. Acquitting himself well, he saw the Town take a 2-1 lead, but with five minutes left he was sent off for a professional foul on Ian Baird. Manager Ray Harford was so incensed with the decision that he too was dismissed.

First and foremost a defender, James could play anywhere along the back and his versatility became a godsend to a succession of Luton Town managers. After making his league debut at Southampton in May 1988, he played thirteen times for the Hatters before making his home debut in January 1990.

Capped twice for England at Under-21 level, he became a feature in the Luton side in 1991-92 and apart from injuries was a regular until a broken leg at Bristol Rovers in April 1998 effectively ended his career. At his testimonial, all his ex-managers who were present used the same words when discussing Julian James. 'Someone you would want in the trenches with you', which summed up his determination and never-say-die attitude.

~~~~~~~~~~

Not surprisingly, Tottenham were not prepared to let Allen move to Luton permanently, so Lennie Lawrence spent the summer of 1998 trawling the divisions looking to bolster his squad. Darren Patterson and David Oldfield left on 'Bosman' transfers to Dundee United and Stoke respectively, while Gavin McGowan and Ray McKinnon came in. Lawrence, however, needed more bodies up front, and although he had high hopes for youth prospect Liam George, he could not visualise a teenager lasting a full season of Division Two football.

Lawrence's prayers seemed answered with the signing of the unknown Frenchman Herve Bacque, who had apparently been understudy to David Trezeguet and Thierry Henry at Monaco. Bacque (or Bactuet as he was known initially) scored in pre-season home games against Arsenal and Coventry and was looked on by Lawrence as 'Tony Thorpe in disguise', although there was a certain element of fan-power responsible for his signing a permanent contract.

Boosted by 'Hervemania', a good number of Luton supporters made the short trip to Wycombe on the opening day of 1998-89 to see if their new French hero could show his talent in the rough and tumble of

Division Two. Unfortunately, he could not, and it did not take long for his star to wane. The team, however, did rather well and by the middle of October were in the top three and had beaten Al Fayed's Fulham at Craven Cottage along the way.

When the long-awaited Kohlerdome Inquiry report was published, all the objections were dismissed by the inspector. The Secretary of State instead blocked the plan. This was due to traffic worries, following the Government's decision not to widen the M1 between Junctions 6 and 10. Kohler was given leave to appeal, which he set out to do, confident that a watered down set of proposals would get the green light.

On the pitch, Luton also enjoyed a run to the Worthington Cup quarter-finals, their best since contesting the final in 1989. This seemed unlikely when the Town trailed 0-2 at half-time at home to Oxford in the first round. Two second-half penalties would have earned parity but for Oxford's last-minute winner. They doubled their advantage in the second leg, only to be stung by three Luton replies.

At Ipswich in the next round, Luton felt they performed better than their 1-2 defeat indicated. David Johnson increased Ipswich's lead at Kenilworth Road, but goals from Andrew Fotiadis and Stuart Douglas forced extra-time. Skipper Steve Davis powered in a header to put Luton ahead, only to undo the good work by netting a spectacular own-goal with two minutes left. The peculiar away goals rule pertaining to the League Cup meant that at that moment Luton were out, but almost straight from the kick-off Marvin Johnson scored a dramatic winner. It is a pity that only 5,655 were there to witness this night of passion and drama.

At least Premiership Coventry attracted a capacity crowd to Kenilworth Road, even though the Sky Blues looked uninterested and lost 0-2 to goals from Phil Gray and Steve Davis. Coventry boss Gordon Strachan was not pleased and blamed big egos and lack of fighting spirit.

Barnsley, relegated from the Premiership, made more of a game of it, but were undone by Phil Gray's 81st-minute strike. This set up a quarter-final tie at Premiership-bound Sunderland at their new home on the banks of the River Wear. Sunderland were going so well they had lost only one game by the time Luton visited. The Hatters felt they had nothing to lose, but referee Eddie Lomas tipped the scales further in Sunderland's favour when Luton full-back Mitchell Thomas – already cautioned for an altercation with Kevin Ball – was sent off, much to the astonishment of the crowd, of both managers, and of Niall Quinn, who Thomas had apparently fouled.

Sunderland's breakthrough was fortuitous, as Marvin Johnson deflected the ball into his own net, but the Black Cats added two more in the dying seconds – through Michael Bridges and Quinn – to distort the score.

The Cup excitement had pushed the league into the background. A rash of injuries, suspensions, and loss of form brought a gentle slide down the table, which gathered momentum when inspirational skipper Steve Davis was sold back to Burnley for £750,000. The Cup run had reaped enough proceeds to delay selling any player, but the loss of Davis was particularly hard to bear because he was a talisman, and without him another struggle was on the cards.

Meanwhile, David Kohler took matters into his own hands. Before learning the outcome of his appeal against rejection of the Kohlerdome project, he resigned the chair and put his shareholding up for sale. He had been subject to much personal abuse, which culminated with an alleged petrol bomb incident at his home. Three days after he stepped down, the High Court upheld the Secretary of State's decision. The Kohlerdome was dead.

The team was dying too. Despite the loan arrivals of Gerry Harrison (Sunderland) and Sean Dyche (Bristol City), seven defeats from eight games – culminating in a 1-3 capitulation at Chesterfield in mid-March – left everyone at Kenilworth Road fearing the worst.

As for the Board, they were no closer to agreement over David Kohler's 60 per cent share-ownership. Faced with an impasse, director Cliff Bassett, who was owed £2 million, called in the receivers. Ironically, this seemed to galvanise the players and supporters. The team won a few games and fears of relegation receded.

Inevitably, the receiver demanded sales on transfer deadline day. Graham Alexander moved to Preston for a cut-price £50,000, while Reading parted with a surprisingly substantial £500,000 for Sean Evers. On the plus side, the receiver sanctioned the ongoing loan of Sean Dyche from Bristol City, plus the return of old favourite Tony Thorpe, also on loan, and also from Ashton Gate. Thorpe was rusty at first but soon found his shooting boots and netted four goals in the last four games to push the Town up to a healthy but unlikely finishing position of twelfth.

On 1st May 1999, for the last home game, the club invited back all ten surviving members of the 1959 FA Cup final team. Some had not met up for years, but they had a good time recounting old memories before watching an uninspiring display against Macclesfield. During a half-time pitch presentation they were feted by the crowd, most of whom had not been born in 1959.

'Fans of Luton Action Group' (FLAG) was established after the club entered receivership. At its first public meeting, 1,500 people turned up, £10,000 was donated, and within a few days another £120,000 had been pledged. The initial aim was to convince the receiver that they could raise enough to buy the club and take it forward as a community-owned trust.

Throughout the summer FLAG made high-profile attempts at fund-raising, but was powerless to prevent the sale of Chris Willmott and Kelvin Davis to Premiership Wimbledon. Despite third-party intervention, the Football League always favoured a straight transfer of shares between David Kohler and Cliff Bassett, except that they could not agree on a price. The brinkmanship went to the wire, with the Football League prepared to pull the plug on the Town's proud history. A deadline was set – midnight on the Friday before the first game of the new 1999-2000 campaign. With two minutes to spare, a deal was finally struck, with Luton fans travelling to Notts County the following day not knowing if they would see a game. The fans did not care that it was a drab spectacle: at least they still had a team to support. No one doubted that the Football League would have carried out their threat.

Considering the youth and inexperience of the new Hatters, it surprised everyone to find them in the top three until the end of September. Seventeen-year-old Matthew Taylor was a revelation, vaulting from youth team to first team with little difficulty. Also catching the eye were teenagers Liam George, Gary Doherty and Matthew Spring, who had also come up through the youth programme.

Inevitably, form did dip, although the long-term injury to Phil Gray did not help as he was one of only a few experienced players left. By Christmas the Hatters were in mid-table. A brief upsurge after the festivities was not maintained and the team drifted down again, though never low enough to threaten the unthinkable. As the season drew to a close, Gary Doherty was transferred to Tottenham for an initial £1 million. Reluctant hero Cliff Bassett sold his majority shareholding to a consortium led by Mike Watson-Challis, who had been a director at Kenilworth Road from 1987-91.

For once, Lennie Lawrence could enjoy a close season not fraught with external worries. He could now focus on bringing in the three free-transfer players he thought were needed to convert the Town into genuine promotion contenders. He had identified several targets when out of the blue he was dismissed by the club's new owner and in his place came ex-Hatters hero Ricky Hill.

Although Lawrence had not been universally popular, it was appreciated that he had shown around £5 million profit in transfer dealings during one of the most turbulent periods in the history of the Town. Hill arrived on a wave of goodwill, built upon his thirteen years as a cultured midfielder at Kenilworth Road. He lacked managerial experience although he came with a fine coaching pedigree. All Luton Town supporters genuinely wished him well.

As the change of regime did not occur until July – after the fixture lists had been published – Hill was not given much time to prepare, but still recruited ex-Town forward Mark Stein, several players the supporters had never heard of, plus Bournemouth goalkeeper Mark Ovendale, who cost a massive £425,000. Hill also brought in ex-Brighton defender and highly regarded coach Chris Ramsey as his assistant.

The opening day of 2000-01 saw the visit of Notts County. A healthy crowd afforded Hill and club owner Mike Watson-Challis a tremendous reception. Ninety minutes later, with the Town having lost 0-1 in a tedious game, the supporters were not quite so up-beat.

With Phil Gray having left under freedom of contract to join Burnley, the Town lacked firepower and as the table took shape they were at the wrong end. Youngsters thrown into the fray before they were ready, panic buys, and rumours of unrest concerning Ramsey's coaching methods made this one of the most depressing periods at the club for decades, compounded by the despair felt by the supporters who held Ricky Hill in such high esteem.

After three months Ramsey was gone, with more ex-Luton favourites, Lil Fuccillo and Brian Stein, appointed as coaches. Sadly the new coaches were unable to stop the rot and after an apologetic 0-3 home defeat by Bristol City – with the club next to bottom, showing two wins from 21 games – Hill was told enough was enough.

The Hatters immediately promoted Lil Fuccillo, who in turn asked John Moore to be his assistant. Brian Stein remained as a coach. Fuccillo tried to reverse Ricky Hill's policy by signing experienced players, but he was rebuffed by most, who did not wish to enlist on a sinking ship. The only players prepared to give it a go were Adrian Whitbread, on loan from Portsmouth, and Lee Nogan on a short-term contract.

Results under Fuccillo were barely better than under Hilll, and by late January the club looked doomed. Never one to mince words, Fuccillo labelled the players as not good enough and the worst squad at Kenilworth Road since 1965.

Rumours then started buzzing that ex-Wimbledon boss Joe Kinnear had been lined up. When he suffered his heart attack, in March 1999, the Dons lay sixth in the Premiership, and Kinnear was admired as someone who could perform wonders on a shoe-string year after year. Given his pedigree, it seemed inconceivable that he could be tempted by little Luton. But the rumours turned out to be true. Kinnear was appointed Director of Football with complete control over all footballing matters at Kenilworth Road.

Despite never signing a contract, Lil Fuccillo was retained. He was purportedly in charge for the visit to Northampton, which marked Kinnear's first public appearance. Kinnear, who was supposed to remain in the stand, could not resist coming down to the touchline where, to the bemusement of Fuccillo, he barked orders to the players. The Town triumphed 1-0, their first victory since Boxing Day, and in a whirlwind few weeks rattled up five wins and sixteen points from seven games. That was championship form, and hope sprang eternal.

Once the honeymoon period was over, Kinnear knew the squad was carrying too much dead wood and not even he could not turn the Town around. After winning at home to Cambridge on 6th March, they did not taste victory in any of the remaining thirteen games, despite signing striker Steve Howard from Northampton on transfer deadline day. With a loud splash, rather than a gentle plop, Luton sank back to a division they had last seen in 1968.

As the bleak reality sank in, the only ray of hope was the purchase by club owner Mike Watson-Challis of the now-notorious wedge of land by Junction 10 of the M1.

Kinnear had his work cut out, but with many of the players he wished to offload being on lengthy contracts, his hands were tied. Helping him to revive the Hatters was ex-Luton hero Mick Harford, who had worked with him at Wimbledon and now came in as assistant manager. This meant no place for Lil Fuccillo. Even within his straitjacket, Kinnear made it a summer to remember. Hardly a day went by without reports of players arriving on trial or signing on the dotted line. In scenes reminiscent of David Pleat's 1978 revolution, five players debuted on the first day of 2001-02, with a further two the following week. By mid-October no fewer than eleven players had pulled on a Luton shirt for the first time.

Given the wholesale changes, it was little wonder the season began tentatively, although the Town never dipped below the top five and the predatory Carl Griffiths, signed from Leyton Orient, took the eye. The season took off with the introduction of French winger Jean Louis Valois for the visit of Torquay at the end of September 2001. Valois proved to be a revelation, with the fans purring in disbelief at his tricks. When he fired a shot into the top corner during the 5-1 win he brought the house down.

Naturally, Valois had to get used to the ball flying backwards and forwards over his head as he acclimatised to the English soccer basement, and he did attract the close attentions of agricultural defenders, but when allowed to play he was a class apart. He was probably the best foreign player at Kenilworth Road since Lars Elstrup.

Although Luton suffered some bad defeats – notably at Mansfield and Macclesfield – they always seemed to bounce back. The loss of Griffiths to a stress fracture of the shin was overcome by signing Dean Crowe from Stoke. But in early December a mixture of flu and injury sidelined 24 players, leading to the decision to pull out of a league game at Kidderminster. Naturally, Kidderminster made mileage out this, and for a time there was a real fear of a points deduction and hefty fine. In fact it was £30,000, but Luton took pleasure in winning the re-arranged game 4-1.

Once everyone was fit, Luton started to chase the incredibly consistent Plymouth, with everyone anticipating the clash at Kenilworth Road.

KENILWORTH ROAD CLASSICS: **Luton v Plymouth** – 2-0

Nationwide Division Three, 2nd February 2002

The collision between the two divisional heavyweights meant a sell-out attendance of 9,585, the biggest since the visit of Southampton in the FA Cup in 1995.

Joe Kinnear, who had purposefully angered Plymouth with some barbed comments after Luton's early-season defeat at Home Park, played the game up, while his counterpart, Paul Sturrock, played it down. Who would be proved right?

Luton were fired up and attacked from the first whistle to the last, hitting the woodwork three times and mustering 24 attempts on goal. They had to wait, though, until ten minutes from the end before prising open the division's most miserly defence. Matthew Taylor was upended by David Worrell for an uncontested penalty and skipper Kevin Nicholls kept his nerve from the spot.

With Plymouth now throwing caution to the wind, Graham Coughlan caused a scare when he too hit the woodwork following a corner. But the game was made safe with three minutes to go. A Valois corner was headed back across goal by Adrian Forbes to Steve Howard, who powered in a header from close range.

'We saved our best display of the season for the team that is top of the table,' said Kinnear, 'It was a 2-0 massacre. They are a decent side and the league proves that but they more than met their match. We had more width and slaughtered them down the sides. They played one up front but we expected that and it suited us.'

LUTON: *Emberson, Boyce, Perrett, Bayliss, Taylor, Forbes, Spring, Nicholls, Valois, Howard, Crowe (Brkovic)*

PLYMOUTH: *Larrieu, Worrell, Coughlan, Wotton, Beswetherick, Phillips (Evers), Adams, Friio, Stonebridge (Heaney), Hodges, Keith (Evans).*

~~~~~~~~~~

The win pushed the Town to within four points of Plymouth, but all the good work was undone when Luton lost their next two games. Kinnear was furious at the loss of impetus and read the Riot Act to the players.

Whatever he said should be bottled and sold, for the Hatters then went on the best run in their history. Twelve wins in a row were recorded, with the tenth, at Swansea, clinching promotion, and the eleventh, a 5-3 revenge home thrashing of Mansfield, cementing second spot.

A 4-0 victory at Hull, with three games to go, actually saw the Town push Plymouth off the top, but Argyle had a game in hand which they won. With Luton drawing at home to Macclesfield in their penultimate game, thus terminating their winning run, they effectively handed the title to Plymouth, whose 102 points and just 28 goals conceded could hardly be begrudged. In any normal season Luton would have run away with the championship. Five club records were broken, not least the total of 97 points, in what was a season to remember.

Joe Kinnear spent the summer up to his normal tricks of wheeling and dealing. As in the previous close season, never a day went by without a rumour being heard of a player coming in. The supporters had to accept the inevitable and allow talented full-back Matthew Taylor to leave for Portsmouth with their best wishes, but they were not pleased when Jean Louis Valois entered into a war of words with Kinnear over his managerial methods and style of play before departing to Scottish Premier League club Hearts.

KENILWORTH ROAD HEROES: **Marvin Johnson**

Wembley-born Marvin Johnson was at school in Aylesbury, playing as a left-sided midfielder, when he was spotted by the Hatters, who moved him into defence for the youth side. After signing as a professional in October 1986, Marvin had to wait until February 1988 before making his debut in a Simod Cup-tie at Everton, where a young Luton side won 2-1. His league debut followed a month later in a defeat at Wimbledon.

As the Town were a top division side at the time, with an established central defensive partnership of Mal Donaghy and Steve Foster, it was natural that he would have to bide his time, but once he got a run in the side there was no looking back. He became a bedrock of the defence until hanging up his boots at the end of the 2001-02 season.

Immensely popular with the Luton crowd for his wholehearted effort, mazy runs from defence and the occasional spectacular own-goal, Johnson has now turned full circle and is youth coach at Kenilworth Road.

~~~~~~~~~~~

The return of old favourite Tony Thorpe went some way to appeasing the supporters, as did the £50,000 signing of midfielder Steve Robinson from Preston.

Giving the promotion-winning side a chance to prove themselves at the start of 2002-03 backfired for Kinnear, as the first four games were lost. The more pessimistic Luton fans were predicting relegation by Christmas. Following another reading of the Riot Act, the players – now aided by tribunal signing from Swindon, Sol Davis – settled down and hauled their way up the table. In the minds of supporters, the season took off with the

2-1 home win over Division One Watford in the Worthington Cup, the first clash between the sides for over four years.

It then became a frustrating campaign, with the Hatters sniffing the edge of the play-off places without ever seeming able to nail one of them. Injuries did not help. Following the loss of Adrian Forbes with damaged cruciate ligaments pre-season, a procession of the sick and lame made sure the treatment table was again in constant use.

Suspensions and injuries permitting, the partnership of Thorpe and big Steve Howard looked promising, but at the other end six goalkeepers were tried out over the course of the campaign, which ended with teenager Rob Beckwith between the sticks. A final position of ninth was, of course, pretty good after the poor start, but Kinnear was far from satisfied.

KENILWORTH ROAD HEROES: **John Moore**

John Moore joined the Hatters in May 1965, just as the club sank into Division Four for the first time in its history: 'I was playing for Motherwell when Luton scout David Hutchinson, who was a Town player in the 1930s, recommended me to his old friend George Martin, who came and signed me without having seen me play,' recalled John.

Moore joined a club in the doldrums, but soon settled, making 43 league appearances and scoring five goals in his first season: 'I only scored thirteen goals in all my career at Luton but in my early days at the club I used to go up for set pieces, hence the reasonable record in my first season. In later years I realised that players such as Terry Branston and Chris Nicholl were rather better in such positions so I dropped back and the goal tally dried up.'

Moore's first tangible success was, of course, winning the Fourth Division championship in 1967-68, when he missed only one game and scored four goals, including the opener in the 4-0 thrashing of Crewe which clinched the title: 'That was a tremendous night, with nearly 19,000 people at Kenilworth Road to see a Fourth Division game, and a fitting end to a great season. Players such as Terry Branston, who was a marvellous leader, and Bruce Rioch spring readily to mind and if you could have coupled the skill of Graham French with my endeavour what a player would have been produced!'

Moore went on to become a rock at the heart of the Luton defence for another five seasons as the Town were promoted from Division Three and then took the Second Division by storm before consolidating under Harry Haslam: 'I was lucky to be in the same team as such players as Mike Keen – who thought so much more quickly than most players on the pitch – Don Givens, another vastly underrated player, and of course, Malcolm Macdonald and John Aston.'

When asked about other memorable games, Moore recalled the famous 2-0 win at Newcastle in the FA Cup in 1973 which set up a run to the quarter finals: 'The press were full of what Malcolm Macdonald and John Tudor were going to do to us and the majority of the 42,000 crowd at St James' Park were convinced that we were in for a thrashing. I had one of those games where even if I was lying on the ground the ball kept on hitting me and I was throwing myself all over the place blocking everything Newcastle could hurl at us.'

After leaving the Town in 1973, Moore had a spell managing Dunstable Town. The call to return to Kenilworth Road came from David Pleat after he took over the hot seat. 'My rock,' is how Pleat described his old playing colleague. When Pleat left to join Tottenham, Moore was asked to pick up the reins and in his sole season in charge, 1986-87, the Hatters finished seventh, their highest ever position.

Moore did not relish the high-profile life of a football manager in the top division and resigned after twelve months, but he was back in 1990 as a coach under Jim Ryan, who he had recruited to his own coaching staff in 1986.

John Moore remained at Kenilworth Road until his sixtieth birthday, serving under several managers, and immersing himself in the job he enjoyed most – coaching and training the youngsters. It is to his eternal credit that two of his youth teams reached the FA Youth Cup semi-final with the second, in 1997, particularly commendable as the Town had to fight against the big city clubs with their expensive academies.

~~~~~~~~~~~

Although the Town had experienced some hectic and bewildering summers over the decades, that of 2003 is unlikely to be surpassed. The previous season had ushered in the nearest to what can be described as a period of consolidation that the Hatters had ever seen. But then the bombshells dropped thick and fast.

It started in late May with the announcement that Chairman Mike Watson-Challis was to retire and sell up to an – as yet unnamed – consortium. The worry that the supporters felt turned to rage when it was learned that management duo, Joe Kinnear and Mick Harford, had been sacked by letter. By the time the 'middle men' arrived at Kenilworth Road to oversee the changes, the fans had mobilised. Angry scenes were reported outside the ground.

Over the ensuing days the front man for the secretive consortium was revealed as John Gurney. A local newspaper, familiar with this gentleman's previous dealings with Bedford Rugby Club, raised doubts in supporters' minds. Bizarre messages started to appear on the club's official website posted in the early hours of the morning.

Gurney intended to change the club's name to London-Luton and build a 70,000-capacity stadium adjacent to Junction 10 of the M1 with a 20,000-space underground car-park. The complex would boast a Grand Prix racing track and be home to an American Football, Baseball and Ice Hockey team under the title 'Team Europe'.

With the club becoming the laughing stock of football, supporters set up the 'Trust in Luton' with 3,000 fans pledging support. Amongst the weapons at their disposal was starving the club of cash by refusing to renew season tickets or purchase any merchandise, with the aim of flushing out Gurney and his still un-named partners.

Seemingly oblivious to everything, Gurney then devised a telephone vote to enable supporters to select the next manager. It did not take a rocket scientist to work out that Gurney's preferred candidate, Mike Newell, was likely to emerge triumphant from the ballot. Ex-Hatters favourite Newell, controversially sacked at Hartlepool a few weeks before, would have obviously preferred to be returning to Kenilworth Road in less hostile circumstances.

'Trust in Luton' meanwhile had brokered a complex deal which brought the short career of John Gurney to a close by effectively placing the club into administrative receivership. Another well-attended 'Trust in Luton' meeting warned that belt-tightening and unpopular decisions were inevitable, but that the club would survive. In the immortal words of Chief Executive Cherry Newbery, who had battled behind the scenes to keep the club afloat while placed in an intolerable situation, 'Don't mess with Luton Town!'

Administrative Receiver Barry Ward became a necessary evil. He demanded major cuts, but in a masterstroke of public relations brought back Mick Harford as Director of Football and first-team coach. This would be hero Harford's fourth coming!

Barred from signing players, and faced with suspicion from the fans, Mike Newell had a massive task to win everyone around. That he succeeded in doing so was to his credit. The circumstances of his appointment may have been bizarre, but he proved himself the man for the job. Although the squad lacked the strength in depth to consistently challenge the leaders, a satisfactory season unfurled which was unimaginable a few months earlier.

The 2003-04 season started with a 3-1 home win over Rushden & Diamonds, but with injuries to a threadbare squad and the controversial exit of Tony Thorpe to QPR, the play-off positions were always tantalisingly out of reach.

Luton were permitted to bring in Coventry starlet Gary McSheffrey on loan and he proved a revelation, netting eight league goals and another in a 4-4 draw at Premiership Charlton in the Carling Cup. Sadly, the embargo meant that the Town were unable to make a transfer bid. After young goal-keepers Rob Beckwith and Dean Brill shipped ten goals between them during October, the Hatters were allowed to bring in the experienced Marlon Beresford on a short-term contract and his steadying influence coincided with the best spell of the season.

In the FA Cup Luton reached the fourth round for the first time since 1995. It was the furthest they had progressed as an associate member since 1933. With Newell registered as a player, the team was down to the bare bones for the visit of Tranmere and lost a disappointing tie 0-1 to opposition that had been beaten 3-1 in a league a couple of months before.

Another consortium, this one fronted by former Town Chief Executive Bill Tomlins, was announced as the potential new owners. But with the club's past record, and new rules introduced to ensure proper accounting, many hoops had to be jumped through before the Receiver could pack his bags. Although the new men were keen to move the club from Kenilworth Road, the Football League barred any takeover until a ten-year lease had been obtained for the old ground. As little had been spent on the ground in the past ten years, funds that could have been spent on the team had to be diverted to repair the roof of the Main Stand.

The Town bade farewell to Matthew Spring and Emmerson Boyce, who joined Leeds and Premiership Crystal Palace respectively, after rejecting new terms at Kenilworth Road. Incoming players were Rowan Vine, on a season-long loan from Portsmouth and, making a welcome return, goalkeeper Marlon Beresford. Paul Underwood, injured on his debut at QPR the previous March, was now fully fit.

Luton supporters would have settled for a mid-table place in 2004-05, but Mike Newell was quietly confident that, barring injuries and suspensions, the team could spring a few surprises. The Hatters opened up with a dogged 2-1 home win over negative Oldham, but followed up with impressive wins at Swindon and Barnsley.

When Torquay were despatched at Kenilworth Road the Town had beaten their previous best start, the first of many records to fall over the course of a remarkable campaign. It was not until the seventh game that any points were dropped (0-0 at Sheffield Wednesday) but the Town were now building up a healthy lead. Even when games were lost – as happened when the Hatters went down to Huddersfield, Walsall and Hull – they bounced back with two emphatic home victories which marked them out as future champions.

With skipper Kevin Nicholls and left-back Sol Davis shaking off their 'bad-boy' images, and the queue for the treatment table shortening, the Town were able to keep a settled side. The emphasis was on teamwork and a never-say-die spirit, which left the supporters unable to believe the rapid transformation. The loss of Mick Harford, who finally joined Joe Kinnear at Nottingham Forest, did not appear to disturb the side's rhythm, and as Christmas approached, a win at Bristol City – the first since 1973 – and a Boxing Day win at Chesterfield – their first home defeat – put everyone in festive spirits.

KENILWORTH ROAD CLASSICS: **Luton v Hull** – 1-0

Coca-Cola League One, 12th February 2005

After the profitable Christmas, the Town wobbled slightly, and a run of six draws from seven games enabled the chasing pack, led by Hull, to close the gap. When Hull visited, Luton were only one point better off, and an all-ticket capacity crowd of 9,500 assembled to witness the clash of the titans.

Top scorer Steve Howard was suspended and in his place came 'super-sub' Enoch Showunmi. City were missing their top scorer, Stuart Elliott. As a bit of spice Hull included ex-Watford skipper Andy Hessenthaler in their line-up, a player the Luton fans loved to hate.

Luton attacked Hull with a will but could not get the ball in the net. In the second period City tightened up without ever looking threatening themselves. The game appeared to be heading for deadlock, but with bare-ly a minute left Steve Robinson, wide on the right, fired in a cross which was anticipated by the 'Croatian Sensation' Ahmet Brkovic, who nipped in between two defenders and headed in at the near post. With the other sides at the top dropping points, Luton had opened up a gap once more. This time they never relinquished it.

LUTON: Beresford, Neilson, Coyne, Davies, Davis, Foley, Nicholls, Robinson, Brkovic (O'Leary), Showunmi (Andrew), Vine.

HULL: Myhill, Stockdale, Cort, Delaney, Edge, Green, Ashbee, Hessenthaler (Price), Lewis, Barmby, Wibraham (Facey).

~~~~~~~~~~~

The win over the Tigers re-vitalised the Town. They won their next three games, among them a 3-2 victory at Hartlepool, who were previous-ly unbeaten at home. Although publicly denying it, the result must have given much personal satisfaction to Mike Newell.

A barnstorming 5-0 home win over Bristol City was followed by a 3-1 home victory over Swindon, which meant the Town had laid to rest two bogey sides from previous seasons. The supporters looked forward to the Good Friday clash with Barnsley, as it gave the chance to show off to the watching millions live on Sky TV. Sadly, the Town got stage fright and went down 1-3. The Town's overall form would have to remain the Luton sup-porters' own little secret!

With doomsayers predicting a late-season collapse, the team bounced back, as it had done all season, with a 4-1 victory at Torquay on Easter

Monday, followed by three more points at home to Blackpool. The Hatters were now in the final furlong and a record crowd packed the Fitness First Stadium in Bournemouth to see if the Cherries could put one over the table-toppers while strengthening their own hopes of promotion.

The Town had not won at Bournemouth since 1969 and their chances of breaking this particular bogey seemed slim when centre-half Russ Perrett was sent off for a professional foul early on. Despite dominating possession thereafter, the Cherries could not find a way through. Given the circumstances, the Luton fans would have celebrated a draw, but they were in seventh heaven when substitute Showunmi stabbed home in the 84th minute. The celebrations went on long into the night because the Town were now back in the second tier – now renamed the Championship – after nine years away.

Promotion was confirmed the following midweek, when Brentford beat third-placed Tranmere and a carnival atmosphere was evident when MK Dons were beaten 1-0 at Kenilworth Road the following Saturday.

KENILWORTH ROAD CLASSICS: **Luton v Brentford** – 4-2

Coca-Cola League One, 30th April 2005

With the Town winning at Wrexham the previous Saturday and clinching the championship in the process – not to mention shattering another bogey – there remained one final hoodoo to conquer. The Bees.

Brentford seemed to have the Indian Sign over the Hatters this season. The 0-2 defeat at Griffin Park in December 2004 came amidst accusations that the Brentford management team had tried to sway the referee. Steve Howard was dismissed in a stormy match and on the final whistle the home supporters greeted the win as if they had won the Champions League.

The two sides were paired in the FA Cup at Kenilworth Road a month later. This time the Bees used every trick in the book to waste time. With Brentford then nicking two late goals, it made it an afternoon to forget. Nor did their manager, Martin Allen, endear himself to the Luton supporters with his posturings, and several scores were left unsettled. Now was the time to settle them.

An early goal from Ahmet Brkovic put the Luton fans in high spirits but the Bees replied twice before half-time through Sam Sodje and Deon Burton. Stringing five men across the midfield in the second period, the Bees sought to hang on to their lead. Luton's Kevin Nicholls and Steve Howard were both denied by the woodwork, but with six minutes left Steve Robinson was brought down by Michael Turner, leaving Nicholls to level from the spot – 2-2.

The drama was not yet over. In the final minute Enoch Showunmi buried a header past Stuart Nelson in the Brentford goal and straight from the restart Robinson side-footed a fourth. Bees boss Allen had presumably been warned not to incite the crowd again. He walked off to a chorus of jeers, vacating the pitch so the trophy could be presented to the players, who then saluted the crowd from the directors box.

LUTON: Beresford, Coyne, Underwood, Davis, Foley, Davies, Robinson, Nicholls, Brkovic (Showunmi), Howard, Feeney (Vine).

BRENTFORD: Nelson, Pratley, Turner, Sodje, Talbot (Harrold), O'Connor, Frampton, Hutchinson, Gayle, Burton (Rankin), Salako (Fitzgerald).

~~~~~~~~~~~

Regrettably, Luton could not break the magical 100 points total. In their final game they could 'only' draw 3-3 at Doncaster. The supporters did not seem to care, and they turned out in their thousands to welcome the champions on their open-top bus ride through the town.

It seems somehow appropriate that the Hatters should end their 100th season at Kenilworth Road in glorious style. This book celebrates all the Luton Town players and teams who have given their all over the preceding century.

The supporters don't need telling, however, that the Kenilworth Road ground has seen better days, and although the tightness of the enclosure may well be worth a goal start in home games during the forthcoming Championship season, it will also be a liability, given its low capacity of just over 10,000.

The club is committed to building a new stadium adjacent to Junction 10 of the M1, and most supporters will welcome a move into a modern arena where there is adequate knee-room, uninterrupted viewing, and plenty of car parking. They will, though, shed a tear when leaving Kenilworth Road for the last time. For all its quirks, it holds a century of memories.

Subscriber	Memorable Match	Season	Competition
Philip Abbott			
Nick Albone	Hull	2004-05	League
Brian Allington	Bristol Rovers	1935-36	League
Nigel Atha	Aston Villa	1982-83	League
Kevin Austin			
Steve Bailey	Crewe	1967-68	League
D C Bain			
Gary Barker	Manchester C	1960-61	FA Cup (abandoned)
Toby Barrett	Chelsea	1979-80	League
Phil Bassill	Sunderland	1961-62	League
Frank Batt	Newcastle	1946-47	League
Chris Beard	Crystal Palace	1989-90	League
Alan Bedford			
Paul K Billson	Southampton	1985-86	League
Keith Blackburn	Halifax	1965-66	League
David Blain	Sunderland	1955-56	League
Pete Bostock	Crewe	1967-68	League
Ian Bottrill	Liverpool	1986-87	League
Karl Bottrill	Newcastle	1993-94	FA Cup
Philip Bourne			
N D Boustred	Chelsea	1979-80	League
Mike Bowley	Crewe	1967-68	League
David Bradford			
Mike Broadbent	Chelsea	1979-80	League
Keith Brooksbank	Hull	2004-05	League
Anthony Brown	Orient	1969-70	League
David Brown	Sunderland	1955-56	League
Jonathan Brown	West Ham	1993-94	FA Cup
J J Browning	Sunderland	1955-56	League
Chris Charman	Southampton	1985-86	League
Tonino Ciuffini	West Ham	1993-94	FA Cup
Peter Clark	Bristol City	2004-05	League
Robert Clarke	Liverpool	1986-87	League
Jeremy Cook	Southampton	1987-88	League
Leigh Coot	Newcastle	1981-82	League
Raymond Coot	Southampton	1985-86	League
David Anthony Cremin			
M R Dack	Wolves	1955-56	League
Andy Davis	Middlesbrough	1962-63	League
Phillip Day	Liverpool	1986-87	FA Cup
Daniel Donkin	Brentford	2004-05	League
Geoff Edwards	Manchester C	1960-61	FA Cup (abandoned)
Graham Farrington	Blackpool	1958-59	FA Cup
Michael Fielding	Newcastle	1993-94	FA Cup
Christopher G Finch	Crewe	1967-68	League
K J Fitzpatrick	QPR	1981-82	League
David Fleckney	Oxford	1987-88	Littlewoods Cup
Matthew Fleckney	Wrexham	1999-00	League

Subscriber	Memorable Match	Season	Competition
Anthony Folbigg	Blackpool	1958-59	FA Cup
Lyn Folland	West Ham	1993-94	FA Cup
David Foxen	Brentford	2004-05	League
Peter John Fuller	Manchester C	1960-61	FA Cup
T L Gascoigne	Cardiff	1970-71	League
Simon Gatward	Newcastle	1993-94	FA Cup
Paul Giddings	Shrewsbury	1981-82	League
Mike Giddins	Oxford	1987-88	Littlewoods Cup
Joan Glenister	Newcastle	1993-94	FA Cup
Clive Goodall	Mansfield	1968-69	League
Barrie Gore	Blackpool	1958-59	FA Cup
Steve Govette	Manchester C	1960-61	FA Cup (abandoned)
Michael Grange	West Ham	1993-94	FA Cup
Richard Gray	Southampton	1985-86	League
Robert John Green	Newcastle	1983-84	League
David Green	West Ham	1993-94	FA Cup
Kevin Griffin	Watford	1981-82	League
J Griggs	Newcastle	1946-47	League
Colin Guy	Liverpool	1986-87	League
Rob Hadgraft	Liverpool	1986-87	FA Cup
Philip Hart	Hull	2004-05	League
David George Hercock	West Ham	1993-94	FA Cup
David Hill	Mansfield	1968-69	League
Jason Hobbs			
Shirley & David Hobbs	Notts Co	1951-52	League
Chris Hodge	Mansfield	1968-69	League
Nigel Holland	Liverpool	1986-87	League
Andrew Holmes	Leeds	1974-75	League
Craig Horseman			
Brian Horsnell	Sunderland	1984-85	League
Peter Houghton	Liverpool	1986-87	League
Brian & Matthew Howe	Brentford	2004-05	League
Tom, Rachel & Denise Hunt	Brentford	2004-05	League
Marie Hyde	Brentford	2004-05	League
Norman Impey	Arsenal	1951-52	FA Cup
Paul Inwards			
Duncan Jackson	West Ham	1993-94	FA Cup
John Jackson	Liverpool	1986-87	League
Jim Jardine	Watford	1968-69	League
David Jellis	Everton	1985-86	League
Paul Jinks	Liverpool	1986-87	League
Bruce Johnson	Watford	1984-85	FA Cup
Graeme Jones	Southampton	1985-86	League
Pete Jones	Mansfield	1968-69	League
Dave Jordan	West Ham	1993-94	FA Cup
Ian Kelly	West Ham	1993-94	FA Cup
Martin Killeen	Grimsby	1981-82	League

Subscriber	Memorable Match	Season	Competition
Andy King	Crewe	1967-68	League
Bruce King	Carlisle	1970-71	League
Russell King			
Trevor King	Chelsea	1979-80	League
Alex Lake	Brentford	2004-05	League
Ian Lee	Birmingham	1970-71	League
Kevin Lennon	Arsenal	1985-86	FA Cup
David Paul Lightfoot	Carlisle	1970-71	League
Steve Lindsay	West Ham	1993-94	FA Cup
B T Lynch	Arsenal	1958-59	League
Aidan McClung	Arsenal	1970-71	League Cup
Mick McConkey	Chelsea	1979-80	League
Paul McDowell	Liverpool	1986-87	League
John E Mackriell			
Chris MacSweeney			
Paul Maddox	Ajax	2004-05	Friendly
Philip Malcolm	Newcastle	1993-94	FA Cup
Neil Marshall	West Ham	1993-94	FA Cup
K Mayles			
S Mayne			
Ann Mercel	Brentford	2004-05	League
Jonathan Miller	West Ham	1993-94	FA Cup
Alison Mitchell			
Tony Molyneux	Manchester C	1952-53	FA Cup
Kevin Morris	Manchester U	1984-85	League
Stephen Murphy	Chelsea	1979-80	League
John Murphy	Southampton	1982-83	League
Daniel Musson	Liverpool	1986-87	League
David Newman	Notts Co	1982-83	League
William Newman	Blackburn	1952-53	League
David Parry			
Julie Parry			
John M Patmore	Bristol Rovers	1935-36	League
Bobby Payne			
Len Pedder	Newcastle	1946-47	League
Rob Piggott	Newcastle	1993-94	FA Cup
Simon Pitts	Newcastle	1993-94	FA Cup
Chris Plummer	Liverpool	1986-87	FA Cup
Daniela Poulton	West Ham	1988-89	Littlewoods Cup
Gez Prior	Fulham	1975-76	League
Craig Purdy	Newcastle	1993-94	FA Cup
Frank Purdy	Orient	1969-70	League
Phil Putman	Liverpool	1986-87	League
John 'the Mad Hatter' Pyper	Liverpool	1986-87	FA Cup
Dave Quinnell	Liverpool	1986-87	FA Cup
Clive Ramsay	Newcastle	1981-82	League
Tony 'Tub' Reynolds	Crewe	1967-68	League

Subscriber	Memorable Match	Season	Competition
David Robertson	Exeter	1964-65	League
Alan Robinson	Crewe	1967-68	League
Danilo 'Dan' Ronzani	Southampton	1985-86	League
Ron Rosson	Newcastle	1946-47	League
P Ryan	Wolves	1974-75	League
Norman Samuels	West Ham	1993-94	FA Cup
Bill Sanders			
Don Scrace	Newcastle	1993-94	FA Cup
Tony Sendall	Blackpool	1958-59	FA Cup
Kevin Shepherd	Liverpool	1986-87	League
Graham Sheridan	Liverpool	1986-87	FA Cup
William Sherwood	West Ham	1993-94	FA Cup
Malcolm Short	Blackpool	1958-59	FA Cup
Mike Simpson	Bristol Rovers	1968-69	League
Roger Smallbones	Blackpool	1958-59	FA Cup
Brian Smith	Blackpool	1958-58	FA Cup
Ian Smith			
Russell Smith	Hull	2004-05	League
Stewart Smith	West Ham	1993-94	FA Cup
David Snaxell	Blackpool	1958-59	FA Cup
Kevin Snaxell	Oxford	1987-88	League Cup
D M Sulsh			
Andrew Swann	Chelsea	1979-80	League
Peter R Taylor	Newcastle	1946-47	League
Philip R Terry	Newcastle	1946-47	League
Richard Tilley	Liverpool	1986-87	League
Thomas Tillier	Brentford	2004-05	League
Derek Tompkins	Blackpool	1958-58	FA Cup
Kevin Tompkins	Liverpool	1986-87	League
Dennis & Michelle Townsend	West Ham	1993-94	FA Cup
Matthew Underwood	Liverpool	1986-87	FA Cup
Colin Unwin	Mansfield	1968-69	League
James Usher	Sheffield Wed	2003-04	League
A R Wallace	Nott'm Forest	1970-71	FA Cup
Michael L Ward	Hull	2004-05	League
Alan Wheatley	Nott'm Forest	1970-71	FA Cup
Jo Wheeler	West Brom	1982-83	League
John Wheeler	Hartlepools	1966-67	League
Roger Whichelow	Liverpool	1986-87	League
Ian White			
Steven Whitehead	Middlesbrough	1994-95	League
Roy Williams	Northampton	1960-61	FA Cup
John Wilson	Sunderland	1955-56	League
John Winter	Hartlepools	1967-68	League
Terence Worrell	Sunderland	1955-56	League
Steve Wurst	Mansfield	1968-69	League
Chris Yates	Crewe	1967-68	League